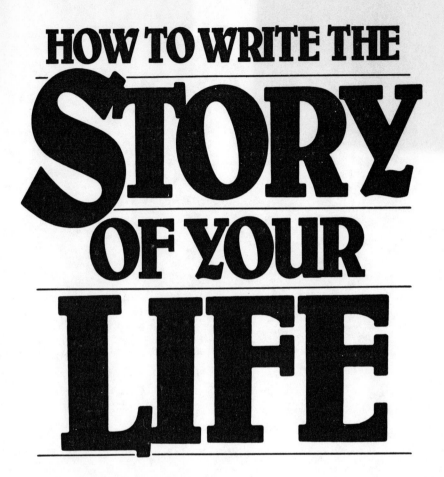

HOW TO WRITE THE STORY OF YOUR LIFE

FRANK P. THOMAS

Writer's Digest Books

Cincinnati, Ohio

Published by Writer's Digest Books, 9933 Alliance Road, Cincinnati, OH 45242.
First edition.
Second printing, 1986

Library of Congress Cataloging in Publication Data
Thomas, Frank P., 1916-
  How to write the story of your life.
  Bibliography: p.
  Includes index.
  1. Autobiography. I. Title.
CT25.T48   1984   808'.066920   84-19527
ISBN 0-89879-160-X

Design by Charleen Catt Lyon

dedication

This book is dedicated to the hundreds of men and women I have been privileged to assist as they penned the story of their lives. In their inspiring pages I have seen a stubborn self-reliance, sacrifice, respect for work, love of God and family, and the triumph of the human spirit over adversity.

contents

Author's Postscript
179

acknowledgments

The minds and hearts of many people have gone into this book. At the outset I want to thank the men and women who have graced my classes in life-story writing. Their enthusiasm has been an inspiration. Sharing their lives has reinforced my belief that I have never met an uninteresting person.

In particular I want to thank those of my writing students who permitted me to use pertinent excerpts from their own memoirs. Invariably I found that they who were writing an account of their lives for posterity were eager to encourage others to do the same. I wish to acknowledge the help of Ellen Tillery, Melisse Meeth, Dr. Bliss Pugsley, and Rose Ledwell for their useful suggestions made during the early preparation of my manuscript. My thanks go also to Beth Hayes for her patient typing of my many pages. I give much credit to Terry Zartman, Dr. Robert Gingery, Edwin Lauth, and others who, in the beginning, urged me to originate and teach a course in memoir writing for adults.

This is a better book because of the skillful and sensitive handling it has received from my editors, Carol Cartaino and Howard I. Wells III. I am grateful to them for their valuable suggestions. Likewise, I want to thank my agent, Richard Balkin, who was the first to recognize the merits of my manuscript. The librarians of the Tampa Library and the New York Public Library were helpful in preparing the list of 100 autobiographies that appear at the back of this book.

I owe a general acknowledgment to the many fine writers I have met and read, particularly my former New York colleagues in the American Society of Journalists and Authors.

Finally, I am grateful to my dear wife, herself a dedicated teacher, who has given me constant encouragement and has always shared my enthusiasm for this uniquely human subject.

I have been on a journey. Not so much a journey back through the past as a journey forward—a starting again at the beginning of it all—going back to Me who was to embark on that journey forward through time.

Agatha Christie, An Autobiography

Introduction:

The How and Why of This Book

MANY TIMES WHEN I have guided adults in the rewarding task of writing the story of their lives, to be left as a living legacy to their families, I have stressed the importance of turning points. These are the fateful bends in the road we journey down that change and shape our lives.

An important turning point of mine occurred seven years ago when my wife and I moved from Long Island, New York, to Florida. Since the tender age of 14, when I first ingested a liberal dose of printer's ink in a newspaper office, I had always earned my living in jobs requiring some form of writing. Now I had plans for my "retirement." Having been a magazine freelancer for many years, I had packed my typewriter and an idea file bulging with writing projects I intended to pursue. But it was not to be.

A local educator, learning of my background, asked if I would consider teaching a writing course at an adult center. Thinking this would not require a great deal of my time, I agreed. I told him I had once, in my spare time, taught an adult course in magazine article writing.

"No, not that," he said. "Can you develop a course that will help adults to prepare their personal memoirs to be passed on to their children, grandchildren, and other family members?"

I was skeptical. Since this project entailed considerable creative effort and soul-searching on my part I decided to interview a handful of community leaders.

"Is there a need for this?" I asked. They were unanimous in their encouragement. One, a clergyman, pointed out that since the family is a keystone of our society, any course that could bring its members closer together by providing a personal history linking one generation to another, would be eminently worthwhile.

So, taking a lesson from the turtle, which never gets anywhere until it sticks its neck out, I now, at close to Medicare age, stuck out mine.

I was hardly prepared for what followed once I took the course to the classroom. The response was immediate. A single announcement about the class in my local paper brought out 42 men and women who wanted to write about their lives. Many said they had always wanted to do this but didn't know how to go about it. Others had tried, but had strayed and then given up in frustration.

Soon I was teaching memoir writing in four adult education centers, including classes in my own town and county, at the University of South Florida in Tampa, and at Eckerd College in St. Petersburg. By now my course was motivating participants so well that I was reading 50,000 words of their manuscripts a week. I went out and bought more eyewash. Local papers ran stories about the course. I was now being asked to talk about it before groups, and being consulted by mail and phone.

I have been so inspired by the warmth and receptiveness of these would-be memoirists that today I continue to teach the course with as much enthusiasm as ever. There are days when I feel that I've become a "hostage" to it. These "students" have ranged in age from 30 to 91, the majority being 50 and over. They have come from all walks of life and every level of education. Some had not seen the inside of a classroom for 40 years. At times their stories reached the heart, bringing forth tears, theirs and mine. They are living proof that anyone can write his or her personal story, regardless of age. I have included selected episodes some of them have written throughout this book. I hope they will inspire you to write many of your own.

Gradually, as I watched these people search backward through their lives, I began to realize they were being doubly blessed. They were not only preparing a valuable family document, but in the process of reviewing their lives, they were also gaining new insights about themselves. They were now looking back more sympathetically on their past and gaining a psychic lift from a better understanding of it. It was a form of mental stock-taking that helped them to see their life's pattern more clearly. This double blessing is such a rewarding part of memoir writing that I decided it deserved a chapter of its own. You will find it in Chapter 8, "Rediscovering Yourself."

There is a saying that God created people because God loves stories. He must have implanted in all of us, too, a desire to recall to others the triumphs and tears of our lives. I have seen in thousands of manuscript pages this fondness for recalling the past. I have also seen an instinctive urge deep in the heart of people to learn more about who they are and where they came from. We are today in the midst of a revival of activity in search of our roots and family history.

The book that follows has grown out of my experience in the

classroom and as a nonfiction writer for over 30 years. I hope you will regard it as a companion as well as a working guidebook. I have included the techniques that most helped others in writing their life stories, long or short. Its object is not to produce Hemingways, Maughams, or Steinbecks, although I can pray for this. Nor do I present myself as a paragon of literary perfection. What writer ever achieves the fluency and clarity he dreams of? Rather, this is a sharing, an attempt to guide you down a practical, tested path around stumbling blocks that have thwarted others. In the process I hope I have managed to dispel some of the mythology associated with writing.

Reflected here is my own philosophy that writing should be a positive experience devoid of nit-picking and that rules can only be guidelines. This is not a book on grammar, although it does seek to make the most of the language already at the writer's command.

The book embraces the five "R's" that I believe are essential to the successful completion and packaging of your life story: Researching, Remembering, 'Riting, Reading, and Reproduction. A series of "Memory Sparkers" will help you to remember at each stage of your life. These, together with the life-revealing topics given, and excerpts showing how other memoir writers have said it, will give you hundreds of ideas for fleshing out your life story. You will also find 50 numbered Writing Pointers unfolded strategically along the way. These can be of value to any writer, beginner or advanced. I have also urged the tender loving care of family photos and documents, and in later chapters, have attempted to answer the questions I am often asked. Perhaps, on completing the pages of your autobiography, you may feel that it is engrossing enough for publication. I have dealt with this subject in Chapter 30 in answer to the question, "Can I break into print with my life story?"

It is said that we humans are happiest when we are creating. I hope that you will find a special joy and fulfillment in writing your life story—a precious document that can live in your family for generations.

F.P.T.

Part One

How to Write Your Memoirs

On a clear day you can see a long ways back.
Adela Rogers St. Johns, *The Honeycomb*

Memory is where the proof of life is stored. It offers material for stock-taking and provides clues about where our lives are going.
Norman Cousins, *The Healing Heart*

The past sharpens perspective, warns of pitfalls, and helps to point the way.
Dwight D. Eisenhower

1

Why a Memoir?

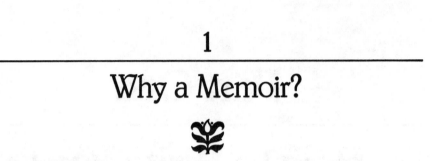

HOW DO YOU VIEW your life?

Far too modestly perhaps. Yet your life is important. It is as unique as your fingerprints. It is a precious piece of time that should not be forgotten. There has only been one life lived like yours in all time and only you can leave an accurate account of it.

Members of your family want to know more about your life than you think. They will treasure every word you write. To them you are the connection, the bridge between the remarkable past and the present. In fact, you are history, and history disappears if you don't record it.

People often say to me, "There's nothing interesting in my life." Or, "Nothing ever happened to me." I always smile and say, "Let's wait and see."

I recall a woman I met socially. When she learned that I was teaching everyday people to write their memoirs she said, "My life has been a disaster. I could never write about it." During our conversation I asked a few questions (much like the ones I'll be asking you). Soon I was able to pick out many facets of her life worth writing about and I pointed these out to her. When we parted she asked me for the starting date of my next class.

One day a man who had worked in a supermarket approached me. "I've always wanted to do this," he said timidly, "but I never was one who could write well in school."

"Don't be concerned about that now," I told him. "You don't need any previous writing experience. I'll just ask you to put down your thoughts in a natural way. You won't be criticized. I have writing pointers that will help you, and when you see how others say it you will start to flow."

He did, slowly at first. As his confidence built he began to pick up a rhythm. Soon he was handing me chapters of seven and eight pages in that scrawly handwriting of his. I still remember the flush on his face when I had him read one of his episodes to the class. When I last saw him he asked me if I knew of a good typist. He had finished his story.

WE HAVE LIVED THROUGH CHANGE.

Most people underestimate themselves. There are golden nuggets of personal history waiting to be mined out of every life. First of all, consider that we have been living through one of the most event-packed periods of our history. We have seen U.S. Presidents come and go. We have been through wars, depressions, recessions, and inflation. We have gone from splitting logs to splitting the atom, from crystal sets to satellite TV, from mustard plasters to heart transplants, and from washtubs, iceboxes, blackboard arithmetic, and crude biplanes to washing machines, refrigerators, computers, and space flights to the moon.

You have seen all this firsthand. You have learned much. You have struggled through it, raised families in the midst of it, and you have thoughts and feelings about it. This now is your chance in a lifetime to tell about it.

It is often difficult to realize how rapidly our world has been changing around us. This makes what we write about our lives now all the more valuable. Winston Churchill recognized this in his book *My Early Life.* "When I survey this work as a whole," he wrote, "I have drawn a picture of a vanished age—the character of society, the foundations of politics, the methods of war, the outlook of youth, the scale of values, are all changed . . ."

Seldom does the average person get the credit for changing the course of history, but it is the average person who transmits it most clearly. In setting down the things you remember you are actually telling those who follow about the kind of homes you lived in, how doctors treated illness, how people traveled, what they wore, what they ate, the games they played, their religious beliefs, what jobs were like, the customs of the times, and how you coped with personal and economic crises of your life.

"One of the best things you can do for posterity is to go home and write your life history," Kentucky historian Dr. Thomas D. Clark told adults attending one of his seminars recently. "It is the only true way for future generations to know what your life-style was really like."

RENAISSANCE OF INTEREST IN ANCESTRY.

Today, more than ever before, people are recording their personal and family histories for posterity. More people are keeping family records, journals, diaries and cherished family letters, photos, and documents. There has been a new wave of interest in searching out and preserving our individual past.

In fact, tracing our personal heritage has today become one of the most avidly pursued hobbies in our land. By word of mouth, and through the printed word, more people have undertaken to search out their ancestry. Thousands of genealogists, many banded together in clubs in towns and cities, are busily questing for their lines of descent. Libraries, where these groups often meet, are providing reference books, and often special sections, devoted to searching out family pedigrees. Many of these genealogists go on to write their life stories.

A number of factors have produced this thirst for ancestral knowledge. Alex Haley's bestselling book *Roots*, tracing his heritage back for seven generations, has done much to revive the interest. The search is more imperative today than ever. The ease of travel and the restless mobility of the American nuclear family have done much to separate generations.

Today the family that stays together is a rarity. A woman who came to my class to write about her family's background told of her six children, a son and five daughters. The son, she said, was working in Argentina. One daughter was living with her husband in Germany where he was serving in the U.S. Army. The other daughters, now out of the nest, were living in Colorado, Ohio, West Virginia, and Maine.

"My husband and I are breathless trying to keep up with our family," she told me. "Unless I pull together something about our lives and about our forebears they will never know much about our family."

WHY THEY DO IT.

I like to ask people who are writing their life stories why they are doing it. I have interviewed over 50 such people asking the question "What made you decide to write your memoir?"

Here, in their own words as I recorded them on tape, is a sampling of what they said:

> "When I was a child our house burned down to the ground and we lost everything including our family documents and photos. I want to recapture the events of my life and my family's struggle."

> "I feel that in doing this I am writing the bible for my family."

"Our family has stories that go back four or five generations. I'd like to put them down for the children."

"I'm writing some things about my life because I want to put some meat on the bones of my genealogy."

"It's a tradition in my family. My husband's grandmother in Texas wrote a souvenir memoir as far back as 1903 and in it she urged her children to do the same."

"I could not attend a reunion of my high school class. So I wrote seven or eight pages of reminiscences and these were read to the assembly. My classmates wrote and urged me to elaborate on my life story. So I'm doing it."

"I've always wanted to do this. My daughters gave me the final push."

"I have a stack of family photos and I want to write my story around those photos."

"I'm writing mine because no one before me in my family ever did anything like this."

"A friend doing a history of our area asked me for my autobiography. That got me going."

"Our twenty-fifth wedding anniversary comes up in April and I'm going to surprise my family by handing out things about my life."

"We did things so differently when I was growing up. I thought my grandsons would like to know about it."

"I have four children and they all want to know more about my life."

"I wish some of my ancestors had written about themselves. They didn't, so I'm going to do it."

"Who's going to tell my family about me and the world I lived in if I don't?"

TEN WAYS TO GET THE MOST OUT OF THIS BOOK.

1. This is a *reading* and *doing* book. The reading (informational) chapters are alternated with the doing (Writing Bite) chapters. One reinforces the other and together they will move you along a productive creative path.

2. To begin with, get an overview of the material covered in the book by glancing through the Table of Contents. Then thumb through the chapters. Having done that, come back to the beginning and move ahead, one chapter at a time.

3. The most important creative chapters are the Writing Bite Chapters. They contain features that others have found to be most helpful.

4. Before you start writing you should read Chapter 10, "The Key to Writing Success."

5. You will find excerpts written by other life-story writers throughout this book. Read them not only to see how others have said it, but also for ideas that may spark some of your own memories. There are more of these excerpts in the Appendix.

6. The Writing Bite chapters will take you through your life stages from birth to retirement. Feel free to break this pattern of writing at any time by tackling other subjects in between. You will find many other topics that can spark you in Chapter 25, "100 Bonus Topic Ideas for Variety."

7. The Memory Sparkers throughout the book are meant to stir up memories for your life story. Although some will jog your memory the first time you read them, go back over them again for more sparks.

8. The 50 Writing Pointers have been selected especially for this book. I have unfolded them a few at a time to meet your needs as you progress. Be sure you review them before you start writing each chapter.

9. We learn by doing. We learn to write by writing. The more we write the better we get. Try to write at least one episode a week, long or short.

10. Autobiography makes fascinating and inspiring reading. Keep the story of someone else's life on your reading table for relaxation and enjoyment. You will find a list of "100 Selected Autobiographies" in the Appendix. I have put this list together with the help of librarians, from personal reading, and from choices suggested by my students.

2

Let's Get Organized

THERE'S A QUESTION I want to ask you. I'm not being facetious. I just want to make an important point. Do you remember the elephant jokes? Here's the question: "How do you eat an elephant?" I'll give you a clue: How do you eat an apple, a banana, a peach, a sandwich, or a piece of pie?

That's right. *"One bite at a time."* And that's the best way to go about writing your memoir. If you do this you will not be intimidated by some of the comments I've heard from beginners such as "It seems overwhelming," "It's impossible," "I panic at the thought of it!"

The secret, as every professional knows, is to cut the task down to size by writing *"one bite at a time"* and to concentrate, for the time being, on only that one bite. This principle will work for you in any creative endeavor, whether you are writing a long letter, a report, or a book.

"HOW MUCH SHOULD I INCLUDE?"

You can't include everything that has happened in your life. If you try that you will become discouraged. Scientists tell us that our brain (I call it our Memory Bank) holds a store of information acquired since birth that would, if we could get all of it out, fill many sets of the encyclopedia. A memoir is hardly an encyclopedia. You just don't have to work that hard.

The word *story* appears in the title of this book and a few words about it are in order. The dictionary defines the word, as we are using it, as "a connected narration of that which has occurred, a description of past events." It comes from the Latin *historia*, from which we get our word *history*. William and Mary Morris, in their book *The Morris Dictionary of Word and Phrase Origins* (New York: Harper & Row, 1971), tell how the word *story* came into being: "Back in the Middle Ages it was the custom in many parts of Europe to paint scenes or print legends on the outside of various floors of a building. Thus each floor represented a different story and, before long, the levels themselves were called stories."

In writing the story of your life you, too, are painting scenes, one story at a time.

In this book I also use the word *memoir* interchangeably. The dictionary helps us here, too. It describes the word as "a history or narrative composed from personal experience and memory; often, especially, an account of one's life, or episodes in it, written by oneself."

The key word is *episodes.* These are the "bites," the stories we need to single out and develop, one at a time. In each we should reach back for the highlights in our lives. One of my students likened these highlights to cooking a pot of stew. "When you stir it up," he said, "the best comes to the top."

Incidentally, for our purpose *memoir* refers to the book as a whole, and the plural, *memoirs,* refers to its contents.

WHY THE STRESS ON "BITES"?

You will note that I have placed a good deal of emphasis on writing your memoir one episode at a time, one bite at a time. This is my own proven method, tested with everyday adults writing about their lives. It is not necessarily the only way to go about the task at hand, but I believe that doing it piece by piece has much to recommend it. By focusing on one subject at a time you can bring forth more about you on that subject. Thus you avoid rambling across many other subjects that may deserve richer treatment than just a few paragraphs in passing.

For example, the person writing about his birth who includes just two or three paragraphs about his mother or father is missing a great opportunity for doing a warm and sensitive chapter on them later. People who simply sat down to write their life story without a plan have come to me in frustration and discouragement because their writing had reached an impasse. I know of no professional writer who doesn't plan his work before starting, its beginning, its middle, and its end. Look at the books in your library. Almost without exception they were written one chapter at a time.

There's another good reason for breaking your personal history down into parts. You make it easier for a member of your family to *read* it, an objective you should always keep in mind. It will also be easier for a relative to refer to different parts of it later because each episode will be listed in your table of contents.

WHAT TO KEEP IN MIND AS YOU WRITE.

Writing has to be aimed. It must have an overall objective and that objective is best realized when we keep the audience in mind. First let us take a look at the objective of some of the people who write about facts and then let's consider what yours ought to be:

The news writer.
Whether he or she is preparing a story for the front page of a newspaper or the evening TV newscast, this writer seeks to *inform.* The writer goes after the *who, what, when, where, why,* and *how* of the story, writes it tightly, and unfolds it quickly, so that busy people can catch up with the news in a hurry.

The magazine article writer (or feature writer).
This writer goes beyond the news article. He not only seeks to *inform,* he also wants to *illuminate and entertain.* He has more time to dig into the background of the story. He can include vivid description, moving narration, and interesting anecdotes.

The nonfiction book writer.
He, too, seeks to *entertain* as well as to *inform* and he has far more elbowroom in which to do it. In effect he is writing fifteen, twenty, or more feature articles that develop the main subject. They become the chapters in his book. Many a book has developed out of a single article that enjoyed unusual reader interest.

You, the memoir writer.
Your objective should also be to *inform, enlighten, and entertain* your audience (your family) as you narrate the high points of your life. Helen Keller gave sage advice to all memoirists when she said at the outset of her autobiography, *The Story of My Life:* "In order, therefore, not to be tedious I shall try to present in a series of sketches only the episodes that seem to me to be the most interesting and important."

On the one hand you need to ask yourself, "What are some of the most meaningful things that have happened in my life?" These facts will inform your family how people, places, and events have shaped your life. On the other hand you need to ask yourself, "What are some of the most amusing, unusual, uncomfortable, triumphant, frightening, ridiculous, and radiant moments of my life?" These incidents will entertain members of your family while they are learning more about you. And in putting down some of these facts and anecdotes you will have anticipated many of their questions.

ORGANIZING YOUR MEMOIR.

Believe it or not most authors find the structuring of a lengthy article or book to be their most difficult task. However, you should have no such difficulty in setting up the pattern of flow of your memoir. This is because you will be writing it in separate bites that can stand on their own. Therefore you can place each in any order that feels good to you, without the need for a transition from one to another.

The novelist Agatha Christie recognized this in writing her own life story. "Autobiography," she said, "is too grand a word. It suggests a purposeful study of one's whole life. It implies names, dates, and places in tidy chronological order. What I want is to plunge my hand into a lucky dip and come up with a handful of assorted memories."

Some writers start their memoirs with birth. Others start with a dramatic episode in their lives, such as a turning point. One woman, I recall, was particularly fond of her grandparents because they had raised her. She asked me if she could include sketches of each. I told her she certainly could because I advocated separate episodes that permitted maximum flexibility. She turned out a very informative memoir that included separate episodes on her maternal and paternal grandparents. She positioned these in the middle of her memoir just ahead of sketches of her mother and father. Others have placed chapters about their parents at the beginning.

THE PARTIAL MEMOIR.

Some people choose to write a fragment of autobiography concentrating on a particular period in their lives. Some have chosen childhood. Others have focused the magnifying glass on their military experience. I have one very nostalgic memoir in my collection written by a man who described his youth on a Wisconsin farm so that his children would get the feel of what life was like then.

Such a partial memoir can be written at any age. Author Leonard Mosley, in his fragment of autobiography, *So Far So Good*, written when he was 24, described seven impressionable years of his early life. "It had been necessary for me to discover what had happened in order to discover what was going to happen," he said.

I mention this at the outset to indicate that the writing of separate episodes makes it possible for anyone to write his or her memoir, long or short, and to ultimately organize it to suit the heart's desire.

LOOK TO YOUR TOOLS.

Make it easier for yourself. This may sound mundane, but attention to a few simple tools can make your writing effort a lot easier. Here are some that will help:

1. *A three-ring loose-leaf notebook.* You will thank me later for suggesting this. Buy one that will take $8\frac{1}{2} \times 11$-inch pages, lined or unlined. This size will give you the room you need to write. Be sure you have your name, address, and phone number in the front of your book in case you lose it. A loose-leaf notebook permits you to organize your memoir in any order you finally choose. It also represents one of the more economical ways to finally package your memoir. (More on this later.)

2. *Setting up your manuscript.* Write on only one side of the page. Leave margins of $1\frac{1}{2}$ inches on the left and 1 inch on the other three sides. Double-space always. Indent your paragraphs uniformly with either five or ten spaces. Make a carbon if you like. It is always good to have an extra copy. Number your pages either in the upper right-hand corner or at the bottom of the page in the middle. Use Arabic numbers such as 1, 2, 3, 4, 5, etc. Indicate the end of an episode with the sign -o-.

3. *A small pocket notebook.* This should be your C.C. (Constant Companion). Memory is fleeting. Capture random wisps of memory as they occur, while they are still fresh in your mind. Many writers keep notebooks.

4. *Paste and scissors.* Don't hesitate to cut up your working manuscript to reorganize it and to make insertions.

5. *A pen or pencil.* And perhaps a colored one to make your editing stand out.

6. *A typewriter,* if you can type. Handwriting will certainly do the job, but the typewriter helps you to see your thoughts in the "clear" so you can visualize them better.

7. *A clipboard.* It is like a portable desk. It enables you to sit back comfortably anywhere while you scribble away.

8. *Large brown envelopes or an accordion file.* To carefully store family photos, documents, clippings, and other family memorabilia you intend to use.

NOW TURN THE PAGE AND WRITE YOUR FIRST LIFE EPISODE.

3

Writing Bite #1—Pick a Topic

THERE IS AN ANCIENT saying that the beginning is half the deed. Now is the time to begin. Here are three topics I think you can do well with. Pick one and concentrate on that one only (you may want to pursue the others at a later time).

Think about the subject you've chosen. You will find "Memory Sparkers" under each topic to stir up your Memory Bank. Jot down some of your recollections on a pad before you start to write your episode. Take advantage of two other aids in this chapter: a selected episode written by another adult and a list of four Writing Pointers that will be helpful as you begin writing. No adult I have worked with has ever failed to produce at least one episode of two, three, four, or more pages from one of these topics. I have chosen them because they will reveal a good deal about you and they can be written mostly from memory.

Don't be concerned now as to where in your memoir you will place your written episode. That will come easily later.

TOPIC 1—A TURNING POINT IN MY LIFE

We all have many turning points in our lives. These bends in life's road can happen at any time. An unexpected event, an opportunity that knocks, a set of circumstances, someone you meet—and your life changes direction. Pick one of your most significant turning points and write about it.

Helen Keller, at 19 months of age, was deprived of her sight and hearing because of a tragic illness that also made her a mute. At the age of six a remarkable turning point occurred in her life. She came under the influence of her teacher, Anne Sullivan, and broke through her world of darkness and silence. She not only learned to read, write, and talk but later graduated from college with honors and then went on to become an author and lecturer.

Will Durant, the historian/philosopher, was in his twenties, a penniless educator and writer of articles, when he started research on his monumental work, *The Story of Civilization.* He had conceived the idea of writing it as he lay ill with dysentery in Damascus, Syria. That turning point recast his entire life.

Memory Sparkers—Turning Point

Can you recall a problem you faced in your life and how you solved it? Often the resolution of a problem can be a turning point. The woman who wrote the episode in this chapter tells how she solved her problem.

Was there some special person in your life that influenced or befriended you? How did this person make a difference in your life? Tell about it.

Have you suffered an illness or accident that landed you in a hospital? While lying there, or later, did you come to some decision about your life? Was that the beginning of a change in your life?

Perhaps marriage was one of your most important turning points. What has it meant to you? How did it change your life? What circumstances brought you and your spouse together? Tell what happened.

Did you struggle to get an education? Tell how you obtained it and what it has meant to you. Could you have gone as far without it?

Moving to a new home, a new town or city can make a big difference in a life. Describe a move that you believe to be significant in your life. What caused you to move? What happened in your new environment?

What career did you choose? How did you happen to get into that line of work? Tell about this. Has it been good to you? Did your first job lead into it or did you make a number of moves before you found your main career?

Did the death of someone very close to you make a big difference in your life? How? How did you cope? What did you do?

Has divorce or remarriage caused serious changes in your life?

Tell about the adjustments you had to make. How has it turned out?

Did your life change when your grown children left the nest? How? What did you do? What were your feelings?

Have there been crises in your life that you had to overcome such as a serious financial setback, being fired from a job, losing your possessions in a fire, storm, or other disaster? Tell about it and what you did to get back on your feet.

TOPIC 2—A HOBBY THAT HAS MEANT A GREAT DEAL TO ME

Your hobby can reveal much about you. You have given it many hours and it has been a pleasant part of your life. It indicates where you turned for relaxation. Have you devoted your spare time to some particular hobby? Tell about it.

Memory Sparkers—Hobbies

How did you happen to get into this hobby? When, at what age? Why do you particularly enjoy it?

How did you develop your knowledge in this hobby? Did you join a club? Did it require special training? Have you subscribed to publications that deal with your special hobby? Have you ever written an article for them?

Does your hobby require special equipment? Is it an expensive hobby?

Have you ever been asked to speak before a group about it? Have you ever placed your hobby on exhibit?

Have you received any awards or honors in connection with your hobby? Have you and your hobby ever been written up? Where?

Have you realized any income from your hobby? If not now, will it become profitable some day in the future?

Sometimes a hobby can blossom into a career. Has your original hobby expanded into something bigger?

Have you made new friends through your hobby? Would you want your children to take up this hobby? Is it a hobby you can pursue at any stage of your life? Will you continue it in your retirement?

TOPIC 3—AN ACCOMPLISHMENT I LOOK BACK ON WITH PRIDE

All of us have rare, triumphant moments in our lives when something we put effort into comes out well and gives us much satisfaction. It does not have to be something heroic or earthshaking. It need only have meaning and importance to you.

Memory Sparkers—An Accomplishment

Raising a family can be one of the most difficult experiences of our lives. Describe some of the highlights of this struggle. Where did you live? What were the times like then? How many children? How have they fared? Have they come up to your expectations? What would you have done differently?

Have you had a career in military service that you are proud of? Or in some other type of service for country, community or church? Tell about this. What was it you did? For how long? Where? What satisfactions or benefits did you derive from doing this?

Is there a particular field of endeavor where you developed expertise? What honors or recognition have you received? How did you happen to get interested in it? What contributions did you make in this area? Have you been consulted about your specialty?

Did you overcome some handicap in life? What was it? How did you go about it? Did you get help from certain individuals? Have you participated in helping others to overcome a similar handicap?

We can take pardonable pride in so many things in our lives: learning a language, making our own clothes, fixing a car, building a house or having one built, overcoming a personal fault, solving a knotty problem, handling a special crisis, achieving physical fitness, losing weight, quitting smoking, handling family finances, running a business, running a home. Choose one that can be revealing and significant to your family.

A MEMOIRIST WRITES:

This memoir writer, a participant in one of my classes, has chosen a meaningful turning point in her life. In describing how she overcame her health and shyness problems she reveals a good deal about herself. Those in her family who read this episode will find that they can easily identify with it. Can you? Her language is simple and down-to-earth, and she has kept to her subject without rambling.

"My Lucky Break—A Turning Point"

On the whole I think I've had an unusually happy and satisfying life. One reason for this was a lucky break that came my way in the mid-1940s.

Years before I had an unfortunate bout with pneumonia which left me with asthma. Both my mother and her sister suffered from asthma throughout their lives, but I thought I was going to escape it. But there I was, skinny as a rail and with no strength to even do the dishes without resting before and after.

I gave up most of the enjoyable extras in my life—the theater, tennis and entertaining. I led a pretty dull life. Reading was about the only pastime I could enjoy, and books were my salvation.

After about ten years of this frustrating experience, Helen, a friend, asked me to consider a part-time job at Rembrook, a private school in West Hartford, Connecticut, where she taught. It consisted of tutoring six children for an hour and a half in reading and spelling.

My husband Pete was afraid it would be too much for me as I would have to drive ten miles to West Hartford. However, I took the job which gradually grew into a whole morning's work, helping second, third and fourth graders. I loved the children and the challenge, and got such great satisfaction in helping these children in the all-important area of reading.

And it was good for me, too. No more sitting around doing nothing and feeling sorry for myself. Each year my health improved and, in time, I outgrew asthma and got fat and sassy. I experienced an extra bonus because I was also acquiring some much needed social ease. I had always been shy and felt insecure with strangers. My close contact with the parents of the children turned out to be so good for me.

I learned to feel at home with all kinds of parents, even those that were wealthy and important. They were all so pleasant and appreciative of what I had done for their children. Over the years I had to speak before gatherings of several hundred people and it was a thrill to feel at ease doing this and to see the pleasure and excitement on the faces of people in the audience.

My association with the head of the school was also a rewarding one. Her high standards and common sense guided the school from an enrollment of 25 students to over 900. I take pride in having been part of this growth. When she hired me she said, "I want someone who has been a teacher and also a mother." These were her criteria and I think wise ones in appointing someone who was to help failing students.

So I have a great deal to thank Helen for. She turned the key which opened the door to my teaching for 22 years at Rembrook—a great joy for me. It was my lucky break.

WRITING POINTERS: 1-4

1. *First, get it down.* Avoid the tendency to become self-critical as you write. Forget about grammar now. The object is to get that first draft down on paper as rough as it may be, or as out of sequence as it may be. What do you do when your car is crossing a railroad track? You keep going. Do that when you start writing—"go with the flow." If you lack a fact leave a space and insert a question mark. You can fill it in later.

"To know how to begin to write is a great art," says author and educator Jacques Barzun. "Convince yourself that you are working in clay, not marble; on paper, not eternal bronze; let the first sentence be as stupid as it wishes . . . just put it down and then another . . ."

2. *Use the pronoun "I" freely.* It is not immodest at all. In fact it is quite appropriate in a memoir. It helps you to write more naturally. Some beginners tend to write in the third person: "He was born in . . ."; "She then moved to Detroit." They were writing about themselves but it sounded as though it was about somebody else. Perhaps you are reluctant to use the first person because you were taught that way in school. Forget it.

3. *Avoid rambling.* Place your title on top of your first page and avoid wandering away from that topic, a common error of beginners. Remember, you want each episode to be a unit that can stand

by itself. Save extraneous material for episodes in which it is more appropriate. You will find many examples of titles in Chapters 20 and 25.

4. *Be confident.* I am convinced that many writers falter because they feel vulnerable. They feel, consciously or unconsciously, that perhaps what they write will not be liked or that it is not good enough. Nonsense. If you have that feeling, shed it now like an overcoat. Just get your words down in whatever way you get them down no matter how squeamish or exposed you may feel. Once you do that you can massage them into the shape you want. And your family will love every word you write.

4

Finding the Facts

MAKE NO MISTAKE about it, the memoir you are writing will be a document of record. It will probably remain in your family a long time. People have shown me yellowed memoirs written by their ancestors three generations before. For this reason it is important that you include in your manuscript a reasonable number of specific and accurate facts.

However, this does not mean that a memoir should be choked with statistics and data. The hard facts such as full names, dates, places, ages, and relationships should be woven into your copy gradually as you go along. This makes for easier reading.

Here are three important methods for gathering the facts you will need:

ENGAGING YOUR MEMORY BANK.

You will be surprised at how much you can retrieve from your memory once you put it to work. More on this in Chapter 6, "Jogging Your Memory."

INTERVIEWING RELATIVES AND FAMILY FRIENDS.

It is a good idea to let your family know that you are writing your memoir. You will find relatives supportive and helpful even if you are not personally acquainted with them. Start with the older members of your family. Which ones tell the best stories as they recall family happenings? Call on them, if you can—grandparents, parents, uncles, aunts, and others. Get them to talk about the family's background and watch for revealing anecdotes. Perhaps there are questions that your children and grandchildren have asked you from time to time. These are important leads in formulating your own questions.

Go prepared with your notebook or a tape recorder. Ask questions when the remembering slows down. As a journalist I've always been guided by the maxim that if you ask a question you may seem ignorant for the moment, but if you do not you may be ignorant forever. It is better to make several visits to gather material rather than one long one that may tire your older relatives. Also, once "programmed," they very often remember more stories the next time around.

While visiting relatives be sure to ask for special family photographs you do not have. Usually they will have a print and not a negative. Borrow the print and have a copy made at your nearest photography store. This does not cost much. Be sure to return the original to your relative.

When relatives live too far away for a personal visit, start a correspondence by mail to obtain the information you need. A woman in one of my classes sent her grandmother a list of ten questions concerning memoir material she needed. Be sure your questions are clear. The fewer you send each time the better. Leave enough space between each question so your relative can answer each on the same piece of paper. Make it easy for them to reply by enclosing a stamped, self-addressed envelope.

When relatives live far away don't overlook the telephone for short pieces of information you need. One memoirist I know managed to include one or two questions each time he made his Sunday long-distance call to an aunt.

Don't neglect to take advantage of those occasions when the clan gets together for an outing or a reunion. This can be a great opportunity for you to gather precious bits of family information.

Also, a nostalgic trip to your old neighborhood may turn up some facts you had forgotten. Streets, houses, stores, churches, and people can stir up memories that could enrich your memoirs. Don't forget to take your camera. Be sure to take a shot of the house you were born in if it is still there.

CHECKING DOCUMENTS AND RECORDS.

With a little effort and patience on your part there are many important family facts you can retrieve from records in your home or that you can obtain elsewhere. To give you some ideas for searching out information you lack I have compiled this list of fact sources. Go over it from A to Z. You may find just the source that will be helpful to you.

A TO Z CHECKLIST OF FACT SOURCES.

A Account books

B Birth and baptismal certificates, Bible records, budget records

C Cemetery records and headstone inscriptions, church records, citizenship papers, canceled checks

D Diplomas, diaries, death certificates, deeds, divorce records

E Estate papers, epitaphs

F Funeral programs, family papers, friends

G Guardianship records, gas mileage records

H Hospital bills, home movies, hometown historical societies

I Immigration and naturalization records

J Journals

K Knowledgeable kinfolk

L Licenses, ledgers, libraries

M Marriage licenses, military records, mortgage records

N Newspaper clippings, naturalization papers

O Obituaries, old letters

P Passports, photos, photo albums, parish registers

Q Querying relatives, hometown chambers of commerce

R Recordings made by family members

S Scrapbooks, school records

T Town officials, town records

U University transcripts

V Voting records, visits to hometown

W Wills, wedding invitations

X Xerox vital documents

Y Yearbooks

Z Zeal—pursue all your facts with it.

HOW RELATIVES REACT.

I wanted to know what relatives said when they received a personal life history written by a member of the family. I chose Clarence. He had such a large family that he sent out 60 copies, typed, photocopied, and staple-bound. He titled it "You Asked for It." He generously allowed me to peek at his return mail and to excerpt from the letters. Here are just a few comments he received from relatives all over the country:

> "We've sure enjoyed your 'autobiography.' Thanks for sending it. My kids have started bugging me to do the same."

> "Thank you, thank you so very much for the book of your memoirs. Both Cliff and I read it and really enjoyed it! I've read some sections aloud to the children. They were amazed at some of the things that had happened and the way life was back in those days. When I finished the book I actually cried."

> "What a nice surprise to receive your memoir and how much we enjoyed reading it! . . . My mother wrote hers several years ago and I wouldn't part with it . . . and I'll also treasure yours."

> "Your memoir 'You Asked for It' was really super. I picked it up with a rather 'ho hum' attitude and didn't put it down until I finished it. I've gone back and read it again. It was a great idea to write it."

> "We very much enjoyed reading and rereading your book, Dad. There is so very much about you and your family I never knew, and I somehow feel I know you so much better having read it. I'm sure I'll read it again and again from time to time."

> "We were very excited and very happy to receive a personally autographed copy of 'You Asked for It.' We sat down immediately to 'devour' its contents. Some of the facts reminded me of some of the stories my mother told me about her childhood."

> "I have read it and will reread it many times and will let my son and daughter read it also so they will get a picture of

their grandparents' background. Not having known my grandparents I had no idea of the type of folks I sprang from. They sound like good, solid people."

"We really appreciate your sharing your life story with us all. What a thoughtful thing for you to do. There were a lot of things that Mom never had told us."

5

Writing Bite #2—Your Birth

EVERY GOOD STORY has a beginning, a middle, and an end. Your beginning is very important to your memoir. At first you may not think there is much you can say about your birth. Actually, when you start to think about it, you will find that you can write one, two, three, or more pages about it. The material that follows will give you an assist. Make notes as ideas occur to you. Watch for additional sparks as you read the accounts of others.

HOW OTHERS WROTE IT.

Here's how some famous people wrote about their births. Note the variety of approaches. Ronald Reagan, in an autobiography written before he became our fortieth U.S. President, stresses his father's reaction to his birth. TV talk show host Phil Donahue, an experienced news reporter, presents the facts quickly, as though writing a news lead. Russell Baker, the *New York Times* Pulitzer Prize-winning columnist, positions the facts of his birth side by side with historical events. Grandma Moses waxes philosophic, and Goethe, the German poet, chooses to link his date and hour of birth with an auspicious horoscope.

> The story begins with the closeup of a bottom in a small town called Tampico in Illinois, on February 6, 1911. My face was blue from screaming, my bottom was red from whacking, and my father claimed afterward that he was white when he said shakily, "For such a little bit of a fat Dutchman, he makes a hell of a lot of noise, doesn't he?"
> —Ronald Reagan
> *Where's the Rest of Me?*

I am Phillip John Donahue. I was born to Phillip and Catherine Donahue (nee McClory) on December 21, 1935, at St. John's Hospital on Detroit Street in Cleveland, Ohio. Through my first eight years of life, I grew physically at about the same pace as America's climb out of The Great Depression.

> —Phil Donahue
> *Donahue—My Own Story*

I was born in his second-floor bedroom just before midnight on Friday, August 14, 1925. Ida Rebecca was there, prepared to deliver me into the world when it seemed that the doctor from Lovettsville would never arrive. He did, however, in the nick of time, and I was issued uneventfully into the governance of Calvin Coolidge. World War I was seven years past, the Russian Revolution was eight years old, and the music on my grandmother's windup Victrola was "Yes, We Have No Bananas."

> —Russell Baker
> *Growing Up*

I, Anna Mary Robertson, was born back in the green meadows and wild woods on a farm in Washington County in the year 1860, September 7, of Scotch Irish paternal ancestry. Here I spent the first ten years of my life with mother, father and sisters and brothers. Those were my happy days, free from care and worry.

> —Anna M. Robertson Moses
> ("Grandma Moses")
> *My Life's History*

On the 28th of August, 1749, at midday, as the clock struck twelve, I came into the world, at Frankfort-on-the-Main. My horoscope was propitious.

> —Johann von Goethe,
> *Truth and Poetry*

THREE STEPPING STONES TO A BETTER EPISODE.

Take advantage of the three valuable aids that follow in this and in each of the forthcoming Writing Bite chapters:

1. Go over the Memory Sparkers and when some of them nudge your memory make notes on a scratch pad.

2. Read the selected episode written by another memoir writer. I have preceded each with a short critique. Perhaps memories of your own will be stimulated by what this memoirist has written. Make notes.

3. Now, before you start writing, go over the Writing Pointers that have been provided for this particular chapter.

Memory Sparkers—Your Birth

A baby is God's opinion that the world should go on

—Carl Sandburg

Do you know the when, where, and how of your birth? The hour, the day of the week, the date, your weight, the town, city, county; other details? (You can find the day of the week you were born, if you do not know it, by consulting a perpetual calendar in one of the almanacs.)

Jot down some of the things your parents and close relatives may have told you (or written) about your birth. Whom did they tell the good news to first? Did they guess correctly whether you would be a boy or a girl?

Were you born in unusual circumstances? In an unusual place? At home, in a hospital, on the way there? Who delivered you? Were there any medical problems concerning your birth? Who was there? Did you learn what your mother's pregnancy and "confinement" were like? Were you born on a special day, on or near a special holiday? What astrological sign were you born under?

Did your parents tell you how they came to name you? How do you like your name? Did it give you problems later?

Were you an only child? Were there other children? How many? Name them and give their ages. Were you the oldest, youngest, in the middle? If you had to do it over again would you be the oldest, youngest, etc.?

How old were your parents at the time of your birth? What work was your father (mother) engaged in? Would you say they were poor, of modest means, well off? Did they keep a "baby" book?

Who was President of the United States when you were born? Were you born at a time of some important or unusual local, national, or world event? (See Appendix for a listing of U.S. Presidents and their terms of service.)

Is there something humorous you always say about your birth? Mark Twain described his beginnings as follows: "I was born the 30th of November, 1835, in the almost invisible village of Florida, Monroe County, Missouri."

Note: Most people have a good deal to say about their birth and the circumstances surrounding it. However, if you do not, try combining into one chapter the facts of your birth with what you remember about the first five years of your life, your pre-school years. You will find Memory Sparkers for these preschool years in the next Writing Bite chapter.

A MEMOIRIST WRITES:

In writing about his birth, this memoir writer has chosen an interesting approach. He has selected a point of view (a slant) that is ably summarized in his provocative title. His writing is natural and his sense of humor comes through. In writing this episode he has also come upon a technique that many professional writers use—he has set up a problem and then showed how he solved it. That adds reader interest. Note, too, that he has used dialogue to good advantage, thus adding more variety to his piece.

"I Was An April Fool's Child"

I was due to arrive April 1, 1909. I must have started my April foolishness then, because I didn't arrive until April 5, 1909. The place was Battle Creek, Michigan.

My mother had an aversion to hospitals. Her five sons came by home delivery. I was the fourth son. If there had been a UPS in those days, she would have been glad to have all of us arrive that way. An expectant mother in those days needed a midwife and, hopefully, the family doctor. According to my baby book, Nurse Parker was there to assist.

As for the doctor, unfortunately he died suddenly a day or so after I was born without recording my birth. This was to have serious consequences later in my life.

On April 5, 1909, there developed one of Michigan's

late raging blizzards. How do I know this? One of my mother's brothers had been blinded in an accident at the age of four. He was a remarkable man and, for a blind man, had a storybook career. He was to become my favorite Uncle—Uncle Jim. At the time I was born Uncle Jim lived over a mile from our house. On the day of my birth, as he often recalled to me later, he started out by himself to call on my mother and me. A snowstorm had started, intensifying as he progressed. There were knee-high drifts before he made his way back.

The fact that my mother's doctor died so soon after my birth without registering my arrival (being born at home there was no hospital record, either) caused many complications in my life.

When World War II came my employer's company was required to obtain birth certificates from each of its employees to prove U.S. citizenship. Mine was not of public record.

My mother then was still alive, and an application to the Probate Court for "Delayed Birth Registration" took care of the problem. This document was sufficient to enable me to get a Passport from an investigative branch of our Government at one time in my career, but later not for Social Security.

Upon retirement, when I went to register with Social Security, the bureaucracy rejected my application for "insufficient evidence" to document my birth. I pointed out that the Government Passport authorities were satisfied with my delayed registration, and that I had been a Security Officer in the Navy in WW II.

"Not good enough for Social Security!"

"What would they accept?"

"A Baptismal Certificate."

I searched the "Baby Book" my mother had compiled. It recorded in her handwriting that for my baptism she had boarded the train from Battle Creek to go to Grand Rapids where my grandfather, on the distaff side, was the Methodist minister.

It was recorded that the baptism was a small family affair in the Rectory and that I promptly drank the Holy Water. However, it revealed no copy or evidence of a Baptismal Certificate. Being a private ceremony in the Rectory, there was no church record.

In thumbing through my baby book, a paper fell out. It was a duly certified "Cradle Roll" record at a Methodist

Church in Battle Creek, showing my arrival as of April 5, 1909, signed by the Enrollment Secretary, and dated only a few months after my birth.

Social Security accepted the "Cradle Roll." I am many thousands of dollars to the good because of that piece of paper. My thanks to the Lord for a mother who was so careful to enter everything in her children's baby books.

WRITING POINTERS: 5-8

5. *Be specific.* Choose precise words over general words. "It was a bright June day" is better than "It was a fabulous day." "He was tall and muscular" is better than "He was a big man." Be specific, too, about names, dates, and places. Doing this sets your life in time and place. Do what a good reporter does. In approaching a story he runs certain questions through his mind. He pays particular attention to what I call (for short) the "5 Ws." Rudyard Kipling, once a newspaperman, has aptly stated them in this little verse:

> I keep six honest serving men
> (They taught me all I knew);
> Their names are WHAT and WHY and WHEN
> And HOW and WHERE and WHO.

6. *Don't skimp on paper.* An artist needs a full canvas for his painting. You need elbowroom on white paper of at least 8½ × 11 inches. Use generous margins, and double-space so that you can easily make insertions and corrections. I've seen beginners writing out copy from one edge of a tiny sheet of paper to the other, leaving no space between lines. This can be frustrating.

7. *Write to express, not to impress.* Be as natural when you write as you are when talking to a friend. The act of writing doesn't demand another you. Avoid being stilted. Some beginners are tempted to show off but that only distracts the reader from what you are trying to say. Throw out the overblown phrase and the cute, fancy language. Be you.

8. *Keep your C.C. Notebook handy.* Capture that glimmer of a memory in your little Constant Companion Notebook the moment it occurs. Otherwise it will slip away from you. Soon (you will know when) you will have enough notes to begin writing the next episode.

6

Jogging Your Memory

❧

IN THAT USEFUL little book *The Elements of Style*, E. B. White describes writing as the bringing down of the bird of thought as it flashes by. This is precisely what we are doing when we are engaged in remembering. Here are a number of techniques that will help you to recapture some of those fond memories of the past.

THE ART OF REMEMBERING.

You are not alone in your effort to recall incidents that are lodged in your memory. You have a very powerful partner—your subconscious. It works in mysterious ways—but it works. Many times you have gone to bed with a problem on your mind. Chances are that in the morning a solution came into your mind. It is the same with memories. Program your mind by focusing it on a particular part of your life and soon that part will pop up in your consciousness. One remembered incident triggers another. You will find that you will get better at it as you go. It's like getting your "second wind." The English author Thomas De Quincey felt that no memory was irretrievable. "I feel assured," he said, "that there is no such thing as ultimate forgetting; traces once impressed upon the memory are indestructible."

Psychologists tell us that we do almost everything better when we relax. Perhaps that is why analysts favor the couch for their patients. At any rate studies have shown that early memories and images are recalled better when we are lying down. So get comfortable when you are in the process of remembering some part of your past. Yesterday seems far away until you start thinking about it. But be assured that your "remembery" is always there, ready to help if you ask it to.

Take the flicker of a memory, turn it around in your mind and let it stew awhile. It will build. When it does be sure to capture it, in whatever haphazard fashion, on a scratch pad or notebook. I am fond of that song "The Way We Were." Do you remember the opening line? "Mem'ries light the corners of my mind. . . . ." They will if you try.

Good memories are usually centered around people, places, homes, family, friends, relationships, and happenings. A nice thing about memories is that you can sort them out in order of importance. Let these memories flow at a quiet time. If they don't come right away go on to something else. The ones you are seeking will probably surface in your mind later when you least expect it.

A recent study found that most people have better memories—at least better long-term memories—in the evening. In this study psychologists tested groups of middle-aged volunteers in the morning, afternoon, and evening for their ability to recall. It was found that the volunteers scored the highest in the evening and the lowest in the morning. So when you beam your remembering searchlight over your past you should favor the evening hours.

What life periods do you find it easiest to recall? For most people it works best to start with the early years and to move forward. However, if it makes you more comfortable to recollect recent experiences, or some particularly dramatic part of your life, by all means begin where you can flow best.

SIFTING THROUGH THE STAGES OF LIFE.

Every stage of a life is important. You may feel that some periods of your life may yield more highlights than others, but all deserve scrutiny. To assist you in systematically mining out the golden nuggets of memory I have set up a "Ladder of Life" with its different stages. A set of Memory Sparkers accompanying each stage will give you a further assist in ferreting out the past. These are the kinds of questions a reporter might ask if he were interviewing you in person about aspects of your life.

The approximate age spans I assign to each stage are of necessity arbitrary. Chronological age does not tell the whole story. Youth has to do with the spirit, not necessarily age. Some people are emotionally and physiologically younger or older at a given age than others. However, this "ladder" does provide a practical framework for climbing each rung of your life in retrospect.

The Ladder of Life

Stage	Approximate Age Range
Birth	(day 1)
Childhood (preschool) Years	(to 5)
Elementary School Years	(5 to 13)
Teen Years	(13 to 19)
Young Adult Years	(19 to 25)
Early Marriage Years	(20 to 30)
Early Career Years	(20 to 35)
Middle Years	(35 to 55)
Later Years	(55 to 65)
Retirement Years	(65 +)

7

Writing Bite #3—Your Preschool Childhood

Memory Sparkers (To about age 5)

> How dear to this heart are the
> scenes of my childhood,
> When fond recollection presents
> them to view.
> —Samuel Woodworth

WHAT LITTLE STORIES have your parents and relatives told you about these early childhood years? How do they remember you as a child?

Where did you live? What was the neighborhood like? Who lived next door? What was your house like? Did you have your own room? What was bedtime like? Did you ever feel abandoned when you had to go to bed, perhaps before everyone else?

What was your greatest fear of those years? Was that fear linked to a person, place, or thing? How did you deal with it?

What are your most vivid recollections of these early years? Do you have any snapshots taken of you then? They make good Memory Sparkers. Describe what you see in them.

When you were especially good, what kind of a treat did your parents give you?

What were some of the games you played as a child? Whom did

you play with? Did you ever have an imaginary friend? Were you ever sent to summer camp? Did you get homesick?

Do you remember when brothers or sisters were born in your family? When? Where? Describe your feelings. Did you get along with them?

Did you receive enough love as a child? Did you attend nursery school?

Someone said they were poor but didn't know it. Were you like that?

Did you have any accidents as a child? Ever go to the hospital? Explain.

Did you have a favorite pet as a child? What was its name? Tell about it.

Did you believe in Santa Claus then? When did you stop believing? What happened?

Did you cherish a particular toy as a child? Did you have one that was your "security blanket"?

Can you remember a particular birthday party that was given for you as a child? Tell about it. What gift did you receive?

What were your meals like? Were you fed alone or with the family? What was your favorite food as a child? Your favorite dessert? Least favorite food?

A MEMOIRIST WRITES:

This memoirist delved back in her memory for most of this episode about the first years of her life. In an easy and candid narrative style she relates the highlights of those days, spicing her piece with anecdotes that illuminate her copy. Her sense of humor comes through nicely. Note how she stays within the scope of this piece— her preschool years—and how she leads the reader into her next chapter with her tag line—a good technique.

"My Preschool Years"

During the first two years of my life in Lorain, Ohio, I remember having my picture taken many times and going by train to Coshocton, Ohio, to see Grandma and Grandpa.

It was when I became three that I was aware, suddenly, of the joy and wonder of Christmas. I wasn't allowed in the parlor where preparations for the big day were made behind the sliding, closed doors but I had been told about Santa and that Grandmother had written a note to him for me.

When the celebrated day finally arrived, the sliding doors were opened, and I was led into a regular fairyland of beauty. The tree that covered one corner of the room was wound round with paper chains and strings of popcorn. On each branch there were candles that looked like blazing stars. Only now, looking back, I wonder what kept them from burning the place down. When I could take my eyes from the beautiful tree I saw Angela, my pretty rag doll, resting in a wire doll buggy that had a high back and a footrest that moved up and down. Grandmother found another package under the tree that she helped me open. It was a pair of red kid gloves. I have saved them over the years and now have them stored with my other loved things.

When I was three years and seven months old my brother Douglas was born. All my short life I had been the center of attention and I know I felt everything belonged to me. When I saw him in my very own white iron bed, covered with my white blanket, I just couldn't stand it. I ran to the kitchen and hid under the sink to cry. When Dad asked what the tears were about, I could only sob, "Nobody loves me any more."

When Douglas was six months old Grandmother was ordered to stay in bed because of a leg injury she received from a fall from her bicycle. Mother was to help with her care which made it necessary for her and Dad to give up their house on 9th Street. We all moved into Grandmother's large nine-room house on 7th Court. I must have been something of a problem at this time for I distinctly remember a few spankings I received.

One evening, when dinner was ready to be served, I tried to swing on one end of the table. It tipped over, throwing food, china and silver on the floor. I was paddled and placed in a highchair to keep me out of mischief.

When Grandmother had visitors, I noticed they were always served something to drink. One day the Pastor of our church came to call on her and I thought I'd be the first to offer him refreshments. I hurried to the basement and came back upstairs to hand him a bottle of beer. It wasn't the time for a spanking but I recall I was sent to the kitchen.

We were at Grandmother's nearly a year when Douglas developed rheumatic fever. I remember they carried him on a pillow, day and night, and there was not much hope of him living. "If he does survive," the doctor said, "he will not live beyond the age of forty." He did live to become a wonderful violinist and teacher at Morningside Conservatory, but, true to the prediction, he died of heart failure at the age of thirty nine.

I was nearly five when Mother and Dad bought a house on 7th Court across the street from Grandmother's. The only means of heating the place was by a large, black, potbellied stove in the dining room that usually roasted us on the side we exposed to it to warm ourselves. We could use the bathroom only in warm weather as the flush box that was near the ceiling had to be drained to prevent freezing in the cold winter weather.

One day, Dougie was placed outside in his buggy for a nap. When mother checked a short time later, Dougie and buggy were nowhere in sight. Mother was hysterical and for two hours the police combed the neighborhood and nearby houses. Suddenly, coming up Washington Avenue we saw three neighbor boys leisurely pushing the big reed buggy with Dougie's blond head, barely visible. The boys had wheeled him down to the breakwater to watch a ship come in. I doubt if the ship had any fascination for Dougie but we were all relieved at the sight of him unscathed.

Dougie and I were told to stay on the back porch to play and I was to watch that no one took him. It wasn't very long before I heard footsteps coming around our house and with mother's warning ringing in my ears I grabbed Dougie and started to scream. Mother said I cried for an hour and never again did she make a statement that would create such fear in me.

Dougie and I had a number of pets but our favorite was Sailor, a large brown spaniel that followed us everywhere. He would tolerate our rough play just so long and then he would move away from us. We also had two bantam chickens, Peter and Betty. One day an egg was found in the nest and, all excited, we showed it to Mother and Dad. It wasn't long until we looked in the nest again and there was another egg. That happened several times that day and later Dad told us he was having fun with us by placing the egg back in the nest each time.

I will tell you of my early school days in another chapter.

WRITING POINTERS: 9-12

9. *There's no need to preach.* Tell your story simply and honestly as you've lived it. Let the story have its own effect. Don't tell the reader what he or she should get out of it. Let them grasp it on their own. You are simply saying, "Here's my life the way I've lived it. Take out of it whatever you will."

10. *Don't waste time waiting for inspiration.* If every writer did there would be very few magazines and books. No, the Muse may not decide to reach out and favor you on any particular day, so go ahead. Thomas Edison once said that genius is 1 percent inspiration and 99 percent perspiration. The only way to begin is to begin.

11. *Reading helps writing.* That's why I've included a list of "100 Selected Autobiographies" in the Appendix of this book. Pick one for your reading table and enjoy it in your spare time. Study how others have written about their lives, and watch for passages and anecdotes that may spark memories of your own. There is no more fascinating reading than reading about the lives of other people.

12. *How to get unstuck.* Here's a tip that will help your writing to flow should you find it hard to get started. Pretend you are writing a letter to someone dear to you, someone you may actually intend to send a copy of your life story to—a son or daughter, a grandchild, a niece or nephew, a brother or sister, a cousin or other relative, a close friend of the family, a lifelong friend of yours. Actually write the salutation at the top of your paper: "Dear Mary" or "Dear John" (you can always take it off later). Now just tell Mary or John what it is you want to say.

I sometimes use this technique with students in my first class. I ask them to write me a letter about themselves. Here's one written in class in about ten minutes. Note how well this woman's words flowed. I pulled a phrase out of her letter for the title.

"My Early World"

Dear Frank:

My families on both sides are Pennsylvania Dutch. I feel most grateful for their special gifts to me, and less grateful for some of their wonderful well-known idiosyncrasies. I grew up feeling love, loyalty and perhaps too much discipline.

Six brothers and sisters followed me, quite regularly, into this early world of mine. So I became a surrogate mother before I was seven. I remember a very happy childhood, never realizing I was taught to be too old too early.

We grew up beside our Church, in a small town named Honey Brook. It was so small that when the local firehouse burned down one night the entire town watched it in their night clothes, the strangest array of sleeping outfits imaginable.

I recall, vividly, Fourth of July picnics featuring hand-churned peach ice cream and baseball games at which my father manned the hot-dog stand. We cut up onions for his stand until we cried. We liked seeing him at work there because he looked so different than he did in the mornings when he left for his job at the bank. We were very proud of him.

The Amish were our neighbors and I recall them bringing in their wonderful produce and chickens. We used to wade in the stream of one of their immaculate farms. We made friends with them although we secretly thought they were different.

Because we lived beside the Church it became the center of our social life. My Grandfather left his horse in our barn while he and Grandma attended services. Church suppers became the center of all news and gossip. We learned about grief then as well as we mourned our departing neighbors.

The village touched our lives forever. When we left for the big city things grew harder. Wars came. We grew up. We managed to get our education through the Depression and through wars. We all fell in love and married. Our children, who had much more than we, are carefully raising their own.

I often go back into our past with Mother and enjoy watching her animation as she recalls many things.

Most Sincerely,
Charlotte

8

Rediscovering Yourself

I SHOULD HAVE anticipated it, but I confess I didn't. I had been teaching adults the fine points of writing their memoirs for about six months. The men and women who came to class, notebooks in hand, represented a real challenge. They wanted to leave "footprints" for their families. Among them were homemakers, nurses, teachers, secretaries, military retirees, former college professors, postal workers, engineers, businessmen and women, social workers, and also two physicians, a clergyman, a lawyer, a county extension agent, and one woman who had been in show business. Many were retired, others were still active in jobs.

We met once a week for two hours. I sent them home each week with an assignment, asking them to reflect on just one part of their lives and to write about it. At home, some shut off their phones, settled down into comfortable chairs, and started to recapture the wisps of memory of another day.

I had been concentrating on techniques, the writing, and the successful completion of life episodes. They were flowing well. So well, in fact, that I had little need for my lecture on "Unblocking Writer's Block." (Once, when I asked if they were having trouble flowing, one woman raised her hand and said, "My trouble is I'm overflowing.")

Gradually, however, I began to sense that more was happening to these "memoir scribblers" than I had realized. Out of the corner of my eye, as it were, I began to see subtle changes in them. They were dressing better. They were coming to class earlier. There was a delightful eagerness in their eyes. They were asking more questions. They were writing me notes and letters. And then (I was surprised at first) every once in a while tears would flow down the cheeks of a man or woman reading a paper out loud. I have always called for volunteers to read their papers aloud in class pointing out that in doing so they could spark the memories of others. They were always generous about doing this. Sometimes they would ask me to read their papers aloud for them. They did spark, for many times as a paper was read I would see them making notes.

There was a lump in everyone's throat the day a man, writing about his childhood, recalled how his father had ordered him to shoot his pet dog. They lived on a farm. His father had bought a hunting dog and the youngster's "mongrel" was interfering with his father's training of the bird dog. The act of firing a fatal shot into his dog had seared the youngster's soul and built up years of resentment toward his father. It wasn't until he wrote out the details of that incident, 40 years later, that he began to forgive his father for that painful memory ("Perhaps I misunderstood him."). He told me later he had cried while writing about that day. Later he sent a copy of it to his two sisters, who, he said, had also cried while reading it.

I recall the hush that came over the class one day when a woman described how her husband had been shot to death one night by a burglar, leaving her in shock, and widowed with a child to support. The incident had happened many years earlier, and now, with considerable courage, she had written her way through it.

There were tears, too, when I asked a husband, and then his wife (they were both preparing memoirs) to read an assignment on their early careers. Their papers describing how they had struggled to get their education during the Great Depression only to find they could not get jobs, left many of us wet-eyed.

Then there was a man I'll call Arthur. He had flown fighters for our Air Force in World War II. He had been shot out of the sky over Yugoslavia and, on the ground, had fled ahead of pursuing enemy to escape capture. One day he came into class and said he wanted to write a fragment of autobiography dealing with this and another near-death experience when he had to bail out of a disabled fighter plane while in training. Week after week, working from clippings and memory, he relived those perilous moments, describing the thoughts that had raced through his mind in the cockpit and as he parachuted to earth. He told me later he had cried while writing it. "I feel more free now," he said. "I've straightened the whole thing out in my mind and released a lot of tension."

I remember one woman who in the middle of the course, had to go to the hospital for a major cancer operation. She told me that her first feelings were of anger that this had happened to her, and that this was interrupting a project for her family to which she was deeply committed. She made it back, coming into class one day on a cane. She went on to finish a superb printed memoir that she later passed out at a family reunion. In an autographed copy she sent me she wrote: "For the past months in your classes I have been very much aware of my own feelings of increased purpose and sense of self-worth, of the joy in creating something uniquely mine."

Soon I began to get other notes and letters from these memoirists as they completed their stories:

"I didn't realize until I wrote my memoirs what a beautiful, privileged childhood I really had."

"In examining my life I realized I was just fumbling along. I can see it better now and feel that I can take hold of it better."

"Writing about our life after my daughter's suicide pulled me through a very tragic period. It brought me peace of mind I had never known."

"Thank you for the opportunity to relive things that really surprised me."

"I think I have many new views of the past."

"Doing this has been one of my proudest accomplishments."

There it was. It began to dawn on me that the process of looking back on one's life and committing it to paper could confer on the writer other salutary benefits—catharsis, new insights, and a rediscovery of one's self. I should have realized this sooner. I have known a number of writing colleagues who have found therapy in the typewriter. I know that at times I have felt a sense of relief after asserting myself on paper.

I recall how Joan Beck of the *Chicago Tribune* once agonized over the death of her dear mother in a column she wrote. "Bear with me please," she said at the outset. "It is the bane and blessing of being a writer that emotions involuntarily form themselves into words in the brain and insist on the catharsis of being written down. Left unsaid, they nag and fester and interfere until there is no escape except to give them substance."

A mother in one of my classes found this cartharsis one day when she finally gave vent to the sad loss of her little baby daughter, a loss that had tormented her for 32 years. Her husband told me later, after she had written about the incident and read her paper to the class, that it was the first time she had ever discussed it openly. The child had been born with a heart defect before the time of open heart surgery. Despite frantic efforts to save the infant at four different hospitals she had died.

"They tried to console me," the anguished mother wrote. "They told me my baby was now an angel in heaven. I had lost my little baby that I had carried for nine months in my body and had given birth to after a long night of pain. My heart was breaking. No one could understand how I felt."

Somerset Maugham understood the value of discharging one's emotions through writing when he said in his autobiography, *The Summing Up*, "I write this book to disembarrass my soul of certain notions that have hovered about it for too long for comfort."

"WHAT GOES ON HERE?"

I put this question to Manhattan psychologist Salvatore V. Didato, author of *Psychotechniques*, a self-help book dealing with everyday problems. Dr. Didato applauded the memoir writing concept. He pointed out that recovering memories of the past has been a basic technique of psychotherapy.

"The systematic focusing on events, as one does when writing a life story," Dr. Didato says, "can bring to light many repressions. Their release can bring new insights into the self. People, it is amazing to know, can take heart and have courage to face these repressions (often false assumptions about themselves) particularly as they look back in later life."

The act of writing about our lives, besides stretching our minds and giving us a taste of creative discipline and satisfaction, also provides us with a form of mental stock-taking that helps us to better understand ourselves. In doing it we begin to discern more clearly what our life has really meant.

"Persons of all ages," says gerontologist Robert N. Butler, "review their pasts at various times trying to grasp the forces that shaped their lives."

The more we review our lives the more our sense of personal identity deepens. We realize then that we have achieved more than we thought we had, and this helps to bolster our feeling of self-worth.

Cardinal Newman spoke of the uncertainty of youth contrasting with the peace of mind of maturity. In refocusing our lens on our lives we more readily come to terms with ourselves. The jagged mountaintops of the past shrink to mere molehills now. We look back more sympathetically, and the where-did-I-go-wrong? feelings begin to evaporate.

Dr. Joseph Sides, a Florida minister who attended one of my lectures, told me afterward: "A lot of times we have been living with a load of guilt over some real or imagined incident. Writing about your life can put it all into the perspective of time. In life, circumstances may determine how you will respond. There's no reason for your feeling guilty because you did what you did. You had no other choice."

From time to time I have been approached by people who, learning that I teach autobiographical writing, have asked me to write their life story for them. Is it any wonder, knowing what I have observed firsthand, that I invariably say: "No, I'd rather show you how to do it yourself. You should not be deprived of the good it will do for you if *you* do it."

DEALING WITH STRESSFUL EPISODES.

Many times in writing about our lives we come to an emotional episode that tends to block us. I recall a woman who had lost her twin sister at the age of 26 in a tragic accident that had overturned her car. This woman's mere mention of her sister brought forth a stream of tears. "I know my memoir won't be complete until I write a chapter about my sister," she told me. "But I can't bring myself to do it." I gave her my usual counsel: "Skip over it. Go on to another part of your life." In due time, on her own, she summoned the strength to write it.

I gave this same advice to the woman whose retarded son, now in his 20s, had turned to drugs and to stealing to support the habit. Sometimes her phone rang in the middle of the night because her son had been picked up by the police. "Is it important for you to include this chapter?" I asked. "Does it really matter?" She thought about it and said, "Yes, I think my family should know the extent of the problem and how I coped. Right now it's a nightmare for me." Finally, after much soul-searching, she wrote that chapter.

Likewise there was the man who had been born illegitimately and who had never met his real father and mother. Naturally he was completely blocked when it came to writing about his beginnings. One day he told me he had spent half of his life trying to track down his natural parents. "That's interesting," I commented. "Tell me how you went about it." A month elapsed. Then one day, his face beaming, he handed me a chapter that described his struggle to live a normal life in society, and the many steps he had taken to learn the identity of his natural parents.

I discussed the handling of such traumatic moments with Dr. Glenn G. Golloway, a Tampa psychiatrist. He confirmed the wisdom of allowing individuals to make their own choices in writing about such events.

"They should feel no pressure," he said. "Rather they should feel welcome to write about it or to avoid it if they wish. Then their own defenses will protect them." Where individuals elect to go ahead in writing about their lives Dr. Golloway believes that "very often people do come to peace with something in their lives as a result."

This is what happened when I followed the principle of "skip and move on" in the case of Margaret, a widow who had lost her husband after many years of a happy marriage. She had grieved over his loss for a year when she started writing her memoirs. I noted that she wrote about many things but never about her married life. I said nothing. Gradually the feeling began to build within her that her marriage was such a high point in her life that she just had to describe it to her children. Two months later she produced an excellent chapter relating how she and her husband had met on a double date and fallen in love. She wrote about their courtship and marriage, the many things they did together, their struggle while raising a family, and the warmth of their relationship. There were ups and downs and tears and triumphs in her pages, but also a realization that things were no longer the same, that adjustments had to be made, and that life must go on.

"Writing this chapter was a catharsis I needed," she told me later. "I have rearranged many things in my mind and found more solace in doing it."

9

Writing Bite #4—Your Elementary School Years

Memory Sparkers (About age 5-13)

> I have had playmates, I have
> had companions,
> In my days of childhood, in my
> joyful school days—
> All, all are gone, the old familiar
> faces.
>
> —Charles Lamb

WHAT WERE YOUR first impressions as you started school? Can you remember that first day? Was it a happy beginning or were you tearful and homesick?

Were you glad to start school? Possibly because a brother, sister, or playmate was going? How did you get along with the other kids in school?

Did you go to a public or private school? Where? How far was it from your home? How did you get there? How many years were you in this school? Were there other schools you went to because your family moved? Did you find that difficult?

Did you go home for lunch, bring your lunch, or was there a school cafeteria? What sort of food did you eat? What was your favorite dessert?

What class did you like the most? The least? Did you have any special interests or talents you were recognized for? Did these influence your career in later life?

Was there anything you really wanted as a child? What was it? Did you ever get it? How did you feel? What present do you especially remember getting?

In the episode in this chapter, George talks about daydreaming in class. Did you? About what?

Did you have any superstitions during these elementary school days? Can you remember any of your teachers? Were you influenced by any particular one? Did you ever have a crush on one of your teachers? On one of your schoolmates?

Did you ever come home with a bad report card? Why? What did your parents say? Did your parents feel that you were being well taught? How did you get along with your father, your mother? How were you punished? For what?

Did any of the children you went to school with later become famous? Are some still your friends? Has there been a reunion?

Did you go to church as a youngster? Tell about this.

Who influenced you the most when you were a child?

What was it like when your family gathered around the dinner table? What did your family do on Sunday?

What were some of the games you played during these school days? Did you learn to ride a bike? To skate? To play marbles, etc.?

Were you awkward as a child? Tall, short, fat, athletic? How did you dress? Were you shy? Did you have a special pet?

How did you get along with your brothers and sisters? Were they going to school, working, etc.? What were some of the chores your parents asked you to do as a child? Which ones did you dislike most?

What odd jobs did you do to earn money especially during summer vacations? Was this the town you were born in? How many years did you live there?

What holiday was the most fun for you?

Here's how a mother has described her children's early school days. Perhaps her remembrances will spark you: "I see lovely homemade Valentines, bruised knees, lots of homework, report cards, PTA meetings, athletic events, Memorial Day parades, Girl Scout cookies, surprise gifts, band and choral concerts, bouquets of dandelions and marigolds, Halloween treats, and dozens of children playing on the 'green, green grass of home.'"

A MEMOIRIST WRITES:

This man vividly recalls the highlights of his school days with a natural style that keeps the episode moving. One can easily identify with his little stories. His sense of humor makes his chapter all the more entertaining. His poetry and quotes add variety to his writing. Children often express a desire to know more about the childhood of their parents. This memoir writer tells his children a good deal about his youth, and he does it with considerable candor.

"Memories of My Elementary School Days"

I recall looking forward to starting school eagerly. I was not disappointed, although it was not exactly what I had expected.

My first grade teacher, Mrs. Towns, was a small, very trim woman whereas I had expected a much larger person who would be able to "handle" me physically when I began to give problems. We had a great year at the West Main Street grade school in Ravenna, Ohio, when I began there.

I've forgotten the name of my second grade teacher, but I can never forget the atmosphere that surrounded her. It made a lifelong impression on me. She was a Catholic and opened each day with a prayer that made me *want* to behave myself. I felt almost as if I was in the presence of God Himself in her room. Needless to say we had a good year. I missed this tender, loving care as I entered the third grade and began to lose interest in classroom studies and my mind started to wander to outside interests.

One thing that led to this, I believe, was the location of our home town which was near Akron where the Goodyear Rubber Company was experimenting with lighter-than-air craft called dirigibles. There was nearly always one of them to be seen in the sky and I was overwhelmed by the great size, shape and beauty of these sleek ships of the skies.

While others in the class were deep in thought, my imagination would let me silently float out the open window where I could be as free as those blimps—free to wander at will to the most exotic places.

"GEORGE!" came my teacher's loud voice, and my dream was shattered. It broke the stillness and I was back in my seat again in the classroom.

Soon the temptation to find relief from my boredom in school began to take on more radical forms. I am reminded of several verses in Edgar A. Guest's poem "Playing Hookey."

> I remember when in boyhood
> Just a step advanced from toyhood
> When in through my schoolroom window
> Floated sweet the wild bird's call.
>
> I would close my desk at dinner
> Like a hardened little sinner
> And the afternooning found me
> Playing hookey from it all.

On another occasion I missed school without realizing it. It was circus day in Ravenna and I was walking back to school after going home for lunch. The parade was on and it went right past the school. I was so fascinated watching the clowns perform on one of the floats that I walked by the school without even seeing it. I continued on to the circus grounds and was sitting in the bleachers observing all the activities when a schoolmate placed a hand on my knee and shouted, "GEORGE!" I came back to consciousness of my real surroundings with a thud and ran all the way back to the school. This time, though, instead of receiving stern discipline everyone had a good laugh.

I got poorer and poorer grades. My father managed a cooper shop with plenty of barrel staves and he knew how to use them in his calling as a father. He gave me many a whipping after I got home from school where I had already been whipped before leaving. I can remember his accompanying remark: "Now son, this is going to hurt me more than it will you." Not until I was a father myself, many years later, was I able to comprehend the meaning of this ludicrous remark.

Had a vote been taken in our class at that time I would have won the distinction of being "The Least Likely to Succeed." Of course I failed to pass at the end of the term and had to take the third grade over again the following year. Overcrowded schools caused me to be transferred to Grant School for my fourth grade, so named because Jesse R. Grant, father of Ulysses S. Grant, had owned the one-room building at one time, and operated a leather goods store there.

Our family was so poverty-stricken in those days that while in the fifth grade I had no underwear. I wore hand-me-down clothing from my older brother Chuck. Many times I didn't even have a shirt so I would put on one of Dad's coats using a safety pin to close it all the way up to my neck. I would not open it all day for any reason. When we went out to the playground at recess I would wait around in order to be last in line to walk up the fire escape steps as I had no seat in my ragged trousers. Neighbors would have helped, but my stepmother was too haughty to accept charity from anyone.

I was getting more than a formal education at this time. The cold, hard facts of experience were beginning to make their impressions on me. One incident in particular stands out in my memory, like a lighthouse in the fog. A coal-burning heater warmed our living room in the long, cold winter evenings and on one occasion, when the coal pail became empty my father ordered Chuck, my older brother, to go refill it.

But Chuck, thinking of that long, dark trip down into the cellar to the coal bin and back, answered, "George'll get it." This aroused me. I responded hotly with, "Why me? Dad told you to get it." Maneuvering into a position where Dad couldn't see, but I could, Chuck showed me his clenched fist. I got the message and meekly replied, "I'll get it, Dad."

As I entered that dungeon to fill the coal pail that night I kept repeating, "For God so loved the world that He gave His only begotten Son that whosoever believeth in Him might not perish, but have everlasting life." I was glad that I had been to Sunday School and I am so glad an appreciation for the Church and its workers was stamped upon my young life. It has stabilized me throughout my lifetime.

Another experience in the home also taught me a great lesson of life. My younger brother Paul, at that time a toddler, seemed to be everywhere at once and everyone else in the family started shouting at him to get out of their road. Finally, Paul stopped, threw back his shoulders and shouted back, "Where's *my* road? Don't I got no road?"

This bit of philosophy caused me to start meditating on the question of, "Do each of us indeed have a road of our own to travel, or must we always seem to be in somebody else's road?"

Entering the sixth grade I began to sense the need of attention, especially from girls. The Ford Seed Company owned a large tract of farmland adjoining our property where they raised many varieties of beautiful flowers just to harvest the bulbs for sale to their customers. They let many blooms wither away and die. So I asked the caretaker if I could have some of the flowers. He told me to take all I wanted.

Filling up my big 4-coaster wagon with the most beautiful of these blooms in season I would haul them a mile and a half to my school—daffodils, tulips, dahlias and the like, passing them out to the girls and giving the rest to the teachers. Did I ever get attention!

You might say I passed that year with flying colors.

WRITING POINTERS: 13-16

13. *You can go to the typewriter too soon.* Writing will come easier for you if you first *think* about your material. Once you have collected your notes, allow a period of incubation and gestation. Let that remarkable gift—your subconscious—go to work for you. Soon ideas will pop out of it on how to approach this piece of writing. Carpenters have a saying, "Measure twice and saw once." Go over your notes, organize them in your mind, then go on to your writing.

14. *Keep it simple.* Use simple, easily understood words. They will help you to express yourself clearly, and your meaning will be better understood by the reader. Don't use a long word when a short one will do. Don't use two words where one will do. Use the familiar word. Avoid the complex. Choose a natural way of saying it. Commenting on clear writing, George W. Ball, a former Undersecretary of State, once said, "I persist in my simple faith that the unadorned declarative sentence is one of man's noblest architectural achievements."

One of the many myths about writing that persists is that big words are a sign of good writing. Nothing could be further from the truth. Abraham Lincoln delivered his Gettysburg address over a hundred years ago, yet his warm and simple words have come down through the years as one of the finest pieces of writing in our literature. "The world will little note, nor long remember, what we say here," he said, "but it can never forget what they did here." The world *has* noted because of the clarity and sincerity of Lincoln's language.

15. *Avoid overloading sentences.* Beginners tend to do this. They try to put too many thoughts into a single sentence. In doing this they lose their readers. Often when I encounter these overloaded sentences, I find it easy to break them up into two or more sentences. You can, too. It has been said that the best sentence is usually the shortest. I hasten to add that this doesn't mean that one telegraphic sentence should follow another. That would make your copy monotonous. You should vary the structure and length of your sentences. Gradually you will achieve a rhythm in your sentences. Generally speaking, a short sentence might contain about 15 words or less, a medium sentence from 15 to 30 words, and a long sentence, 30 or more words.

16. *Don't switch tenses.* Changing tenses in midcopy is not only confusing to the reader, it is also bad form. The best tense for a memoir is the past tense: "We moved to San Francisco on May 17, 1946." Of course, if you are quoting someone who speaks in the present tense you have to go along with it. If you should choose to use the present tense in one of your episodes to create an intimate or dramatic tone, then you should stay with that tense throughout that episode.

10

The Key to Writing Success

A FEW YEARS AGO John Kelley (the elder) finished his 50th running of the 26-mile Boston Marathon. He was then 73. After the race he was interviewed by reporters.

"What keeps you going like this?" he was asked.

Kelley mopped his brow and replied: "I believe in the 3 Ds."

"What are the 3 Ds?"

"Desire, dedication, and determination," he replied.

Most successful professional writers possess the 3 Ds. They know how to make time, how to set up a schedule, and they have the determination to stick to it. If you possess these qualities you will most certainly succeed in completing your memoir, and you will do it sooner. Do you remember this little poem?

> God gave us two ends,
> One to sit on and one to think with;
> Success depends on which end we use the most;
> Heads we win, tails we lose.

The fact that you are holding this book in your hands indicates that you have the desire to write your memoirs as a gift for your family. Now add dedication and determination and you are on your way. Here are seven tips that can help you to make time, and to use it more productively:

ORDER YOUR PRIORITIES.

Time is the precious stuff of life. However, there are too many distractions around nowadays that can rob us of time. We need to simplify our lives, to get down to essentials. One way of sorting out activities that eat up our time is to keep an hour-by-hour record of what we do for an entire week during our waking hours. The little chart that follows will help you to do this. Fill one out for each day. Seeing your week's activities at a glance on a piece of paper makes it easier for you to decide what is and what is not important in your life.

ACTIVITY RECORD

Activity	Date:
8-9 A.M.	
9-10	
10-11	
11-12	
12-1 P.M.	
1-2	
2-3	
3-4	
4-5	
5-6	
Later	

Now, having thrown out the unessential, set up a "Must Do" list of the important things you want to do. Place the most important one at the top and list the rest in order of priority. Then tackle one at a time starting at the top and think only of that one until you've completed it. Once you have set up this kind of a list you will find that you have avoided that swamped feeling, and the anxiety that goes with it.

Surely you will place the completion of your memoir high on your "Must Do" list. After all, it is a project you undertake only once in a lifetime.

SET UP A WRITING PLAN, AND THEN WORK YOUR PLAN.

The pros do this. If they didn't most of what you read wouldn't be in print. During what part of the day does your mind work most clearly? Are you a "Lark" (an A.M. person), or a "Nightingale" (a P.M. person)? Or are you perhaps an "Owl," a person who likes to work in the quiet of the wee hours? Decide on the hours when you can be most creative. Then pick one day of the week and write at that time. You need only schedule yourself for two or three hours, one or two days a week, for your memoir work. But regularity is the key.

If you stick to your schedule you will find that your writing will come more easily. This is a case where what looks like the hard way is really the easy way. Regularity not only helps you to write better, it also keeps you from going "cold" on your subject. When you put it down and pick it up, after skipping weeks, you have a lot of wasteful catching up to do.

So go to your calendar and make an appointment with yourself for one day each week of the month. Pencil it in: "9 to Noon, Memoir Writing Time."

CLOSE THE DOOR.

Writing is a personal matter. You have to do it alone. Set up a quiet, comfortable writing nook somewhere in your home. Take your shoes off if that makes you feel more relaxed. I do when I'm writing. Take the telephone off the hook, or have someone else answer it. Don't let anything interrupt you during the few hours you have set aside for this creative effort. The Russian composer Tchaikovsky recognized the need to create without distraction and he meticulously hoarded his time. He had a villa outside of Moscow, and the story is told that he put up a sign: "P. I. Tchaikovsky, Receives Monday and Thursday, 3 to 5. Otherwise not at home. Please do not ring." You do not have to be that exclusive but you do need to cherish every hour of your time and to put it to good use.

CLEAR THE WORK PLACE.

Avoid clutter. Keep a clear desk or writing table. Newspapers, magazines, correspondence, or other extraneous material at your elbow confuse and distract. You should see only your notes and other papers pertaining to the particular episode you are writing about. This helps you to focus down and to stay on track.

THINK AHEAD.

Each week, perhaps on the weekend, decide what one chapter in your life you will write about next. This will tune in your mental "computer." Say you have decided to write a paper on how you met your spouse. Before you know it you will be jotting down things you remember about your courtship. Then, when you get to your scheduled writing time, you can plunge in. You know the subject and you have given it thought in advance. Now you're ready to *get it down.*

KEEP A WRITING RECORD.

If you do this you will be encouraged, if not surprised, at the progress you are making. Seeing what you have already written, at a glance, will inspire you to do more.

Set aside a page in front of your notebook for your Writing Record. Here's how you might set it up:

MY MEMOIR WRITING RECORD

Week No.	Date	Subject	Hours of Writing Time	Pages Finished
1	Apr. 2, 1985	Birth	3	3

SET YOURSELF A DEADLINE.

Many writers work better with deadlines. I think it wise for you to set yourself a reasonable date for the completion of your memoir. What that date will be depends on a number of things: how long your memoir will run, the number of hours you devote to it each week, and how well you stick to your schedule. I have seen a few memoirs completed in eight weeks. On the other hand, where there have been interruptions, I know people who have taken a year or more. Some memoirs run 50 pages (on $8\frac{1}{2} \times 11$-inch pages, typed, double-spaced). Others have gone two and three times as long.

A professional writer can turn out a nonfiction book of average length in about a year. My own feeling is that a beginning writer who adheres to a schedule should be able to turn out a memoir of average length for his family in about six months. If you work only one day a week, producing only three typewritten pages (or the equivalent) you will have produced 78 pages in six months (26 weeks), an ample size for the average memoir. Writing one more page of copy a week could shorten this time of completion.

I hope I have given you enough of a guide to set your own deadline. Whether or not you finish "on the button" you will find that setting a goal in advance will help you to be more productive.

11

Writing Bite #5—Your Teen Years

Memory Sparkers (About age 13-19)

> It is not possible for civilization
> to flow backwards while there is
> youth in the world.
>
> —Helen Keller

WHAT WERE YOU like as a teenager? What impression does your family have of you as a teenager?

As you look back, would you say your teen years were your most difficult ones? Or the most fun? Did you have trouble "finding yourself"?

What are some of the things that happened in your teens that you remember to this day? Embarrassing, funny, sad, or otherwise?

What was your family life like at this time? What work was your father in? Did you resent authority? How did you get along with your parents, brothers, and sisters? Were you close to your relatives?

What were some of the rules your parents set up for you in your home?

How did you like school during these years? What were your favorite subjects? What school activities did you take part in? Did you receive any special honors? What teachers do you especially remember? Who were your special friends?

How did you spend Saturday nights or Sundays as a teenager?

What part-time jobs did you do for extra money? Which was your first? Which was the one you liked the best? Tell about it—the pay, the hours, your feelings. Did any of these jobs lead to something bigger for you?

Did you date much? Where did you go, what did you do? How much did you spend? What was your parents' attitude regarding dating? How did you learn about the sex facts of life?

During this period can you pick out one or two people who had the greatest influence on your life? Tell about them. How did they help you?

Who were your idols during these years? In sports, in the movies, in school, in your neighborhood, etc.

What was it like when you went to the movies then? How often did you go? What was the price of admission? What kind of movies did you like most?

What were your favorite sports, hobbies as a youth? What did you excel in?

Did you like dancing? What kind? Who taught you? What was your favorite kind of music? Did you sing or learn to play an instrument?

Can you remember how you learned to drive a car? Describe this. Whose car was it? What kind? Who taught you to drive? Where did you go?

Were you particularly conscious of your appearance at this time—your clothes, your hair, etc.? What did you do about it? What did you most like or dislike about yourself?

Was your family religious? Were you? Did you go to church on Sunday? Have your feelings about religion changed since then?

A MEMOIRIST WRITES:

The author Thomas Wolfe wrote a book entitled *You Can't Go Home Again* implying that when you do, after a long time, it is never the same. This memoir writer, using an imaginative approach, decided to go back to the scene of his youth to write this episode. The result is a very moving, nostalgic piece that conveys a picture of an era gone by. His writing is simple, yet powerful. Note that he has chosen a theme for this chapter and that he does not stray from it. Sometime after he wrote this I learned that he had passed away while on a summer visit to friends in the Midwest. Yes, he had by then completed his memoir for his family. When I asked his widow later for permission to include his piece in this book she replied, "Yes, he would have liked that."

"The Teenage Street I Once Knew"

I stood upon a street where, sixty years ago, I lived my teenage years.

One block south was a boulevard, profuse with shrubs and trees, where we would often lazily loaf on summer days and share our youthful dreams.

One block north was a quiet, yet busy street of small family-owned shops where the butcher might give you a free slice of salami or where, at the grocer's, you could buy a large spicy dill pickle for a penny, right out of the big wooden barrel.

Six blocks to the east, which we trudged with dragging feet and frequent moans, was our old grammar school. Here were learned not only our ABCs but also woodworking and printing.

Six blocks west, and how much shorter they seemed now, was our nickel movie house. Here, with thrills of joy, we went each Saturday matinee to see what happened to our serial Hero who had just fallen off a cliff the Saturday before.

Thus, bounded on all sides, our world bloomed. No asphalt jungle this, but a peaceful area of close-set homes with a few having two flats for accent. It was a place ruled by a combination of sternness and love.

Long before the United Nations was conceived, we had it. Jew, Gentile, Catholic, Aryan, Latin, Slav. It made no difference to us. We asked not race or creed, only who had the bat and ball. New families in the block brought us but one concern—was there a boy our age and how well could he pitch.

Such was the block I knew. But now it is no more. The street on which we played seemed narrower now, compressed still more by cars, parked bumper to bumper at both aging curbs. The cars were aging, too, as were the once well-cared-for houses.

Yet once this street was free, free to use as our baseball diamond, except for a chugging Ford or a high-wheeled dray that might stop our game momentarily, giving our underhand pitcher a minute's rest.

Our bases were marked by pilfered bricks. First and third hugged opposite curbs while second and home stood dangerously in the street's center.

Our out-of-bounds, being automatic outs, were the kerchief-sized lawns that patiently withstood our many transgressions.

So life, and our game, flowed on, accented at modest intervals by broken glass and fleeing feet, to be later rectified by pennies we collected for payment and hat-in-hand apologies.

Now as I look back I can but wonder. Where are the teenagers today? Where do they play? Not on this street to be sure, so closely clenched within the fist of automation and strangling in neglected decay.

I asked the buildings, which I once knew as being brightly scrubbed and whitely trimmed, what had happened. Where were the boys, and the girls, too, who wheeled creaky carriages to and fro, and marked their hopscotch on the walks with worn-out arc-light carbons?

But the buildings stood in silence, looking back at me through grimy dull-paned eyes. Yet I knew these buildings were alive. I knew they contained more humanity than in my youth.

But humanity in what sense? The real humanity of life, love and laughter, as I had known? This I can not say. I only know that life, for me, was good in those teenage years as I carefully put my street back in the soft cotton batting of my youthful dreams.

WRITING POINTERS: 17-20

17. *Watch your paragraphing.* Solid blocks of writing on a page make it difficult for the reader. I have seen entire pages of a manuscript without a single new paragraph. White space gives the reader eye relief; it makes it easier for him to grasp your thoughts. A paragraph is a distinct portion of your writing that deals with a particular point. In it you state your idea, you explain it, and you

conclude. Your idea may require a number of subparagraphs and that is fine. When you come to a new idea, or an aspect of it, pause for a paragraph. Try for at least three or four paragraphs to a page.

18. *Five more tips on how to get unstuck.* They call it "writer's block." Erma Bombeck once described it as that time when your fingers show up for work but your mind is out to lunch. I have never taken this alleged hindrance to creativity seriously. Most memoir writers I have worked with have not had this problem.

I have already mentioned one technique that will ease you into your writing—pretending you are writing it as a letter to a member of your family or a friend. Here, just in case you need them, are five more tips on how to get unstuck:

- Throw out the critical you. Let your words and ideas rush in. Don't reject what you want to say too soon.

- Skip a difficult part and go on. Come back to it later when you are fresh.

- Reread what you wrote yesterday. Or read passages from a book by your favorite author before you start.

- Limber up. Somerset Maugham, when he had trouble starting, would type his name over and over again on a blank page. Try stream-of-consciousness writing (whatever comes into your mind) but do it for no more than five or ten minutes.

- Set up the diving board so you can plunge right in the next time. Stop in the middle of a paragraph you can easily finish when you begin again. Or, leave yourself instructions as to where you are to start the next time.

19. *Avoid clichés.* To keep your writing fresh try to stay away from hackneyed phrases and clichés such as "cool as a cucumber"; "light as a feather"; "like two peas in a pod"; "happy as a clam at high tide"; and "right as rain." These are stale phrases used by others. Dare to be original. Say things with your own words in your own way. That will make your copy more interesting, and your reader will see more of you.

20. *Never lose sight of your reader.* Sometimes we get so absorbed in our writing that we forget our reader. Then we go off the track. Constantly keeping the reader in mind helps you to aim your writing better. If you do this you will find that you will explain things better as you go along. Another thing happens—you begin to anticipate questions your reader might have. In answering them in your copy you most certainly will capture his or her attention.

12

The Outline—a Valuable Tool

IT HAS BEEN SAID that when the gifted Michelangelo started a sculpture, he would look at the block of marble before him and "see" the figure in it that he wished to create. Then he would set to work with his chisels to bring that figure to life. Similarly, when he painted, he first sketched the rough outlines of his proposed art on his canvas.

The writer, too, needs to visualize beforehand the outlines of what he proposes to write. Most writers I know prepare an outline in advance of some kind, even if it is one that they keep in their heads. When you are writing a longer piece, such as an article, a chapter in a book, or a memoir episode, some kind of outline is a must. Simple or detailed, it helps to organize your thoughts and to make your writing flow more easily. It eliminates the groping and resultant frustration. With an outline you know where your writing is going.

Keep in mind, however, that there is nothing rigid about the outline you prepare. Regard it as a guide, a road map. As you write you may find that you will want to make detours, putting this segment up higher, or inserting that paragraph down lower. Or, you may want to include an entirely new thought that just occurred to you.

There are many ways to prepare an outline. Here are five versions. I urge you to use one, or some variation of one. I assure you that an outline will be well worth your time.

HEN SCRATCHES ON A PAD.

News reporters often use this method when not taping an interview. As memories occur to you about the particular episode you are writing on, scratch out key phrases or sentences on a pad or sheet of paper. As you start to write, all your reminder notes are there before you and you can work them into your copy as you go. I use this method on short pieces. I take a legal-sized yellow pad and scatter phrases around the page at different angles so they will stand out. I use a red pen for very important ideas and a black pen for the rest. I use all capitals on some key words, and upper and lower case on others. As I work each thought into my copy, I cross it out. I often have leftover phrases I decided not to use.

THE PASTE-UP OUTLINE.

Here you write each of your notes on separate slips of paper (I like 3x5-inch memo sheets that come in pads or boxes of 100). Then you paste them down on a long sheet in the sequence you wish to follow as you write.

THE BALLOON OUTLINE.

I like to use this one when writing articles. I'm sure you are familiar with the balloons in comic strips that carry the dialogue. I take a yellow pad, put the working title of my article at the top, and then make balloons all the way down the page, connecting them in the order I plan to write. Then I insert my key phrases in each balloon.

Here's how, using this balloon method, one might outline the memoirist's episode that appears at the end of the next chapter: "The Walk That Changed My Life." The notes for fleshing this outline out would, of course, be on a separate scratch sheet at the writer's side. (See following page.)

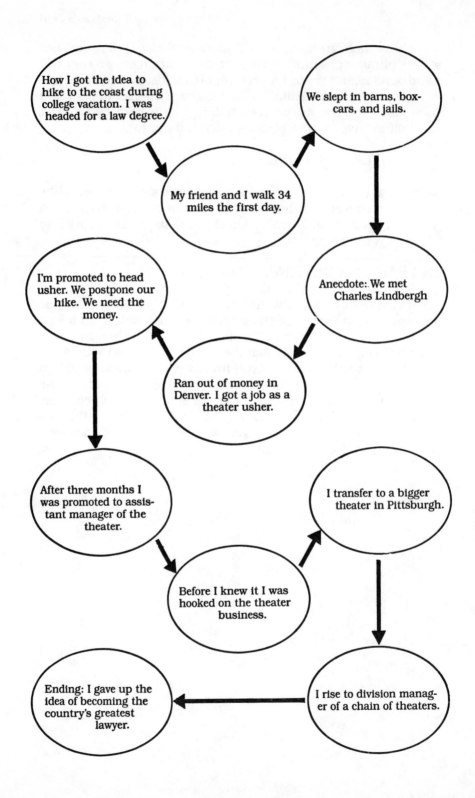

THE FORMAL OUTLINE.

Having decided on your subject you now break it down into parts, one under the other: the title, the lead, and then the subtopics. Each subtopic is given a number and each gets an outline of its own. Again either reminder key phrases or sentences are used on each line. This is the skeleton on which you will proceed to build your episode.

THE SPOKES OF A WHEEL OUTLINE.

Here you take a sheet of paper and draw the rough outline of a wagon wheel with its hub in the middle of the page. Place your intended title for the episode in the middle of the hub. Then write your key phrases or sentences along each spoke of the wheel going around the hub in what appears to be the best pattern for you. In this way your notes are neatly arranged in a circle and are visible to you at a glance.

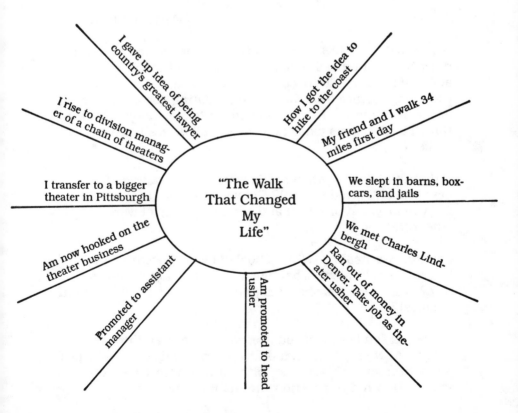

13

Writing Bite #6—Your Young Adult Years

My salad days,
When I was green in judgment.
—William Shakespeare

"DECISIONS, DECISIONS." That's how one memoir writer has described that crucial time in life when you leave your teens and enter young adulthood. Schooling, housing, finances, a car, independence from family, dress, dating, jobs, deliberating on a career and the future—all enter into our thoughts at this time. The decisions made here could well have shaped your later life.

Did you finish high school? Did you go on to college? A business school? A trade school? Did you enter military service? Did you drop out of school and enter the world of work? Any other direction?

Continued schooling: What school did you choose? Why? Where was it located? What major or what subjects did you take? What were your best subjects? What teachers helped you the most?

Where did you live? Did you work to put yourself through this school? At what jobs? What did you earn? Did your family help you with finances? Were they pleased with your choice of school? How did you spend your summer vacations?

Were you active in any sports, clubs, plays, or other extracurricular activities? Did you make many friends? Who were special friends?

What was life like in school? Did you enjoy it? What level of schooling did you enjoy the most? Did you do much dating in school? Did you meet your mate there? (More on this in the next life stage, "Early Marriage Years.")

Did you receive any special honors in school? What was said about you in your school yearbook? Did you graduate? With what degree or certificate? If not, tell what happened. What do you think this higher schooling did for you?

Have you ever been back for a class reunion? What graduation day stands out the most in your life? Why? Was your family very proud? Was it a real "commencement"?

Do you recall what goals you set for yourself during these years? How close did you come to realizing your dreams? Were you very idealistic then? How did those ideals fare in the light of later experience? Did you think about politics or causes then?

Military Service: What branch were you in? Why did you go in? How long did you serve? Where were you living when you entered the service? Where did you undergo basic training? Where did you travel to in the military? What was your rank? Your pay? What were your duties? Were you in combat? Where? Did you study while in service? What? Did you continue your education on the G.I. Bill? Looking back, how do you value your military service? Was it helpful to you?

The world of work: Why did you leave school? What were the circumstances at home? What job did you take? Where? Doing what? What were you earning? Did you help at home?

Did you like this job or did you move on to others? (More on this in the upcoming "Early Career Years.")

Were you living at home or away? If at home, what was your family life like? What advice did your parents give you? What rules of the house did they have? Did you have brothers and sisters? Were they going to school, working?

Who were your best friends in those days? What sort of leisure things did you do?

A MEMOIRIST WRITES:

In writing about his young adult years this writer has put his finger on a very crucial episode in his life. Fate knocked and he responded. He has dramatized this experience with an excellent title. Note how well the story flows, as natural as though he is writing a letter to his family. Note, too, that he is comfortable in using the pronoun "I." Some beginners shy away from it. His story builds with pertinent details as he goes, thus holding the reader's interest.

"The Walk That Changed My Life"

I was a young man attending the University of Chicago and when summer came I returned to my home in Milwaukee, Wisconsin.

The past several years had been very strenuous both mentally and physically. I had been taking pre-law courses in the morning and during the afternoons and weekends I was selling Fuller brushes.

One day as I was reading in the public library, I picked up a book about a man who had spent a lot of time hiking around the country. I became so fascinated with his adventures that I said to myself "Why don't I do that?" I had decided to continue my law education at Stanford University in California and I decided I would get there by hiking. I talked it over with my buddy, who was a bank teller, and he was agreeable to starting out with me. Our parents and friends thought we were crazy, but that did not deter us.

We went to the Mayor's office in Milwaukee and asked if he would give us a letter stating that we were respectable citizens and that he would appreciate any courtesies that might be extended to us. He was happy to give us such a letter, which attested to the fact that we were not vagrants, when we told him we expected to send back accounts of our progress to our local paper.

In the spring my friend George and I, with signs on our backs reading "Lakes to Coast," started on our eventful journey of approximately 2,000 miles. The weather was clear and cold. We were dedicated to hiking and not to accepting rides, except in emergencies.

At 9 P.M. that first night we reached Oconomowoc, Wisconsin, 34 miles from Milwaukee. We were both foot-sore and exhausted and stretched out on benches in the railroad station. We fell asleep only to be awakened a short time later by the police who took us to the station. After reading the letter from our Mayor we were treated with respect and invited to spend our first night out in a jail cell as guests of the city. The next morning we were treated to a breakfast by the police which was most wel-come. After friendly goodbyes and best wishes we started on the second day of our journey. The day was eventful, as were all the days of our hike.

Two days later we reached Madison where we present-ed our credentials and were ushered into the office of the Governor who gave us a warm welcome. Upon leaving he gave us a letter of introduction to the Governor of Califor-nia, presenting his personal respects. We felt flattered and grateful.

We averaged 35 to 40 miles a day. Since we had very limited resources we slept in barns, boxcars, jails and on gym mats in various YMCAs, as well as on the ground. We were invited into some farm homes for lunch and bought bread at bakeries.

On the eighth day we crossed the Mississippi at Du-buque, Iowa. News of our hike preceded our arrival and newspaper reporters met us. They ran a story and we were treated as celebrities. As we walked through the town people stopped to talk with us and to ask ques-tions. It was a warm feeling for us. Since our finances were very low we remained for a week doing landscape work for one dollar a day.

We hiked on and reached Omaha three weeks from the time we started. We bussed and washed dishes for our meals at the YMCA and slept on their gym mats. We picked up several odd jobs to replenish our lean exche-quer.

One night in front of the YMCA, a young man joined us and introduced himself as Charles Lindbergh. I remem-bered his name because I found out that we were both Scandinavians. He said that he was a mail pilot and had watched our progress from day to day as he flew over us from Chicago along the highway. It gave us a cheery feel-ing that our progress was being watched from the air.

Finally we reached Denver, Colorado. We slept at the

YMCA on gym mats for a few days and bussed and washed dishes for our meals. We decided to stay a few weeks and I got a job as an usher at the Isis Theater on Curtis Street—Denver's Great White Way. It was called that because the fronts of all the theaters for three blocks were covered with electric lights. My partner got a job at a bank so we were able to afford renting a room.

After ushering for a week I made such an impression on the manager that he promoted me to head usher and raised my salary from $10 to $14 a week. In the weeks to come I began to enjoy the motion picture theater business. The Isis was the flagship of the four theaters in the Fox circuit in Denver.

My buddy and I decided to postpone the balance of our hike to the coast for several months to build up our capital. We finally earned enough money so that we were able to buy suits at a second hand store.

After three months as chief usher I was promoted to Assistant Manager at the Rivoli Theater which had been closed for the summer and was reopening with top new feature attractions for the fall and winter season.

Three months after being at the Rivoli I was given my first managerial position at the Strand Theater, and three months later I was transferred to our Plaza theater. A year after starting as usher at the Isis theater I returned there as manager because the current manager was transferred to New York.

By this time I was earning the munificent sum of $35 per week which in those days was a handsome salary. My buddy became homesick and returned to Milwaukee. I was still determined to go to Stanford to get my law degree but I kept postponing it and before I knew it I became "hooked" in the theater business.

After two years my boss accepted a position in a Loew's theater in Pittsburgh which produced big stage shows and presented top national stars. Soon he wired me to join him as Assistant Manager and I accepted, starting an exciting career with Loew's Theaters that lasted for the next 45 years.

Thus, a young man who yearned to be the country's greatest lawyer became a veteran Theater man who rose from usher to Division manager.

WRITING POINTERS: 21-24

21. *Get people into your life story.* People have a great interest in people. We are fascinated by the lives of our fellow human beings. This accounts for the great popularity of biography and autobiography. You have encountered many people during your lifetime and many have meant a great deal to you. Why not recognize them in your memoir by paying tribute to them, or by giving them credit for what they contributed to your life? Also, it is said that the sweetest sound is the sound of one's own name. Your relatives would love to see their names in your pages.

22. *Use complete sentences.* A sentence, too, has a beginning, a middle, and an end—the subject, the verb, and what follows the verb. Sometimes when we get careless, or when we write as we speak in conversation we may use a sort of shorthand English: "Went on then to Los Angeles." "Talked to my mother about it." "Wish we were back in Massachusetts." These sentences are incomplete because they lack a subject. This is improper grammar that can confuse the reader and fail to communicate clearly.

Until now I have not discussed the subject of *grammar*, the science that deals with the way language works. There's a reason for that. I want you to give your highest priority now to content, to getting down on paper the essential facts of your life. Whether you know it or not by this time in your life you have absorbed a working knowledge of how to arrange words in combinations in order to communicate your thoughts to others.

Don't let the subject of grammar scare you. No one is perfect at it. Our language is subject to frequent change. Even those who teach and write English have a difficult time keeping up with it. Editors do, too. I learn something about grammar every time I sit down to write. I've forgotten most of those grammatical terms I've learned in school such as the "introductory adverb clause," "a dangling participle," or "a subordinating conjunction." You probably have, too. I think you can do pretty well with English without knowing all those terms. I certainly don't think of them when I write. I just apply some of the rules of grammar instinctively, and I think that is true of most other writers.

In writing your life story you should strive for a reasonable standard of good English. Well-turned-out sentences and paragraphs that convey your meaning clearly not only give you creative gratification, they also make an impression on your descendants. The language a person uses tells you something about that person. Besides, since your story will undoubtedly have a long life in your family, you surely want it to be clear in meaning no matter when it is read and by whom.

Many of the Writing Pointers in this book have been designed to guide you in the path of better English usage. The simpler you write the less trouble you will have with grammar. Reading good authors and listening to good speakers can be helpful. In the next Writing Pointer I have suggested that you read your finished episodes aloud so your ear can help you to catch errors.

There are a number of good books on grammar it would be worth your while to consult. Start with that little classic written by William Strunk and E. B. White, *The Elements of Style*. *Errors in English* by Harry Shaw is a handy quick-reference guide to correct usage, sentence structure, and many other features of grammar. Jacques Barzun's *Simple and Direct* is another excellent guide to the art of writing what you mean. I have listed other worthwhile books in the Bibliography. Also, in the next chapter in my answer to a question I have suggested another step you should take before you "go to press" to ensure that you have used basic good English in your life story.

Who knows, someday a generation or two hence a descendant of yours may say, "He (or she) sure knew how to use the King's English."

23. *Read your sentences aloud.* Often, after you have written a sentence, you may have some doubt about it. The sentence may be lengthy or involved, or you aren't sure that it will be understandable. Try reading it out loud. Put your ear as well as your eyes to work. Or, put it on your tape recorder and play it back a few times. This is an excellent way to simplify awkward sentences.

24. *Try it another way.* Sometimes you find yourself trying to squeeze out a sentence and it just won't come. Get around the roadblock by trying it another way. Peg Bracken, author of *The I Hate to Cook Book*, recalls a writer who struggled with the sentence "That morning in the yard he saw two mongooses." It did not sound right so he changed it to "That morning in the yard he saw two mongeese." This still was not right so he tried it again: "That morning in the yard he saw a mongoose. Almost immediately then, he saw another mongoose."

"Surely there are ten ways of saying anything, everything," says biographer Catherine Drinker Bowen in her thoughtful book *Biography, The Craft and the Calling*. She cautions against regarding our every written word as sacred. You will find that being flexible pays off.

14

Questions I Am Often Asked

❧

Do I have to start my completed memoir with my birth?

Not necessarily. You could start with an episode that deals with a revealing turning point in your life, or one that you believe is especially dramatic. If you have written episodes on your mother and father or your grandparents you may wish to start with these and then pick up your own life.

I find that beginners are overly concerned about the final organization of their memoir, especially at first. Also about transitions. Of course there should be some general continuity that parallels the progress of your life. But if you have written each episode so that it stands on its own you will find, as you near completion, that you will instinctively place the episodes in a logical order. This is your memoir and it should reflect your own taste and judgment.

Should I get a "reader" to go over my copy?

Yes, but you should choose that person carefully. Remember that friends or relatives tend to overpraise, and others may criticize merely to impress you with their knowledge.

What you are looking for is impartial, objective criticism. Pick someone who cares about writing besides caring about you, such as an English teacher, a teacher of writing courses, or someone in your local writers' club. As you hand your edited manuscript to your reader (never show a first draft) ask specific questions. Are there any passages that will not be clearly understood? Are there any omissions or inaccuracies? Are any parts of the manuscript repetitious? What parts did you like best? Least? Are there any glaring errors of grammar or spelling?

You may want two people to read your memoir copy. However, bear in mind: They are not passing final judgment on what you have written. You are. Nor are they to tamper with your general style. In the end, pick and choose from the comments made only what *you* believe will strengthen the memoir—then discard the rest.

How long should my memoir run?

Abraham Lincoln was once asked how long a woman's skirt ought to be. He replied: "Long enough to cover the subject but short enough to be interesting." Lincoln's statement would be a good guide for any writer. However, the memoir writer does have a special freedom. He is writing for an audience that will love every word. He is writing a document that will become part of the family's history. The task here is far easier than that of the professional who is told by his editor that he is to provide a specified number of words.

An episode in a memoir can vary in length depending on its content. I have seen some that ran a page and a half, and some that ran to 30 pages. Too short is as bad as too long. A good rule of thumb is that what is most important receives the most space; what is least important receives the least space.

I was once asked by a man if 28 pages were too long for one of his episodes. After I read it I said, "No, it is not." He had written with great feeling about one of the most terrifying experiences of his life—the day a raging hurricane had swept away his family's home and everything they owned.

Don't be concerned with length in your first rough drafts. Let your thoughts flow forward without interruption. At times this can result in more length than you need. But I would rather be in that predicament than to be very lean. You can always edit your copy later to remove needless words and paragraphs, providing you have not fallen so much in love with them that they appear to be engraved forever on paper.

The length of the completed memoir can only reflect how active your life has been and how well you have described it. I have seen a memoir that ran 16 typed pages, stapled in one corner and handed out at a family reunion. One man had his printed and library bound. It ran to 105 printed pages. A mother of seven children completed her life story in 216 pages.

I recall one of my student writers who had lived a very active life here and had also worked in countries abroad. He decided to record his personal history in two volumes totaling over 300 typewritten pages. He titled it "A Backward Look at a Fulfilled Life." One day, after he had packaged his memoirs, my phone rang and he invited my wife and me to a reception in his home. At the proper time he assembled his many relatives (and their children) around the living room table where we had partaken of refreshments. He made a little speech and then very proudly presented each of his kin with autographed copies of his memoirs. He was 84 at the time. The love and the pride that I saw in that family's eyes that day will live with me forever.

I have seen memoirs that contained no photos or documents and some that included as many as 30 photos and six documents. One day a student showed me six packaged copies of her memoir. Each contained 52 photocopied pages and 11 family photos neatly arranged in a red-covered three-ring loose-leaf notebook. She told me they were to be gift-wrapped and presented to members of her family on her next visit.

Your completed memoir can be as big or as small as you want it to be. First and foremost, though, it should communicate the most important facts about your life and times. After you've written that, you should place at the end of the last sentence what a newspaper editor once called "the greatest literary device known to man," a dot like this.

Should I "write" my story on a tape recorder?

Unless you are a public person accustomed to speaking into a microphone, or someone especially skilled in verbal communication, I do not recommend this method. I believe you get more depth into your story when you sit down and write it. In writing it you think about it more. You work at your own pace. Also, it is easier to make changes, to reorganize your material, or to work in additional facts.

Of course, where because of age, infirmity, or injury to the hands, a person cannot manage to write it out, the tape recorder can be very useful.

Some memoir writers pick out a favorite episode they have written and read it into a tape recorder. They then turn that cassette over to relatives, along with the written memoir, so they will also have a record of their voice.

Should I include the tears as well as the laughter?

A woman in one of my classes described her 33 years of marriage this way: "Those 33 years were full of love and pregnancies and births, struggling and achieving, work and play, and the accompanying joys and sorrows."

Do you want your memoir to be interesting and readable? Then let it honestly reflect life as you lived and observed it. When the average person begins to write his or her life story there is a tendency to become self-conscious. Because of this holding back, some of the more human bits and pieces that round out one's personality are lost.

Candor adds human interest. The more you reveal of yourself the more readily your reader can identify with you. Constant sweetness in your copy may cause the reader to wonder if you have lived in the real world. That kind of treatment in either fiction or nonfiction would turn any editor off. Look at some of the most successful novels and you will find struggle, conflict, disappointment, obstacles, anger, suspense, and human problems that need to be resolved.

An artist does not paint his canvas with only one color. He uses many colors and his painting has contrasts and shadings. Reality is showing the warts as well as the dimples. All memories can't be sweet—some are bittersweet.

"Tell the bad news as well as the good," says Leonard L. Knott discussing autobiography in his book *Writing for the Joy of It*. "Don't worry about shocking the grandchildren. Kids are pretty near shockproof today. . . . Your grandchildren may love you—but they'll suspect you weren't a saint all your life, and they don't much like saints anyway."

In advocating that you let your hair down I am not referring to very personal, traumatic moments or circumstances in your life that you cannot bring forth. I simply suggest that you allow your reader to see you just as you were during those moments of give-and-take as you struggled through your life. I do not urge that you write anything that would hurt or embarrass others. There is also no need to include material that might provoke family quarrels. Nor is it necessary to name names or to be gory in a memoir. I have seen some of the most heartbreaking moments in a life described with balanced, tactful writing. Remember, you can use delicate language about an indelicate subject.

When you come to parts of your life that you find difficult to decide on, ask yourself questions like these: "How significant is this event in my life when I compare it to all the others?" "Has it changed the course of my life?" "Do I tend to exaggerate its importance?" "Is it something my family should really know about in order to understand me better?" "Is there some point I want to make here that could be a valuable lesson for my descendants?"

I recall a woman who included an account in her memoir of how her grandfather had come to lose a fortune at the hands of unscrupulous business partners. After he died, his partners had exploited his unsuspecting widow and before she knew it she had signed away the rights to everything he had owned, including the family home. This writer not only wanted her family to know about this but she was also saying in effect: "Beware how you manage your financial affairs as you go through life."

Sometimes a hurt or injustice we suffered in our past festers, and it comes to mind now as we go about preparing our life story. If it doesn't seem to go away perhaps there may be catharsis in writing it out in all its details and then placing it in your notebook, or in a desk drawer, to cool for a while. Such was the case of a man who had been fired by his boss early in his career. He had despised this boss and believed he was fired out of jealousy. Now in his later years the memory of this still rankled him. He asked me several times in class whether he should include an account of the incident. I could see from the expression on his face that it really bothered him, so I suggested he go ahead and put it to paper.

One day he handed me four pages on the subject. After reading it I penciled some of the questions I've posed above at the top of his paper. In the end he tore it up and went on to other segments of his life.

Can a husband and wife write their memoirs together?

I know many couples that have done just that. In doing it this way they give each other reinforcement, and get to learn a great deal more about each other.

Here are two ways for a couple to approach it: In the first method the partners work independently, starting at the beginning of their lives and progressing to the present. What happened before they met will be new material. What happened after they met on a given subject will be the point of view of each.

In the second method, a dual autobiography, the partners blueprint the pattern of proposed chapters in advance (the Writing Bite chapters in this book can be helpful here). They can then decide who will write what chapters. Where both want an input on a chapter, that part is prefaced with his or her name. This latter method was used by Will and Ariel Durant in their book *A Dual Autobiography.*

If you like sports you may want to read an unusual father and son dual autobiography, *A Farewell to Heroes,* authored by sportswriter Frank Graham, Jr. It deals with his and his father's life and the legendary sports heroes they had met. His father, Frank Graham, who had died many years before, was an eminent sports columnist and author.

In the book the lives of the living (the son) and the dead (the father) are brought together side by side. The younger Graham achieves this by first blueprinting chapters dealing with their lives. He then lets his father speak through appropriate columns he had written while he (Frank, Jr.) fills in his own chinks of memory. The result is a colorful autobiography of two lives in the same book.

(More questions are answered in Chapter 30.)

15

Writing Bite #7—Your Early Marriage Years

Memory Sparkers (About age 20-30)

> Marriages are made in heaven
> and consummated on earth.
>
> —John Lyly

CAN YOU VIVIDLY recall your wedding day? When and where did it take place? Describe your feelings. Who attended? Were you nervous? Did all the arrangements go smoothly? Sometimes the things that went wrong become memorable. Are you still in touch with members of your wedding party? Look through your wedding album for more sparkers.

How did you happen to meet your spouse? Was it love at first sight? What were you both doing at that time? How did you propose? (Or how were you proposed to?) Where? What was it that attracted you? How long was your courtship? Describe some of the things you did on dates.

Did your family like your intended spouse? What was the reaction of your parents when you told them you were getting married? How did brothers and sisters react? Your other relatives?

Did you have a honeymoon? For how long? Where did you go? How did you travel? Did you have good weather? What are some of the things you did? Did you take pictures? Did you spend a great deal of money?

In what ways were you and your spouse alike, different? Did

you find marriage a difficult adjustment? What was the first year of marriage like? What did you most have to overcome? Were you both working?

Did you begin your married life modestly in a small apartment? By renting or purchasing a home? Where? Were your relatives helpful? How did you happen to locate there? What were some of the first things you bought for your new home?

Were there children? How soon? How many? Name them. Where was each born? When? Who delivered them? Tell what changes took place in your household when they were born. Did the first children reject later ones? How did they get along? What were their personality differences?

How do you think you performed as a parent in these early years? If you had it to do all over again, what would your ideas about child-rearing be now?

Describe a few of the best rules you set up in your home for your children's discipline: chores, behavior, finances, dress, and so on. Were you a strict or permissive parent? Which rules did you have the biggest problem with?

If you did not have children, discuss your feelings about this. Was it by choice or circumstance? Explain. Do you regret not having had children?

If you did not marry describe what the single life was like. Were you single by choice or circumstance? Were there advantages in being single? Did you have family obligations? Were there periods of loneliness? Did you find making decisions alone difficult? Did you pursue a career? Doing what? Did you find your career satisfying? Did you miss having children?

Did you live at home or away from home? Where? If away, did you have a roommate? How did you meet? How did you get along? Did you share the rent? The cooking? How did you get along with your parents and other relatives?

What were your free-time activities? Music, reading, TV, the theater, art, dancing, sports, etc. Were you active in any groups? In church? Socially? In volunteer work? Did you have a car? Who were your friends? Where did you go to meet people? Did you travel? Where did you go on vacations?

A MEMOIRIST WRITES:

This woman tells the story of how she fell in love in an interesting manner. Note that she is quite candid in revealing her inner feelings. She uses natural language and takes you there by including the 5 Ws: who, what, when, where and why. She builds suspense as she goes and her subtle humor comes through in the telling. Her episode pivots nicely on the train ride and her title provokes just enough curiosity to make you want to read on.

"Sometimes It Pays To Miss A Train"

It certainly wasn't love at first sight between the Professor and me. He considered me a "high hat," the only student at Lynchburg College who didn't speak to him on campus. And, as far as I was concerned, he was just another teacher. This put the gulf between us as wide as the much-quoted generation gap. Yes, he was good-looking and young, though scarcely two years older than I. I had been out of school for two or three years.

In 1930 Lynchburg College at Lynchburg, Virginia, was very small. It had only 195 students, so by mid-October of that year the Professor, the new head of the Chemistry Department, knew most of the students by sight. It was then that something new was added: a strange female student who wouldn't speak to him.

At first I didn't know who he was. Being a month late in returning to college for my Junior year, I had missed the assembly at which the new professors were introduced to the student body. Later, noticing the good-looking young man with burnished brown hair, deep blue eyes and bouncy step, I asked a classmate who he was. She told me about him and the tragedy that had befallen him. On the opening day of school his young wife had died, the result of an embolism following childbirth.

Now I knew who he was but having once adopted my non-speaking policy I was loath to change it. One evening in January the famous Polish pianist, composer and statesman (once Prime Minister of Poland) Ignace Jan Paderewski gave a concert in Lynchburg. I had heard so much about him ever since I was little. This was a memorable event for me, an aspiring pianist, and I was quite excited over going to the concert. Nancy, a classmate and fellow music student who lived in town, was driving to the concert and she invited me to go with her. I was surprised when I saw her other two passengers, the Professor and his sister Dorothy, a freshman at the college.

Although Paderewski was then 71 years of age, he played a beautiful program. On the way back from the concert Nancy and I were extravagant in our praise. This meeting between the Professor and the "high hat" student did nothing to dispel the former's impression of me and certainly did not change my feeling toward him.

Easter vacation, spent with my mother in Washington, D.C., was a refreshing respite from my classes. At its close I went to Union Station to catch the train to Lynchburg. This particular train was on time, but I wasn't. Trains, like time and tide, wait for no man—or woman, either. Fortunately trains were plentiful in those days and I had only two hours or so to wait for the next one.

As I entered one of the coaches I looked around to see if there was someone else from the College on board with whom to pass the time during the five-hour journey. There were only two candidates: a big, beefy, not exactly refined, football player whom I disliked, and the Professor. I chose the Professor as the "lesser of two evils" and selected a seat directly in front of him. A few remarks now and a few remarks then soon grew into a friendly conversation. It wasn't long before the Professor came to sit with me. We chatted pleasantly as the miles rolled by. He told me that he had had a wonderful married life and showed me photos of his beautiful baby daughter, then about six months old.

Mother had packed sandwiches and cookies for me to eat on the train instead of spending scarce money for the dining car food. It was now time to eat and I was hungry. But what would the Professor think? Would sharing a sack lunch be beneath his dignity? I finally asked: "Would you be so plebeian as to share some chicken sandwiches with me?" He was and he did. (And many times since then he has teased me by repeating this question.)

After arriving in Lynchburg, the football player, the Professor and I took the same trolley car, which at that time went as far as the college gate. Although the Professor's stop arrived a half mile or so before the college he offered to go with me to carry my luggage to the dorm. I thought this was very thoughtful of him since he would then have to walk and carry his own luggage the half mile to his apartment. I thanked him but assured him that the football player could help me without much inconvenience.

To me, even after this journey together, the Professor was still just that, although a very pleasant and friendly one. However, I will always believe that missing my train was good luck instead of bad. It was a distinct turning point in both our lives. Without this train journey together it seems hardly likely that the two of us would have ever been more to each other than just a Professor and a music student who was decidedly "high hat."

Of course you know the ending. We were happily married.

WRITING POINTERS: 25-28

25. *Watch "downhill" writing.* Sometimes toward the end of a writing session we tend to get tired. When that happens our writing begins to lose its sharpness and it does not compare with what we wrote earlier. It is wise at this point to stop for the day and to pick it up the next time, when we are fresh. If you did finish an episode during the tail end of your last writing session, go over it the next time to see if it can be improved.

26. *Link your life story to history.* You have lived during a time of important historical events. When you link what was happening to you to such events you are positioning your life in time and place. The reader can then quickly comprehend the period of your lifespan. Who was President when you were born? (See list of U.S. Presidents and their terms in the Appendix.) When you graduated from high school? Where were you when Lindbergh crossed the Atlantic, when Prohibition ended, when the zeppelin *Hindenburg* was destroyed by fire, during the Great Depression, at the time of Pearl Harbor, D-Day in France, V-E and V-J Days, the stock market crash, the day President John Kennedy was shot, the day when U.S. astronaut Neil Armstrong became the first man to walk on the moon? When opportunity allows, you can add more color to your memoir by showing how your life has paralleled such important historical happenings.

27. *Are you comma-prone?* I've read many manuscripts written by beginners and if there is one punctuation mark that I see flying around in my sleep it is the comma. I think it is overused. When it is I believe it can puzzle the reader. Rather than rely on it to straighten out heavy sentences it is better to rewrite the sentence so that it flows forward with less interruption. The comma is appropriate to indicate a slight pause in the sentence. You can hear this pause if you read it out loud. Too many such pauses in the sen-

tence can slow down the flow of thought. Of course the comma comes in handy to separate words in a series, clauses, inserted parenthetical expressions, and parts of sentences that are out of their customary position. Some of these can be simplified by rewriting the sentence. I see many sentences that flow nicely when I eliminate the commas. Check the sentence. If it flows smoothly without the comma, eliminate it. The trend is toward fewer punctuation marks. You will find more on this subject in Harry Shaw's excellent book, *Punctuate It Right!*

28. *Get your feelings into it.* Your inner reaction to what has happened to you, how you perceive a situation, can help to give your memoir more warmth, depth, and meaning. Many of us, because of the times in which we were raised, deny our feelings. We find it difficult to reveal our inner thoughts, to express our emotions, beliefs, and attitudes. The memoir, written from the vantage point of a lifetime of experience, provides us with an ideal opportunity to express how we feel about life, love, and our loved ones. It provides us with a chance to say some of the things we have always wanted to say but never have. Here we can express our gratitude to those who gave us a boost along the way. Here, when opportunity presents itself, we can reveal our convictions regarding the world we live in, marriage, religion, health, death, relatives, friends, and life's values. The poet says, "Gather ye rosebuds while ye may." There is no time like the present. Trust your feelings—they are usually right. Allowing them to be reflected in your memoir will add another dimension to it.

16

Treasure Your Family Photos and Documents

SOME PEOPLE I MEET give their family photographs and documents tender love and care. Others, unfortunately not realizing their value, store them in old shoe boxes or in dusty attic trunks. Believe me, they deserve better.

PROTECTING YOUR PHOTOS.

First of all, family photographs are Memory Sparkers in themselves. The material in many a memoir has been forthcoming simply because a faded photo has triggered remembrances of days past. A photo is a living record. People and events are preserved in it. Photos should be carefully organized in plastic dust jackets in a 10 × 12-inch manila envelope or in an accordion file. These can be found at a stationery or office-supply store. File your photos and negatives (if you still have them) chronologically. Then decide which ones you will include in your memoir package. I have seen a few memoirs that did not have any photos (they were lacking), and others that included five, ten, twenty-five, and more snapshots.

Remember that you can have copies made of photos you treasure even though you do not have a negative. Your photography store can make a "copy negative." You can have old, faded photos retouched and renewed. Shop around for the best prices. Keep all of these precious photos you intend to use separate from the others.

Black-and-white photos last longer than color prints. Color prints and slides may fade in time. However, you can have a black-and-white print made from a color slide. It loses a bit in the translation but it still serves the same purpose. Some of the better copying machines reproduce photos surprisingly well. Ask your photocopying center to show you a sample.

Photos should be protected from sunlight, heat, insects, water, and excessive humidity. Keep them in a dry, cool, dark place. Keep them in transparent plastic sleeves that you can get at your photo store. Some are made to fit three-ring binders. Avoid using rubber cement or white pastes that contain water or penetrating solvents as these may come through your print. Mount your prints with adhesive sprays such as Kodak Rapid Mounting Cement or 3M's Photo Mount Spray Adhesive. These will not stain your prints. Avoid mounting your prints facing each other on opposite pages in a scrapbook if they are not under transparent vinyl sheets. Humidity could cause them to stick together. If you do not use plastic sleeves you can protect your prints from surface scratches by spraying them with a clear spray. Ask your photo or art-supply store to recommend such a product.

IDENTIFYING YOUR PHOTOS.

I have often heard people bemoan the fact that they had albums full of pictures but some of the people in them were a mystery because the photos lacked identification. To stand the test of time and to be complete, photo captions should include some of the five Ws. They should indicate where they were taken, when they were taken, the names of all the people pictured, and on what occasion the photos were taken.

Identify each photo in your memoir with a few lines placed below it or to the side of it. The caption can be informal, but it should be complete. Use names and dates: "Uncle George Smith, my sister Gladys, myself, Mom and Dad, taken at my graduation from St. Edward High School, Cleveland, 1938." Or, "Celebrating my seventh birthday in Boston, January 9, 1923. My sisters and brothers, left to right: Barbara, Ralph, Marian, David, Diane, and Eileen. I'm in the middle, blowing out the candles."

Photos can also be mounted on one page in your memoir and their captions can be placed separately on the opposite page simply by numbering each photo on the left and numbering each corresponding caption on the right.

The photographs selected can be bunched together in the center of the memoir, or distributed singly in appropriate chapters.

Do not write on the backs of photographs with a pen. The pen digs into the print paper leaving an impression that comes through on the photo side. Also, since the paper cannot absorb ink it may mar the face of the next print. If you must write on the back of a print use a felt tip pen, write very lightly, and do it at the bottom where it is less likely to hurt the picture. Never use paper clips or pins to attach a caption to a photo. Attach it to the back, at the bottom, using a spray adhesive or double-stick tape.

CHOOSING YOUR PHOTOS.

"I have a whole drawer full of family photos," one woman told me. "How will I ever decide which ones to use?" I suggested that she use the same process of elimination that she had used to select the episodes of her life. In choosing your photos you are looking for highlights—the ones that have the most meaning to you, the ones that trigger the greatest remembrances, and the ones that best help to tell the story in the chapters you have written. You should always choose the ones in which you appear most natural and attractive. Choose also the ones that will reproduce best. Tiny, fuzzy snapshots will not. A good test to see how sharply your photo will appear is to photocopy it.

Since this is *your* memoir you certainly should be represented with pictures taken at various stages of your life. Also appropriate, if you are lucky enough to have some good ones, are photos of parents, grandparents, brothers, sisters, spouse, children, other relatives, and special friends. If you lack such special family photos write to your relatives and ask to borrow them so you can have copies made. Promise that you will return the originals. Photos taken on special occasions, such as birthdays, school graduations, weddings, vacations, and holiday gatherings, should be considered. Others might be photos of the house you were born in, of you with a special family pet or the family's favorite car. If you are retired a photo of you and your spouse in front of your retirement home would be appropriate.

In making your selection you must also consider the quality of your photos. Will they reproduce well? Can they be restored so that they will show up clearly? Is the photo large enough or is it so small that its details would get lost in reproduction?

After you have made your selections spread them out on a table. Edit them down to "the most precious few." If you do not your memoir could get bulky. Ask yourself: "Will this photo add to the story I want to tell my family?"

HANDLE YOUR FAMILY DOCUMENTS WITH CARE.

Original papers are a precious part of your family's history. Documents such as wills, wedding announcements, letters, birth and death certificates, diplomas, mortgages, journals and ancestral charts are irreplaceable. You have seen them, yellowed and crumbling at the edges, or cracked in the middle where they were folded.

Recently a man preparing his life story showed me a precious letter written by an ancestor several generations before. It was clipped to a piece of cardboard, completely unprotected. The paper clip had rusted and it had left its outline on the brittle, yellow paper. Incidentally, most papers yellow because of the acid used in their manufacture. I have seen pins pushed through documents to hold them together causing rust stains and further damage. It is also unwise to use staples or rubber bands. If you must use clips, use a plastic paper clip.

One cardinal rule in preserving family papers says that you should not do anything to them that is irreversible. Laminating them, using heat-sealing, self-adhering laminates, is an example of what not to do. Avoid using regular cellophane pressure-sensitive tape. It gets brittle and leaves stains that work through the paper over the years. The experts use a tape for temporary repairs such as 3M's Micropore surgical tape. It can be removed without leaving a residue. Rubber cement or the white glues are not recommended for use on precious documents. They can bleed through the paper. If possible you should try not to paste down at all. But if you must, then experts recommend that, to withstand the test of time, you use a paste made from wheat flour and water in the proportion of one to six. Mix an ounce of the flour with six ounces of water and heat in a thick-bottomed pan. Stir constantly until the mixture becomes a smooth cream. Let it cool. Apply it thinly, and then go back and apply it again. Do not use the paste again as it tends to get watery after standing.

Flattening a document should be done with care. Avoid using heat such as that given off by a clothes iron or a dry mount press. A simple method would be to insert it between two clean sheets of paper, or between blotters, and to sandwich this between any flat objects such as books or pieces of plywood. A light weight should then be placed on top until the paper flattens. Paper that was rolled must stay pressed for a longer time.

As a first step in preserving your family papers I would recommend that you photocopy them and that you finger these copies instead of the delicate originals. This also assures that you will have a record should the original deteriorate further.

Remember that documents have some of the same enemies that photos have: heat, insects, light, and humidity. They should never be kept in yellow manila folders or tucked away in old Bibles. These may be highly acidic and this could be transferred to the documents. Acid-free folders are obtainable from the Hollinger Corporation, 3810 Four Mile Run Dr., Arlington, VA 22206. I prefer protecting a valuable document in a separate, transparent plastic folder. The paper should be laid out flat to avoid cracking at the folds. Stationery or photography stores carry these plastic folders including the type that will fit into a three-ring loose-leaf notebook. If you have difficulty finding them write to 20th Century Plastics, Inc.,

3628 Crenshaw Blvd., Los Angeles, CA 90016. They have vinyl sheet protectors, fitting standard three-ring binders, that are sealed on three sides so papers cannot fall out.

The restoration of precious documents that are seriously damaged is an art that had better be left to the experts. Some of the major libraries have restoration laboratories and they may be able to recommend a restorer. Ask your local librarian if she knows of one. They are scarce. Also, if you are near a university with a rare books department inquire there. They do a good deal of restoration work. Above all, cherish and preserve your valuable family records of the past.

17

Writing Bite #8—Your Early Career Years

Memory Sparkers (About age 20-35)

> Make the most of yourself for that
> is all there is of you.
> —Ralph Waldo Emerson

WORK, THEY SAY, is essential to our well being. What kind of work career did you choose? Did you work for someone on salary? Or were you self-employed? At what? How did it work out?

Did you take a number of smaller jobs before you arrived at what was to be your main career? What were they? Which one led to your main job? How did you get it? Was this what you studied for in school?

Describe what you did in your career job. What were your duties and responsibilities? What did you like the most about it? The least?

Were you happy doing this work or was it the kind of work you fell into and carried on in order to earn a living? Were you able to balance the demands of job and home? Are there stories you like to tell your friends about those days on the job?

What accomplishments in your work career are you most proud of? Did you receive any special honors, raises, promotions?

Describe some of the toughest problems you faced on the job and how you solved them.

Mark Twain once said he would rather have been a preacher instead of a writer of humorous stories. If you had it to do over again would you have chosen the same field of work? If not, what?

Did your career serve you well? Did it give you the wherewithal to raise your family properly? Did it enable you to grow personally?

What did you think of some of your bosses? Why did you leave jobs? Were you ever fired? Did you go on to better things? What did you learn from that experience?

If you became a homemaker after marriage, did you find the adjustment difficult? What job or jobs did you hold prior to marriage?

What household chores did you like the most, the least? Were you taught many of the skills required of the homemaker by your mother? Other?

Describe a big problem you faced in the home and how you solved it. Did the family think you were a good cook? What was your favorite dish? What was the recipe for it? What dishes did the family like the most? Were your children and your husband helpful around the house?

What were some of the things you learned about shopping? Did you put aside the food money in a separate envelope as some housewives do? Did you run short at times? What system did you use?

What kind of stores did you shop in? Compare the stores and prices of your early years with those of today.

Do you think it is easier to be a homemaker today than it was in your day?

A MEMOIRIST WRITES:

When I saw the first draft of this episode dealing with one's early career years I sent it back. I felt that it was too conservatively written. Reading between the lines I saw that what this woman had omitted could be far more interesting than what she had written. After asking some questions to draw her out I urged her to let her hair down, to get more of her feelings into it. I also told her that it was perfectly human to include the confrontation with her father and that it would add human interest while revealing more of herself to her family. She agreed and, together with a new title, turned out an excellent episode.

"I Chose My Own Career"

When I was 19, I was working as a file clerk with General Electric in Schenectady, New York, and I hated it. My father had preordained that I was to go to Wellesley. To enter there you had to have at least two years of Latin and two years of French. I suffered through two years of these in High School and flunked both. My father called me a "puddin' head." I did graduate from High School and then my father, an Engineer with G.E., got me a job as a file clerk with the hope that I would eventually become a secretary. But that wasn't what I wanted either.

I had been talking with Elsie who was visiting her Aunt in the neighborhood. She was a nurse and encouraged me to quit my job and go into nurse's training. "Don't go to a local hospital," she said. "Go to a good hospital in a large city." She helped me to send away for catalogues in New York, Boston and Philadelphia. I chose St. Luke's Hospital in Manhattan and was accepted.

My father was furious. He just didn't want me to be a nurse. My mother, too, disapproved mostly because she felt that New York was a big, wicked city and that harm would come to me. "It won't if I mind my own business," I told her.

With my trunk packed I called a taxi to go to the train. As I left our front porch my father said: "If you go through with this I never want to see you again."

He later changed and became very proud of me. In my heart I have forgiven my father who was a strict disciplinarian of the Victorian school. I can never remember sitting on his lap. He was trying to be a good father but he didn't know how. At the time, he alienated me when I could have been a very loving daughter if he had handled me right. I can see all this now.

The girls in my nursing class at St. Luke's were great. The motto inscribed on our nursing pins on our caps (in Latin) was "To heal a body and save a soul." I tried hard on the healing side. Though we worked long hours for very little it was a very happy time in my life and I have never regretted it.

We were on duty 12 hours a day from 7 A.M. to 7 P.M. with two hours off for classes. No pay. We were nurses because we wanted to be—not for pay. My father was sending me $10 a month and that helped.

I remember one funny incident. I was on night duty and was relieved for two hours by another nurse. I could have gone to my room to sleep but instead I piled pillows from the linen closet in a bathtub and went to sleep. When the night supervisor made rounds she discovered me. I had to go up before our Directress the next morning but I got off with just a reprimand.

Once I had a date with Russell, the man who was eventually to become my husband. You had to be back by midnight but we went to a movie on 42nd Street and then we walked through Central Park to 110th Street. I was late and tried to sneak back in but got caught by the night supervisor. The next day I was up before Mrs. Bath, our Directress, again. "You have worn a path to my office," she said. "You have got to learn to conform." I cried. But she was wonderful. She loved her nurses. She put her arm around me and said, "You are a good nurse and I want to keep you."

I liked the care of surgical patients the best. One day in ethics class, taught by Mrs. Bath, she said: "Why did you choose St. Luke's?" I replied, "I sent for catalogues in three cities and I chose St. Luke's because I liked the picture of the hospital building the best." All the class roared with laughter.

We had a resident chaplain who came to each ward each day for prayers from the Episcopal Prayer Book. On Sunday a small organ was wheeled into each ward, hymns were sung and we had a short service. Our chapel was, and is, of white marble and there was a vespers service every afternoon. If we were off duty we went. This was an uplifting influence on our relationship between nurse and patient.

Speaking of that, I recall something a minister, a friend of our family, told me. I never forgot it. "Never lose your smile," he said. "No matter how many skills you learn in your nursing they will never do more good than your smile."

Graduation for us was at St. John the Divine, across the street. The Cathedral was not completed at that time. None of my family came. Only one other nurse did not have any family there. We got black velvet bands on our caps, and our pins.

Fifty cents an hour for twelve-hour duty was our earned income as graduate nurses. Forty-two dollars a week.

In 1938 we had a reunion of all classes for the 50th Anniversary of St. Luke's Training School. It was elaborate and was held at the Waldorf-Astoria Hotel. Our class had the largest delegation. Strange, some had changed so I did not recognize them. Others had not changed at all. Many of us have remained close friends all these years. I have always been glad I chose nursing and St. Luke's.

WRITING POINTERS: 29-32

29. *When you describe your travels.* Have you ever visited a home and been bored stiff as your hosts flashed hours and hours of slides about their trip to this place, and then that place, and then to that place? There is that danger, too, if you try to describe in your memoir one of those long "If it's Tuesday we must be in Belgium" tours that you took. A better way to handle your story is to pick out one, two, or three highlights of the trip and to focus on these with information you picked up on the spot, together with additional data you obtained in your local library later. When you look back what stands out? Was it the Passion Play at Oberammergau? Then dwell on it. What does it depict? In what year did it start? Why? How often is the Play given? When? How many people attend? What is the little town of Oberammergau in Bavaria like? What were your feelings about the Play?

Did you also visit the ancient city of Babylon in the Euphrates Valley? Then you walked in the footsteps of history, of Hammurabi, Herodotus, Nebuchadnezzar, and Alexander the Great. Here you saw the ruins of a city that had reached its zenith of wealth and power centuries before Christ. How did it fall? What went on in the Tower of Babel? What were the Hanging Gardens of Babylon? What was the Processional Way? Describe your feelings about this. In focusing on the highlights of a special trip you took you have an opportunity to be educational as well as interesting.

30. *Prefer the active voice to the passive.* It makes your writing more direct, more vigorous. In the active voice you would say: "Mother cooked delicious meals." In the weaker passive voice it would read: "Delicious meals were cooked by Mother." "I loved her" is better than "She was loved by me." "We enjoyed those days at the lake" is a stronger sentence than "Those days at the lake were en-

joyed by us." It may not always be possible to use the active voice but you should use it more often than not.

31. *Use exclamation points sparingly.* When an editor sees a heavy sprinkling of exclamation points in a manuscript he knows he is dealing with a beginner. The same goes for too frequent underscoring of words, or capitalization of entire words in the body of your copy. Instead of relying on these devices, try to achieve the real emphasis you want through the choice of your words and the content of your sentences.

Although I have singled out a few of the more common errors beginners make in punctuation and grammar in these Writing Pointers, I hardly intend to nit-pick on these subjects. This is not a book on grammar and punctuation, nor do I profess to be an authority on these sciences since by now I employ them mostly by instinct, praying that I am right. I assume you have a working knowledge of grammar and punctuation and that if you wish to learn more you will pick up appropriate books in the library. Some of these are listed in the Writing Bibliography in the Appendix of this book.

32. *Write as you talk?* There are several schools of thought on this. I go along with what this advice seeks to achieve: the avoidance of stilted or ponderous writing. But I don't believe that we should write precisely as we talk. Spoken language transferred to paper can sound choppy, with many contractions, incomplete sentences, vague words, and repetitions. Also many of the thoughts we convey in speaking receive an assist from our tone of voice, our facial expressions, and gestures. The written word can receive no such help. Actually I go along with those who advise that you should write as you *think.* If you do this I believe your writing will have more clarity and depth and that you will derive still another bonus—you will find that you are putting more of your feelings into your writing.

18

Twenty-five Ways to Achieve Variety

❧

PEOPLE LIKE VARIETY. That's why they enjoy weekends and take vacations. That's why they like variety shows and why they twirl their TV dials. They like to be surprised, enlightened, and entertained. Variety is truly "the very spice of life."

There are many ways to get variety into your memoir. It is not that difficult to do. Here are 25 ideas for achieving variety in the preparation of your life story. I don't by any means expect you to use all of them. I just want you to be aware of the possibilities and if you manage to work just a few into your manuscript pages this chapter will have been worthwhile.

1. *Poetry.* Use it at the beginning of an episode or in the middle or at the end. If it is your own poetry, all the better. If you use someone else's always give credit. For publication use you must obtain the author's permission.

2. *Family sayings.* Quote those quaint phrases that were spoken in the bosom of the family day in and day out. Every family has had some original expressions you can recall. "Use it up, wear it out, make it do." "Anything worth doing is worth doing well." "You can move a mountain with a teaspoon."

3. *Quoting from family letters* or reproducing them in their entirety where they fit into one of your episodes.

4. *Recipes* your mother or grandmother used for main dishes. Recipes for drinks, desserts, or candies that you particularly liked.

5. *A family tree.* If you have worked up such an ancestral chart, particularly of your immediate family (space is a problem), include it at the beginning or in an appendix.

6. *Humor.* Surely you can think of some amusing moments or situations in your life, even if you have to tell a story on yourself.

Here's an amusing incident one memoirist recalled that occurred when he was a little boy living in Queens, New York:

> One day when I was four my two little cousins and I decided to take a look at the wine barrels in our landlord's cellar. He made his own wine. Soon we proceeded to sample each of the four barrels. Everything was fine until Rudy came across this large 100 gallon barrel. Its spigot was different from the others, the off position being straight up and down. He turned it to the right like the others and the wine flowed. He turned it to the left and it still flowed. Right, left, right, left and then the panic set in as the 100 gallons of precious wine gurgled out on the floor. We took off in terror as fast as our little legs could go.
>
> Needless to say our parents gave us the paddling of our lives. But the landlord, God bless him, forgave us as naive children and never raised his voice to us. But he did raise the rent.

7. *Photos.* Do get some of the more important ones into your memoir. They are a part of your history and they convey information that you cannot always put into words.

8. *Dialogue.* When you show two people talking you create more interest. The quotes provide realism and they break up the solid text. People always like to know what other people said. Here is a bit of dialogue extracted from one episode written by a woman describing the early struggle of her family:

> One day in late spring Dad made his announcement at the supper table. "I've started an egg route."
>
> "An egg route!" Mother gasped. "We don't have chickens."
>
> "Don't be foolish, woman," Dad snapped. "I know that. I'll *get* the eggs."
>
> "How?" I dared to break the rule that children should speak only when spoken to, especially at the table.

9. *Clippings.* There may be some valuable newspaper clippings in your life such as your wedding announcement or a story concerning an award or some achievement. Clippings usually reproduce very well. Insert them in appropriate chapters or in an appendix.

10. *Quotes from a diary.* If you have kept one, or if you have access to one written by another family member, extract pertinent quotes from it. Indicate where the words came from and mention the year in which they were written. I have seen passages quoted from memoirs written by one's ancestor.

11. *Statistics.* Yes, they can be dry but if sprinkled judiciously here and there they can give substance to your writing. The population of your town, of the United States then, the cost of things back then, mileages between places, the number of houses you have lived in, the number of U.S. Presidents who have been in office during your life-span, the dates when events occurred, and so on.

12. *Maps.* A small map that focuses on a particular area can help to tell your story of where you lived and where you traveled. It can be photocopied or hand-drawn.

13. *Calligraphy.* Some people use this attractive method of printing to make their chapter titles stand out. It could also be used to illuminate a special phrase or passage in the text, or on the name of a relative above or below a photo.

14. *Vital documents.* Birth certificates, marriage certificates, wedding announcements, diplomas, commendations, and other special papers can be photographed and included in appropriate chapters or in an appendix.

15. *Famous proverbs, axioms.* Don't hesitate to sprinkle in some pithy proverbs by famous persons expressing a familiar truth you want to get across. Benjamin Franklin had many of them. You no doubt have acquired some favorite ones. Your librarian can help you to find many more.

16. *Drawings.* Your memoir will say a little more about you if you can use some of your own drawings in it, assuming that you have that talent. If not, why not have a friend or someone from your local art club make up a few drawings for you? One memoir writer, having few family photos, had an artist draw sketches to illustrate particular segments of his memoir. In another case a man engaged an artist to draw his family's crest for the cover of his life story.

17. *Anecdotes.* These are little stories that can brighten your big life history. Sometimes they are handed down in families. The Bible is full of little stories. Short human-interest incidents from the story of your life always make for interesting reading. Here's an anecdote written by a man who recalled his boyhood on a Wisconsin family farm:

> I remember most vividly Mother placing me against the
> wall opposite the kitchen sink at a point where the kitch-

en hardwood molding ran from floor to ceiling. Then holding my head still with one hand she used the other which was holding a huge sharp kitchen knife to make a notch in the molding just level with the top of my head. Each of my brothers was measured for height also and the height notched in the same manner.

At first I recall surprise and even shock that Mother, who was neat, proud and careful in every detail of household management, should be doing such a thing—carelessly starting to carve up our unmarred woodwork.

But then an explanation of what was really happening gradually emerged. Snatches of conversation and the look in Mother's eyes and her manner told the story. "How much did I grow?" "Who grew the most?" "How much are you supposed to grow?" Mother then showed us a second notch for each of us taken a year before. The distance between the two revealed the growth of each of us and who really grew the most. But no one showed keener interest and pride than Mother.

18. *Dialect.* Don't hesitate to use it as long as you put it in quotes.

19. *A chronology.* Your life in brief, highlighting your important years, can make a big contribution to your memoir. It adds another dimension to your memoir helping to make your life journey more understandable in time and place. It can be positioned at the very front or at the end. (See Chapter 22, "The Chronology—Your Life at a Glance.")

20. *The lyrics of a song.* There's a great deal of nostalgia in recalling the words of a song. Why not quote a line or a verse to set the mood for what you are writing at that particular time? The same applies to hymns you have loved. Use of a song's lyrics for commercial purposes requires the permission of the music publisher.

21. *The names of people.* Be a name dropper. Get names into your memoir, especially the names of those in your immediate and past family. Your descendants will be pleased to see their names.

22. *Special awards.* Certificates indicating a special honor received for community or other service; special invitations received from high places; school, athletic, and business awards. Do not hesitate to let your descendants know about these. They tell a great deal about you, they can set an example, and can indicate where some of the family strengths lie.

23. *Lists.* Where appropriate it may be more convenient for you to list certain things. This not only breaks up the usual format of the page, but it also adds information in a smaller space. Such lists might include books you read as a youth; songs you sang then; family sayings; the homes or towns you have lived in; excerpts from a ledger or from printed ads showing the price of food and other items years ago.

24. *Titles:* These can add variety to your memoir. A good main title and provocative titles for each of your chapters can give the reader a sense of interesting things to come. Also, I have known some artistic memoir writers to hand-print their titles or to reproduce them in calligraphy to give their finished product a more distinctive look.

25. *The way you structure your memoir* can add variety: varying the length of paragraphs and sentences; alternating long chapters with short chapters; alternating more serious chapters with lighter ones; starting each chapter with a fresh, new subject; opening your life story at some dramatic point rather than opening with your birth. These are all techniques that can add variety and interest.

19

Writing Bite #9—Your Middle Years

Memory Sparkers (About age 35-55)

> Middle age is not the beginning of
> the end; it is the end of the
> beginning.
> —Eric Butterworth

SOMEONE HAS SAID that middle age can be looked upon as a time of second flowering. Do you agree? Did you like your mid-years better than your earlier ones?

Looking back, how do you view the experience of raising your children? Was it a big struggle? Are boys more difficult to raise? Can you remember a particularly dark day, a sunny day? Did some funny things happen? Would you do it differently to-day?

Was it a jolt for you when the children left the nest? How did it happen? What were your feelings? What new interests did you find to fill in the extra time?

Now that you have been a parent yourself, how well do you think your parents did?

They talk about a midlife crisis. Have you had one? Describe it.

What are some of the thoughts about marriage that you would like to pass on? What ingredients most make for success in marriage?

What sort of relationship did you have with your parents at this time? With your brothers and sisters and other relatives? Did you have to help your parents financially? Otherwise? Did you lose a parent at this time?

Did you notice any change in your appearance at this time of your life? First signs of gray hair or wrinkles? What were your feelings? Did this cause you to review your life, to assess your progress? Did it give you your first intimation of mortality?

How busy were you in these years? What sort of activities were you involved in? What were your hobbies? What did you do for recreation? Were you a sports enthusiast? Which ones?

Have you played a musical instrument? How did you get started? How far did you go? What is your favorite kind of music?

Have you been involved in a favorite charity? Were you in volunteer work for your community, your church, your country? Tell about this.

How has your feeling about religion developed? Have you been active in a church? Has religion played an important part in your family, in your marriage?

Were you married more than once? Was divorce a jolting experience for you? What were your feelings? How rough was your adjustment? How did it seem to affect the children? Your friendships? Where did you live? What did you learn from this experience?

Were you satisfied with the schools your children were attending? Did you work closely with their teachers? How did your children do?

What reading have you done in your lifetime? What authors do you like the most?

Did your parents emigrate from another country? Have they described their journey? Give some of the details. How did they feel when they arrived in this country? Why did they leave their old land? What were their first jobs? What stories do they tell about those days?

Do you remember the Great Depression? Prohibition? The various wars? How did they affect you, your family? What was it like then? Did you ever lose a member of your family in a war?

Have you suffered any natural disasters such as hurricanes, fire, flood, earthquake? What happened?

Does a particular wedding anniversary, birthday, holiday, graduation day stand out in your memory? Describe it.

A MEMOIRIST WRITES:

Before writing this chapter this woman had many doubts about whether she should include this subject in her memoir. She asked my advice. The crisis had occurred many years before. I asked her if she felt that she could now deal with it in writing. She said she thought she could. I pointed out that there were many positive aspects to her story and that she should emphasize these while dealing with the crisis itself as factually and as objectively as she could. She went on to write one of her best chapters, a warm account by a loving mother.

"My Midlife Crisis And How I Coped"

It was during our middle years that my husband Mack and I decided to adopt a child. I really can't recall exactly why we waited so late in life to make up our minds. Maybe the reason was that we were constantly surrounded by children. Mack was a high school teacher of science, chemistry and agriculture. I was an elementary school teacher at heart although I was certified to teach English, social studies and physical ed in High School.

We both adored children and often brought them home from school with us. On one occasion I brought William home with me. He was one of my second grade pupils. Mack was teaching agriculture at Gibbs High School in St. Petersburg during this time so he asked William to help him propagate plants for his school. Mack had built a greenhouse in our backyard.

William's mother was delighted to have me bring her nine year old son home with me each day. She had six children and was happy to let us enjoy one of them. Mack paid William by the hour for the work he did. He encouraged William to take charge of his own time-keeping and salary figures. I furnished him with hot, wholesome meals and helped him with his home assignments. We always delivered William to his home each evening.

William was shocked beyond words when he first laid eyes upon our beautiful, three-day-old adopted baby Karen. He was a little jealous of our bundle of joy at first, but he soon learned to love her as his little sister.

As he grew up, William, whom we regarded as a foster son, continued to visit our home each day. When he was about 16 years of age he told my husband he intended to get married. He asked Mack to tell me about this because he knew I wanted him to complete his education first. After we learned that William was really serious about getting married, we consulted with his mother and gave him and his fiancee a lovely little wedding at his mother's church parsonage. We are very proud of William who is now the father of six children and a dedicated church and community worker.

Our daughter Karen was enrolled in a Nursery School at the tender age of two. This was a very good school which boasted of teaching its pupils everything from toilet training to the ABCs. Karen entered public kindergarten at our Elementary School at the age of five. Her early school years through senior high school were spent in various parochial and public schools in St. Petersburg.

Then, while all was going well, tragedy struck. Karen was eight years old and in the fourth grade at St. Joseph Catholic School when her father was shot and killed by an armed robber. This was a most traumatic experience for all of us. Mother Childs, Mack's mother, was devastated as he was her only child. Karen found it hard to believe that anyone would want to harm her Daddy. She was especially fond of her father as he had devoted so much of his time to her. He often took her fishing with him on his motorboat "The Princess." He had just purchased a new and larger boat prior to his death. I often shut my eyes and tried to blot out the awful truth.

After Mack's death I had to pick up the pieces and go about the business of living. Mother Childs came to live with us after the first year of Mack's untimely death. Karen begged to spend her sixth year with me as my student at our Elementary School. To this frantic plea I reluctantly agreed. However it was not to be, because the sixth graders were transferred to another school where she spent her middle school years.

Since all public high schools, ninth through twelfth

grades, were on double session during most of the seventies, I sent Karen to St. Petersburg Catholic High in ninth grade where she remained through eleventh grade. Tuition fees climbed higher and higher during this time, especially for non-Catholics. After a few discussions Karen finally convinced me that she wanted to complete her high school years at Gibbs High School, near us. She stated that she was now mature enough to spend the lengthy afternoons alone until I arrived home from school at about 3:30. She graduated in June of 1977 with a very high average.

She then attended Bethune-Cookman College for four years, graduating in 1981 with a Bachelor of Arts Degree in Sociology. I am proud to say that she is presently employed as an assistant manager of a branch of the Neighborly Center in St. Petersburg. She hopes to return to school later in this term and work toward a Master's Degree in Sociology.

In 1967 I was one of the first black teachers selected to teach in an integrated school in St. Petersburg. My principal was a wonderful Christian woman who had evidently prepared her staff, the Parent-Teachers' Association, as well as every student, for the arrival of two new black teachers, of which I was one. There were about 25 black pupils enrolled in our school of 860 pupils. Everyone was so kind to us that we soon felt at home in this new environment. It was so rewarding to experience the sincere love and the kindly deeds which were bestowed upon my family and me by my principal and staff, the PTA, and my beloved pupils.

After my husband's death I realized that I had to shoulder greater responsibilities. Mack had always taken care of the business at hand. Now it was I who had to pay such bills as: property taxes, insurance, lights, water and the telephone. It was I who had to make major decisions such as purchasing a new car, dealing with legal matters, selling our rental house, and selling Mack's recently-purchased motorboat.

It was with the help of the good Lord and the wise advice of my attorney along with the loving support of my sisters, Hallie, Hazel, Frances and Rose, that I survived my ordeal. My daughter Karen has been a constant source of comfort and inspiration. Without her I don't know what I would have done. She is so protective of me.

The biggest thrill of my middle years was to receive my

Master of Arts Degree from Catholic University of America in Washington, D.C. in June of 1969. I had completed my work during the summer of 1968. I am sure that I would have graduated with honors but no honors were bestowed on graduate students.

It was a proud moment at the graduation. Unfortunately Mack was not there to witness it. But I am sure that he smiled down on me as I received my degree for it was he who encouraged me to settle down at one school and work toward a degree. Every living relative was present at my graduation: my mother, mother-in-law, four sisters, Karen and all my nieces and nephews as well as my Uncle and Aunt.

It was while I sat in my graduation group that I vowed to take advantage of Catholic University's offer of applying my extra 60 graduate hours toward a Doctor of Education or Philosophy Degree. I had earned them from the University of California in Berkeley; Howard University in Washington, D.C., and Tuskegee Institute in Alabama, prior to my admission to Catholic U. The policy was that I could apply them toward a Doctorate, but not toward a Masters.

However, I had to face one reality. Since Karen had recently lost her father she was quite lonely. So I agreed with her that I was needed at home during our summers. I put my dream of a Doctorate on the back burner. But I may still shock everyone and get it at the age of 80. Who knows?

WRITING POINTERS: 33-36

33. *Use picture words.* Try to get a touch of color into your writing. It takes a little extra effort to turn a plain, general word into one that can come alive in the mind of the reader. It is not just a bird, it is a meadowlark. It is not just a sky, it is a cloudless, azure sky. It is not just a tree, it is a graceful elm. It is not just a sunset, it is a scarlet sunset. It is not just a flower, it is a beautiful yellow rose. "She looked into his calm blue eyes" says more than "She looked into his eyes."

Wilfred J. Funk, editor, author, and lexicographer, was once asked to choose ten words in the English language he thought were the most beautiful. He chose: chimes, dawn, golden, hush, lullaby, luminous, melody, mist, murmuring, and tranquil. Note that many of them bring images to mind.

34. *Interviewing with the tape recorder.* You can acquire a good

deal of rich family history from relatives if you use the tape recorder properly. Sometimes people "freeze" when confronted with a tape recorder. So your objective should be to put your relatives at ease and to make the tape recorder as unobtrusive as possible. Place the recorder a little to the interviewee's side. Don't keep looking at it. I lock in the other person by making eye contact and by referring to a list of questions I have jotted down in advance in a small notebook I am holding in my hand. Sometimes, even though we are being recorded, I put down a few notes and the subject watches me doing that instead of looking at the tape recorder. When the conversation bogs down I go to my next question. If the interview is running long it can tire your subject. Take a break or ask if you can come back on another day. Be sure to practice with your recorder in advance so you have mastered it mechanically. Failure to push down the "record" button can result in valuable material going unrecorded or being erased.

35. *Do you suffer from semicolonitis?* Many beginners do. When in doubt they throw in a semicolon as they would a comma and then go merrily on. Or they use it instead of starting a new sentence. The semicolon signifies a greater break than the comma. Unless you use it to separate two closely related thoughts, it would be better for the reader if you used separate sentences. Incidentally, the word "semicolon" can mislead you to believe it is half a colon. But the two have different uses. A colon is mostly a mark for introducing or saying "Watch what is coming" as in this sentence: "To sum up: Work hard, save your money, watch your health and trust in God." The semicolon calls for more of a pause than a comma. It is used as a mark of separation between sentence elements of equal rank: "I walked down the street where I once lived; the faces were no longer familiar there."

36. *Handling numbers.* There are several styles that can be used with numbers to attain uniformity throughout your manuscript and to save space. I recommend the following guideline: Spell out numbers 1 through 10, and use numerals from 11 on. There are exceptions, of course, and here are some:

• Use numbers for dates: "December 7, 1941."

• It is not good form to use numbers at the beginning of a sentence. If you must start with a number, spell it out: "Fifty years ago."

• Use Arabic numbers to number the pages of your life story.

• Use numbers to indicate time: "7 A.M.; 11 P.M."

• In a sentence or paragraph, do not use both figures and spelled-out numbers. Keep them uniform. Use numerals throughout, or spelled-out numbers throughout.

20

Titles Are Worth Your Time

❦

SOON AFTER I STARTED working with beginning memoir writers I realized that I would have to solve a problem. I found, too often, that they were committing a common mistake—they were rambling across many subjects in a single episode, ending far afield from where they had started. I saw, for example, that the writer would start with an episode about his childhood and soon he was writing about his mother, his grandfather, an aunt, a special friend, and about incidents that took place many years later in his life. In wandering away from the main topic of a chapter the writer not only loses the unity of his piece, he also "throws away" good material that could later enrich other episodes. In some cases this material, casually dropped in passing, could actually suggest themes for separate episodes.

In a class in magazine article writing I once taught I found a similar problem. The adults in this class who aspired to selling their pieces to editors, were collecting many rejection slips. Editors do not want a lot of general information about a subject. The editor wants the story to be sharply focused, to have a theme. This is also called "a slant," "an angle," or "a viewpoint." A general, wandering piece tells him instantly that he is dealing with a beginner who lacks discipline in his writing.

Instead of a broad story about exercise, the editor might be intrigued with a sharply focused article entitled "20 Ways to Flatten Your Stomach." He has seen tons of material on dieting but he might express interest in a story with such a title as "Fighting Fat at Fifty."

Focusing down is just as important in memoir writing as it is in the writing marketplace. A memoir episode entitled "Our Family's First Car" makes far more interesting reading than "Different Cars We Had and the Bad Roads We Traveled."

"The Love I Once Jilted" (about a career the writer wished he had chosen) and "My Father—Born Too Soon" are other examples of successful memoir episodes that have a point of view.

To guard against this tendency to ramble, I advise that you start every episode by placing a title (headline) on top of your first page as a guide to keep you from straying. In composing it, ask yourself "What is it I am really writing about here?" Narrow your broad idea down to a specific one. Can you state your theme in a single sentence? Your title should be short, say no more than ten words. Be sure it is an accurate, honest statement of what is to follow. Don't mislead or exaggerate. Write the title out in capital letters (upper case). Fix that title in your mind as a guide while you write. It will give your paper cohesiveness and greater readability. This focusing down need not limit you, nor affect the length of your episode. You can wander as far as your memory will take you providing you stay within your theme.

Your title can be a temporary one. You can refine it later. Professionals call it their "working title," one that gives the editor a quick idea of how the article is slanted. Often the editor will change it before it gets into print. You can do that, too.

There are many kinds of titles. (Sometimes they will pop up out of your own text when you reread it.) Suit your title to your subject. If your paper is on a serious subject use a straight title. If it is written in a humorous vein, try for humor.

Here are examples of titles actually used in memoirs that I have seen:

The summary title:	"The Three Wars in My Life"
A striking statement title:	"The Day I Was Shot out of the Sky over Yugoslavia"
The narrative title:	"The Teenage Street I Once Knew"
Humorous:	"I Was Born a Girl but They Kept Me"
The question title:	"Remember Castor Oil and Camomile Tea?"
Direct Address:	"You Pick Your Friends, Not Your In-laws"
Alliterative:	"Memories of Mama"

While on the subject of titles, you might start thinking now on what your main cover title will be. I will give some examples in an upcoming chapter.

21

Writing Bite #10—Your Later Years

Memory Sparkers (About age 55-65)

> Age is opportunity no less
> Than youth itself, though in another
> dress.
> And as the evening twilight fades
> away
> The sky is filled with stars invisible
> by day.
> —Henry Wadsworth Longfellow

A MEMOIR WRITER I know has written these encouraging words: "One of the things I have learned that I hope I can make use of is that life can begin at any time if you want to begin from where you are and go on from there." Do you feel that way?

Have you found that the things you once thought were important are no longer important now? What are some of these?

As one grows older, friendship becomes all the more precious. Have you kept in touch with your closest friends? Tell how you met and about some of the experiences you have shared.

What are some of the favorite stories, humorous or otherwise, that have been handed down and told in your family?

How have you fared with your health? What in the way of a health history would you want younger family members to know: disabilities, allergies, surgery, accidents, doctors? What formula for living a healthy life would you recommend?

When you look back, what is it you remember the most about your mother and father? Do you see them differently now than you did originally?

Can you remember some home remedies that your family used on you as a child? Some may seem hilarious today. Describe them.

What U.S. Presidents do you especially remember during your lifetime? How did they influence your times? (See list of U.S. Presidents in the Appendix.)

Have you been widowed? Are you, or were you, a widower? Did you feel like a "fifth wheel?" Were you lonely? What were some of the adjustments you had to make? Did you go back to work? Did you volunteer in some organization? Did you remarry? What attracted you? How did the children on both sides react?

How were you affected by wars: World War I, World War II, Korea, Vietnam? What are your feelings about war?

Who are some of the people who have most influenced your life? Write about one or two. Tell what aspects of your life they influenced, how they did it, and what it has meant in your life.

What are some of the technological changes you have witnessed since your youth? We have just been through what has been described as the most amazing 60 years in history with progress in science, medicine, education, entertainment, modern living, and the arts.

Looking back, do you think you have done as well as your parents? Do you feel that they achieved as much as they could have, given the conditions that existed then? What are some of the greater advantages you have had?

How did your family celebrate some of the big holidays: Christmas, Thanksgiving, Halloween, Fourth of July, New Year's Eve, etc.?

Of all the places you've lived, which holds the fondest memories for you?

Do you plan to retire? What are your plans? How are you looking into this?

Do you recall the Great Depression? How did it affect your life? Where were you living then? How did you cope?

What are your personal feelings about life and the purpose of life? Have your values and beliefs changed over the years?

A MEMOIRIST WRITES:

This very readable chapter is written in simple unstilted language, the kind one might use in writing a letter to a friend. The writer shows the "warts as well as the dimples" in describing his father and this "telling it like it is" makes for interesting reading. Note that this memoirist has chosen a theme for his chapter and that he develops it throughout, thus avoiding rambling into other subjects that might make good episodes in themselves. Though he has described his father with revealing candor, can there be any doubt about his affection for him?

"My Father—A Man Born Too Soon"*

I do not ask myself, "Who was my Father?" but "What was my Father?" In answering this second question I come up with two answers. First, "He was a loser." And the second one is hinged closely to the first, "He was born too soon."

Financially he invested in the mountains of shale oil before there was a process to refine it. Healthwise he had diabetes before insulin was discovered. There are more "born too soons," but let's digress.

Father was born in Norway around 1865. Immediately his "born too soons" began as he grew. He had one leg shorter than the other by about two inches. These inches he could not afford to lose as he was only about five five as an adult. Anyway, they put him in agonizing traction to try to lengthen the short leg with no luck. Today something could be done.

He was born in Norway "too soon" because Norway, at that time, was ruled by Sweden. The rivalry between these two countries, which today is just in fun, was serious then. So when he reached draft age, he sailed to the USA to keep from being drafted into the Swedish army.

---

*This episode, written by an adult student, appeared in the *Tampa Tribune* as part of a feature article dealing with the author and his memoir writing course.

So at age 18 he arrived in Chicago with little money and without English as a language.

Fortunately he had served as a goldsmith's apprentice and was quickly gobbled up by Marshall Field doing gold work. One of the jobs he had at Field's was making solid gold spectacle frames for their well-to-do customers.

Making the frames aroused his curiosity about the lenses that went into them. This led him toward an unnamed and almost completely untried trade of opticianry. This, in turn, led him into an even more unexplored field which, in later years, became optometry. As this specialty began to grow Father went to night school to study the mysteries of the human eye while still keeping his job at Field's.

These studies led him into opening a part-time office in our home to supply a need that was springing up, especially since people were living longer and needed glasses to enable them to read. This he did easily as no specific training or license was needed to be what was then called an "Optician."

But Dad was not satisfied and continued studying. In fact he joined with other men wishing to advance their craft into a profession. And it happened. Father took a state board examination and was among the first men in Illinois to be licensed as a Doctor of Optometry.

With this Father quit Field's, mortgaged the house and opened an ethical upstairs office. However, he again was "born too soon." By then most jewelers had stolen into the "eyeglass business" and were dispensing glasses without the training. They got a license not by examination but "by exemption."

But Father struggled along, as did others, holding to the high ideals of this fledgling profession and finally made it pay. It was a tough grind and I recall that he seldom came home from his office until around eight o'clock.

This might be a good time to digress a moment and tell you more about my Father, physically. As he'd come home to his late supper I could see him coming in through the door. By that time I was 13 and we'd moved to the apartment across the street from our old house.

First I'd hear the thump of his cane as he labored up the flight of stairs to the apartment. I usually tried to be at the upper door to greet him. He would usually sit down on a chair in the living room where I would put on his slippers after removing his shoes that laced up over his ankles. He then gave me his cane to put away. I remember it well. It was of ebony wood with a slightly curved, engraved silver handle.

As I said before, Dad was only five five. However, when I knew him he weighed about 225 pounds. He was quite bald, with a round face and several chins. Mother said he was very slender when they were married but her good cooking had about doubled his weight. His fatness was a great problem as he could not sleep lying down but spent the night sitting in a chair with his head on a pillow placed on the back of another chair in front of him.

Dad wasn't the only one "born too soon." So were most of his children. Twin daughters were born at seven months. Though there were no incubators then, they still lived for two weeks, bedded in cigar boxes. A third died as a baby from diphtheria, and a fourth as the result of a fall from a buggy.

Though four of us arrived at adulthood, one sister died of peritonitis and another of tuberculosis—things unheard of today. That just left my brother and myself, and he died at the age of 70.

Then diabetes struck Dad. There being no insulin, he had to go on the strictest of diets with foods tasting like sawdust. He lost weight constantly until his clothing hung like sacks. Mother was kept busy altering them. But diabetes took its toll and after five years, with as many strokes, he passed on.

Such is the tale of a loser. Being born too soon he lost his children and his life.

Yet he was a man of faith, faith in his adopted country and its future, faith in his chosen profession and faith in his family. He was not of heroic stature, except to me when I was young. But I think he is very representative of millions of others who came to this melting pot to discover the freedom that meant more than life itself.

WRITING POINTERS: 37-40

37. *When in doubt, change it.* In reading over your manuscript have you ever come to a word and hesitated? Have you wondered if it was the precise word you wanted? In that case follow your instinct—change it. That intuitive something inside of you is probably right. If you have trouble with it so will the reader. And it is so easy to change. If you can't think of a better word look for one in

your thesaurus or dictionary. Sometimes you have this doubt about a word the moment you put it to paper. If you are in a first draft just put a question mark after it and go on. Come back to it later and make the change.

38. *Appeal to the five senses.* Your writing will hit home to your readers more if you look for words, phrases, and anecdotes that will appeal to their sense of tasting, smelling, seeing, hearing, and touching. Here, for example, is the way one memoir writer evoked the sense of taste in a chapter dealing with her family:

> Most families have a dish or two that is a sort of love med-
> icine offered to a family member who is feeling a bit un-
> der the weather. Ours was milk toast, a favorite of my fa-
> ther's: thick slices of bread, oven-toasted and buttered,
> and then drenched with good hot milk. It was comfort-
> ing to the spirit as well as the tummy.

There are many tempting images that we can call on that will communicate quickly with our reader through the senses: the scent of a flower, the pungent aroma of herbs and spices, the whistle of a train, the chirping of birds, the rustle of branches in a breeze, the spicy aroma of Grandma's russet apple pie as it comes out of the oven, the sweet smell of fresh-cut grass, the softness of a kiss.

Here's how one memoir writer managed to call upon most of the human senses as he vividly recalled what he saw when, as a boy, he visited the village blacksmith in Virginia:

> Long before I got to the blacksmith shop I could hear the
> Smithy's hammer making a bell-like ring as it struck his
> anvil. There was a fascinating rhythm as the huge man
> bounced his enormous hammer on the anvil before he
> began the ching, ching, ching of striking the glowing red
> hot iron he held by a long-handled pair of pliers. Cas-
> cades of sparks flew with each ringing blow.
>
> I was virtually hypnotized by the process of shoeing a
> horse. In that wonderland of marvelous odors made up
> of a blend of horseflesh, leather and burning coke in the
> forge, I watched as the blacksmith approached the
> horse, always from the head. He had a way of calming the
> most excitable animals by talking and smoothing them
> along their necks as he walked back to look at their feet.
>
> First of all he would take the old shoes off by holding
> the hooves between his knees as he stood with his back
> to the horse. This he did with one mighty wrench of a

pair of pincers. Then he would cut out the growth around the center of a horse's hoof, known as the frog. After that he smoothed the whole area with a large rasp. I was told it didn't hurt the horse any more than cutting fingernails hurts humans.

Taking a long bar of iron, he measured it by eye across the hoof to be shod. Then the bar would be thrust deep into a bed of coke and the bellows turned causing sparks to rise under the hood of the forge while the coke was brought to a white hot glow.

When the iron was sufficiently hot, the blacksmith would lay the glowing end of the metal across the forge and, grabbing his hammer, he would begin the ringing rhythm of beating the iron into shape. Almost as if by magic, the shoe took shape under the shower of sparks. Only then did he cut the new shoe off the bar with one well-aimed blow of a hammer with an axe-like edge. After more shaping he fitted the reheated shoe to the hoof of a horse. This he did for only a moment so as to burn the fit into the hoof. Then he would chuck the shoe into a tub of liquid to cool. In the meantime, the odor of burned hoof filled the shop with an acrid smell, as the hissing metal hit the water and oil mixture.

39. *Avoid abbreviations.* Remember that they may be familiar to you but not to members of your family. They may not know the meaning of D.A.R., S.A.R., A.M.A., NRA, CCC, D.A.V., WACS, WAVES, and others. It takes only an extra minute to spell it out and you save the reader the trouble of looking it up. The abbreviation "etc." is another that should be outlawed in clear writing. Instead of the nebulous "and so forth" you convey far more to the reader when you take the time to state specifically what you mean.

40. *Shun slang.* Your memoir deserves better. Slang is often used in flashy speech: "beatnik," "scram," "wacky," "cut no ice," "put on the dog," "goof off." It has no place in a document such as yours unless you are quoting someone, or unless you plan to do a humorous episode explaining the slang terms of your day. Slang words are beneath good English. Many pass out of use and therefore become obscure to later readers. Furthermore, they keep you from seeking out more exact words to say what you want to say.

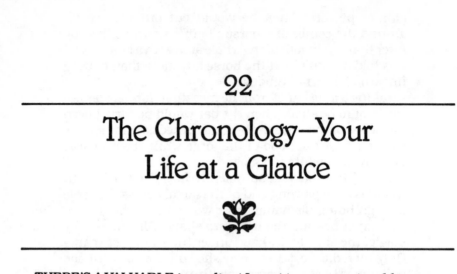

22

The Chronology—Your Life at a Glance

THERE'S A VALUABLE ingredient I want to urge you to add to your memoir—a chronology of your life. This informative feature can be placed at the beginning of your life story or at the end. My personal preference is to position it at the end. It certainly should be listed in your table of contents.

With a little effort you can compile this chronology gradually while you are working on your episodes. This chapter will show you how to prepare your chronology, and you will find a completed example of one as a guide.

Remember that you are writing your life story in separate and independent episodes. These episodes may or may not necessarily be placed in chronological order when you are finished. Even if they are, there would be gaps in time between them. The chronology— highlighting the journey of your life in short summary sentences— fills in these gaps. By scanning the two pages or more of your chronology your descendants will see at a glance the outline of your life path. There is a greater comprehension of a life when it is seen in this fashion. The chronology also becomes a valuable family document of record because it shows date, places, and events.

If, along the way, you manage to weave in a few historical facts that parallel the years of your life (such as who was President when you were born) you will make this document even more interesting.

To get started, take one of your loose-leaf pages and at the top write the title, "MY LIFE CHRONOLOGY." Then draw the lines as indicated in the example that follows. Write in the years on the left, and the important changes and events of your life on the right. Be sure that only the year appears on the left. The month and date, if you have them, go on the right.

You can enter as many items as you wish under each year. One method of working out your chronology is to take several work sheets and to list every year of your life along the left side. Then start putting down changes that occurred in your life next to the relevant years. Leave space between years because several events may have occurred in a particular year. Work on your chronology from time to time until you have it filled in to your satisfaction. If there are years where you have no entries, drop these from your final draft.

Here's a checklist of some important events and changes you may wish to note in your chronology. Some of these are actually turning points in your life. You will no doubt think of others.

Your birth
Entering your first school
Moving
Graduation (elementary school)
Moving again
Entering another school
An important birthday
An accident, injury, or illness
A death in the family
Moving again
Entering another school
Graduation (high school, college)
Your first job
Another job
Another death in the family
Births in the family
Marriage
An award
Another job
Births of children and grandchildren
Military service
Volunteer service
A promotion
A commendation
Buying a house
Buying your first car
Moving again
Anniversaries
Special birthdays
Special holidays
Retirement

OBTAINING HISTORICAL FACTS.

You can find these by consulting any of the world almanacs. There are other references your librarian can help you with such as *Timetable of History*, by Bernard Grun, and *This Fabulous Century*, by Time-Life Books.

A FEW TIPS.

Keep your items short. Save the details for your episodes. Be specific as to names, dates, and places. Choose either the past or present tense, whichever you are most comfortable with, and stay with it throughout. Take your time in filling it out. You may have to look up some documents for dates. Leave blanks where facts are missing and fill them in later. Remember, this is *not* an outline of the episodes you are going to write. However, your chronology can serve as a Memory Sparker helping you to remember important events you do choose to write about.

A little humor doesn't hurt once in a while. I have seen such light items as these in chronologies: "1933—We took in a cat." "1963—Caught a ten-pound northern pike less than 150 feet from my office during the lunch hour." "1948—We moved to Danbury, Connecticut. This makes the 26th different address we have lived at. Wow."

The chronology that follows is a composite put together to illustrate a sample format and style. How long should a chronology run? There are no limits. It can run two, three, four, or more pages depending on how much living you have packed into your life and how well you can recall events.

My Life Chronology
Dorothy Ann Smith

Year	Important Life Change Or Event
1922	I was born on September 3rd to Mary and Arthur Wilson in the French Hospital, Los Angeles, Calif. Warren G. Harding was President of the United States. The population of the U.S. was 110,000,000.
1927	I started in Kindergarten at the 97th Street School in SW Los Angeles. Charles Lindbergh completed the first solo

transatlantic flight from New York to Paris.
I started my first piano lessons.

1929   The U.S. stock market crashed in October. It was the beginning of the Great Depression.

1930   My mother, father, my brother Robert and I, moved into our new home in SW Los Angeles.

1931   I won a gold cup in a musical talent contest and my picture appeared in a Los Angeles newspaper.
We took in a beautiful Collie and named him Shannon.

1933   I continued taking piano lessons.
Prohibition, in effect since 1919, was repealed on December 5th.

1934   I graduated from elementary school and started at Bret Harte Junior High in Los Angeles.

1935-36   Nothing earthshaking.

1937   We had two graduations. I finished Junior High and my brother Robert graduated from Fremont High. In September I started at his school.

1940   I graduated from Fremont High and took a job as a secretary at the General Electronics Company, L.A.

1941   Sunday, December 7th. There was great excitement today. The Japanese bombed Pearl Harbor, Hawaii. President Franklin D. Roosevelt declared it an act of infamy and we entered WW II.

1942   On January 9th I married James R. Smith, my schooldays sweetheart. He had a job as an engineer with the Acme Materials Handling Company, L.A.
We bought our first car in June, a used 1939 Dodge.

1943   Our first child, James, Jr. was born on February 6th at the Bon Air Hospital in L.A.
Three months later Jim was called into active service with the Army Corps of Engineers and was first stationed at Camp Pendleton, Calif. I took my child and went to live with my parents.

1945   President Roosevelt died in Warm Springs, Ga., on April 12. He had been in office since 1933. He was succeeded by Vice President Harry S Truman.
V-E Day, May 7; WW II hostilities ended in Europe as Germany surrendered.
V-J Day, Sept. 2; Japan formally surrendered aboard the U.S.S. *Missouri*, ending WW II.
Jim was discharged from the Army as a Captain in November after serving in Africa and Europe. We took an apartment in L.A. and he went back to work with his old company.

1946   We bought our first little home in L.A. in April.

1947   Our second son, Charles, was born on June 10th.

1948   My husband surprised me on my birthday, September 3rd, with the first piano I ever owned, a spinet.
Jim Jr. entered the Manchester Avenue Elementary School. He had the same teacher that once taught me.
I volunteered to play the piano at a local Senior Citizens' Center.

1950   I was in an auto accident. I got off with two broken ribs and bruises.

1953   Our son Charles entered the Manchester Avenue Elementary School. That's three of us who've gone there.
General Dwight D. Eisenhower, hero of WW II, was inaugurated as the 34th President of the U.S. on January 20th.
The Korean armistice was signed in June ending the Korean War.

1954	Young Jimmy graduated from elementary school and followed my footsteps into Bret Harte Junior High.
1957	Jimmy graduated from Junior High and entered Fremont High. In July we took a trip to Florida with my folks and our two sons. We drove from L.A. to Tampa to buy property. We bought a double lot in NW Tampa.
1959	Charles graduated from elementary school in June. In August we moved to Tampa, Florida. My husband took a job with the Tampa Machinery Company.
1960	Jimmy graduated from High School. He was awarded a medal for excellence in history. In September he enrolled at the University of South Florida as a political science major.
1961	We moved into our new Tampa home on Linebaugh Avenue in April. Jim designed it and we did a lot of work on it ourselves.
1962	Charles graduated from Buchanan Jr. High in Tampa and entered Chamberlain High.
1963	John F. Kennedy, 35th President of the U.S., was assassinated in Dallas, Texas, on November 22. Vice President Lyndon B. Johnson became President on the same day.
1964	Jimmy graduated from USF with a BS degree in political science. He left home in August to go to Washington, D.C., for a career in the F.B.I.
1965	My mother, Mary Wilson, died on September 5th of cancer at Tampa General Hospital. Charles finished at Chamberlain High and enlisted in the U.S. Air Force. He was first stationed nearby at MacDill Air Force Base. Everything they say about the "empty nest" is true.

U.S. planes began combat missions over South Vietnam in June. By year's end we had 184,000 U.S. troops there.

1967   Jim and I celebrated our 25th Wedding Anniversary. The children treated us, and my father, to dinner at the Kapok Tree restaurant. I started as church organist at our local Community Church.

1968   My father, Arthur F. Wilson, died on December 10th at Memorial Hospital in Tampa after a long illness. He was 69.

1970   On April 11th my brother Robert died as the result of an auto accident.
I joined the American Red Cross and began volunteer work at the VA Hospital.

1974   Richard M. Nixon resigned as President as a result of the Watergate scandal. Vice President Gerald R. Ford of Michigan was sworn in as the 38th U.S. President.

1975   American troops were evacuated from Vietnam in April, ending the Vietnam War.
Jim Sr. underwent a stomach operation at Memorial Hospital in March.

1976   Jimmy (James Earl) Carter was elected U.S. President in November defeating President Ford.

1979   My husband retired from his engineering job and went into business for himself as a general contractor.

1980   The population of the U.S. was 226,500,000. It has more than doubled since I was born.

1981   52 American hostages, captured by Iran in the seizure of our U.S. embassy in Teheran, were released in January and returned to the U.S. They had been held for 444 days.

1982   Charles left the Air Force and joined his father in his business.
I traded in my spinet for a baby grand piano. I love it.

23

Writing Bite #11—Your Retirement Years

Memory Sparkers (About age 65 plus)

> Don't simply retire *from* something;
> have something to retire *to*.
> —Harry Emerson Fosdick

IN THE MEMOIR episode that appears at the end of this chapter the memoirist describes retirement as "anxiety, fear, frustration, joy, peace, hope, and time to reflect."

How do you view retirement? Do you see it as an opportunity to "make the rest of your life the best of your life?" Did you say "Hooray" to retirement? or "Good Lord, retirement already?"

Were you reluctant to retire? Why did you? Was it sudden or did you have time to plan ahead? How did you go about it? How did you choose where you would live?

How difficult has retirement been for you? Any surprises? Are you living on less? Describe the adjustments you have had to make.

Do you think now you retired too soon? Too late?

With both of you now at home have you found the relationship with your spouse more difficult? How have you worked it out?

How are you using your leisure time? Have you taken an interest in books, music, TV, sporting events, athletics, exercising,

other recreational activities? Have you found a second career?
A part-time job? A new hobby?

Have you turned to travel since retiring? Describe some of the
trips you have taken. Did you go with a tour group?

What do you do to avoid loneliness? Have you made new
friends? What do you do together? Do your children visit you?
How often? Do you take trips to see them?

How is your health? What do you do to stay in good health?
Have you had to drop any of your activities?

How have you been managing financially? With inflation ramp-
ant are you afraid you will run out of money before you run out
of breath?

How many houses (places) have you lived in during your lifetime? Tell about your first house or the one that has meant the
most to you.

Do you enjoy being a grandparent? How many grandchildren do
you have? Where are they? Do you see them often? What do
you do together?

Have you been in touch with your former coworkers? Have you
visited with them? Have you visited your former company?

Describe a day, a week, or a month in your life as a retiree.

Have you been active in your religion? How?

What advice would you pass on to your children, grandchildren
about life, raising children, religion, getting along in a career,
with people?

There's a saying, "You can be all you can be." Have you been? If
you had your life to live over again would you live it the same
way? Any regrets? What would you change? Ben Franklin said
he would live the same life over "only asking the advantages authors have in a second edition to correct some of the faults of
the first."

Do you fear old age? Do you have a fear of being a burden, of
having to go to a nursing home, as some do? What do you worry about the most now?

What are your views on death and dying? The philosopher Will Durant called it the wisest of inventions. "When it comes," he said, "I hope I shall have the wits and grace to look back gratefully upon life and say to my children and grandchildren, 'It was good.'" May that be your blessing, too.

A MEMOIRIST WRITES:

This man's family will get a very realistic idea of what retirement can be like when they read this chapter. He has written an honest and well-organized account of many aspects of his retirement life providing the reader with many valuable insights. Putting one sentence after another he allows you to see his life very clearly, just as it is. His thoughts flow easily. He writes to express, not to impress. Toward the end of his chapter he uses the excellent device of summing it all up in a single paragraph that opens with the question: "So what then is retirement?"

"Retirement—a Shift in Lifestyle"

If, as some people believe, it is a blessing to be "retired" from the business of the work-a-day world and the quest for the rewards of gainful employment, then I am thrice blessed.

However, just because I was able to retire three times does not of itself mean that my economic benefits grew in proportion. In fact, somewhat the reverse is true.

One might say I was caught unprepared. My employment with the Allis Chalmers Corporation in Pittsburgh still had six years to go before I would reach the age of 65 and the "normal" retirement benefit my 40 years of service entitled me to. However, dark clouds, in the form of union troubles, began to gather. Finally the company advised the union it could no longer meet union demands and that it would have to close down the plant. The union didn't believe it! It closed down. And I came away with severely reduced pension benefits. So my first retirement was "forced."

At the tender age of 59, still with financial needs beyond my meager pension, I sought other employment. Who would want to hire a person of my age and assume pension responsibility? But I was able to "shop from strength" and succeeded in obtaining a job as a Senior Buyer with a large engineering/construction company in Pittsburgh with a large backlog of orders, mostly of an international nature.

After only six months in Pittsburgh I was assigned to work out of the Paris office, purchasing for a direct ore reduction plant then being constructed in Iran. I spent most of seven months working on this particular contract. It was challenging and afforded my wife Ruth and I an opportunity to see some of western Europe.

Returning to Pittsburgh I worked on other contracts. Then things began to happen. One job after another was pigeon-holed for reason of international politics. In 1978 I was sent to Indonesia to purchase for a reduction plant being built in conjunction with a huge steelmaking complex. After almost a year my wife and I returned to Pittsburgh. We had again had a chance to see parts of the world we would otherwise never have seen.

By May of '79, with no new orders added to the backlog, the company felt the need to reduce the work force. I, being a newer employee, was among those affected. Lay-off again. How many times can this happen? By now, however, I had worked enough to be covered by their company policies concerning employee-vested pension rights. I could not collect for a year, but would be eligible for unemployment compensation for much of that time. How much pension benefit can one expect, though, for so few years of time worked? Not much to be sure.

By now I was 62 and eligible for Social Security at the reduced early level. Ruth and I took vacation time and visited friends in Florida. They suggested that we look around at the opportunities there. Florida was wonderful. Without really intending to make a commitment on this particular visit, we did find a condo of our liking and took the plunge.

Returning to Pittsburgh we then involved ourselves with the sale of a lifetime of accumulation, keeping only those most treasured of things. Our condo was not going to hold too much. We kept our trailer in a campground resort near Pittsburgh as a northern terminus when we returned to that part of the country. Then we sold our home in which we had spent the greater share of our married life.

In 1979 we officially relocated in our condo in an adult community in Florida. It was the first winter that I didn't have to shovel snow or suffer the biting cold temperature. Christmas came and went. Our grandchildren visited us in the spring and everything seemed to be going along fine. Then the phone rang.

My former boss asked that we return to Pittsburgh for an interview in connection with a job offer in Algeria. In short, we went for the interview and accepted a contract offer to work in Annaba, Algeria, for a period of one year with option for a second. It sounded so inviting—Annaba, a Mediterranean coastal city with a deep water port, on the northern coast of North Africa. It offered once again an opportunity to travel to parts of the world we had not yet seen.

We closed up our new home in Florida with all its nice new furnishings and packed off, first for an overnight in Paris, then on to Annaba and the unknown. The work there was slow getting started because of government red tape (Algerian style). The cars we were to have been provided did not materialize for months, nor did the housing. The natives, in dire need of western technology, gave the impression they'd rather we weren't there. On three separate occasions we were the victims of robbery.

While we lived in a hotel built in 1974, and modern by most standards, the natives lived in high-rise hovels or tin shacks mostly without sanitary facilities. Cars were old and mangled. To drive was an immense risk. We went back and forth to work in a company bus. We became virtual prisoners of the hotel in which we lived. We did manage, though, to get to Tunis, other parts of Algeria, Switzerland, Greece and Italy.

While we were in Italy my company was sold and the new owners had us return to Pittsburgh after only seven months (no tax break for us). So in 1980 our third "blessing" of retirement came about, this time enhanced slightly by foreign service.

Having been "blessed" three times, I figured my string had run out and I'd better just begin living the "life of Reilly." Sure we have alarm clocks but we don't use them. Most certainly we enjoy the Florida climate change, the opportunity to swim in January and to picnic on the beach. We play cards more frequently, assume minor roles in civic affairs and in organizations we now have time to enjoy. Our community clubhouse offers forms of entertainment or activity we have not found time for: for example billiards, painting, lapidary, photography, dancing and other hobbies.

But what is "retirement" all about? If I were to say I had

planned for it I would be fibbing. Throughout most of my life my efforts were directed toward earning a living for wife and family, keeping the roof over our heads and a car with which to get around. Our life was not on a lavish style then, nor is it now. Family vacations through most of the years were both brief and minimal in cost outlay. Not until recent years did I feel able to join a fraternal organization. Most of our friends were of long standing. Some are no longer among the living and others are now scattered about the country. The same goes for relatives.

So things change. First our residence, then church membership, followed by a whole new set of friends and associates. On rainy days—of which we have relatively few—we endeavor to do our shopping, laundry and such, thus saving the next good days for pleasurable pastimes. This alone is a luxury only those "retired" can enjoy. Exercise comes in a variety of forms including walking, bicycling, golfing, swimming, dancing, and occasionally, bowling.

Trips to a nearby town provide us an opportunity to shop for clothes (needs are minimal in this climate), to go to the cinema or to enjoy dining out. Otherwise our time is spent in and around our community with little need to go outside. Our slogan here is "The town that's too busy to retire." That is true. There are simply not enough hours in the day to accommodate all the things we could wish to do. For certain "that ole rockin' chair" is not a problem.

I remarked at the start of this chapter that three-times retired didn't mean three times the retirement income. However, Social Security and a minimal draw upon our savings have sustained us to this point. My wife now also qualifies for Social Security which we hope will let us breathe a little easier. The pension monies available to us were rolled over into one of the IRA funds now so very popular. This we plan to leave untouched as long as possible. The nervousness experienced when making that first decision is now eased somewhat we are pleased to say.

Since we continue to travel to the Pittsburgh area to our trailer facility we are afforded the chance to visit with old friends and the few relatives still living in that area. We have entertained some of them here in Florida and look forward to further chances to do more. "Ya'll come, ya hear?" Just call first.

As for my being around and under foot all day long, I must say Ruth and I appear most compatible. Perhaps this stems from the fact that we are together much of the time on the golf course where we have ample opportunity to vent our frustrations on the ball instead of on each other. I try to help her where I can—loading the washer or dryer, preparing morning coffee, watering the indoor plants, getting rid of newspapers and other refuse, and other small jobs. She, in turn, concentrates on all the big jobs like making the bed, loading the dishwasher, vacuuming, sorting the laundry and such. Of course she's the expert in the cooking department.

So what then is retirement? It is anxiety, fear, frustration, joy, peace, hope, time to reflect, time to enjoy, time to travel more leisurely, time to visit, time to appreciate the past and friendships developed along the way, time to read, study, partake of hobbies, share new experiences with others, time to "put your house in order" as much as possible, and a whole host of other things. Oh yes, time to be bored but only if you let or make it happen.

Just as it never occurred to me to think back or place great value on things of the past (until now), thoughts of death and dying have never held a prominent place in my mind. I don't think I am afraid, but that is an experience one cannot anticipate with any degree of certainty. We don't yet own cemetery property, nor do we have thoughts presently of buying. In fact, with the passage of time, thoughts of cremation vs. burial have injected confusion into my mind. This, I must clarify and stipulate for the guidance of my survivors.

Being "retired" is also being "unemployed." I'm a person who likes to be active and have things to do, a purpose for getting up each morning. While I relocated in Florida so as to enjoy all its benefits and to pursue some of the activities I've mentioned, I'm not opposed to a job for say two days a week, two hours a day with two hours for lunch, payday every day and twice on Saturdays, with all the federal, state and local holidays observed. If you know of such an opening for a person of superior qualifications, call me "collect" by all means.

To end this, I would urge everyone to "retire" at the earliest possible moment, enjoy life to the full, and by all means embark on the program of writing your own memoirs. It is fun to do and hopefully a source of pleasure to all who will eventually read about those things which were the highpoints as well as the disappointments of your life.

Whatever you do, don't sit in a rocker. There's too much to see, do, enjoy and share—all just waiting for you.

WRITING POINTERS: 41-44

41. *Keep it moving.* Veteran baseball player Dizzy Dean, speaking of a slow teammate, once said: "He runs too long in one place. He's got a lot of up and down, but not much forward." To hold the reader's interest your story should have a considerable amount of "forward." When your story stays in one place too long you have a tendency to overemphasize it, to overwrite it, to put in unnecessary detail and, perhaps, to ramble. That tires the reader who has already grasped your idea and is looking for the next turn of events. Move it along.

42. *Spread your copy out.* When you have finished a chapter try placing the pages side by side on a table or a board so you can see all of them at a glance. This helps you to see your episode more clearly from beginning to end. Now you can quickly see if this paragraph should go higher or lower, whether the chapter moves along smoothly, whether you have strayed from your topic, or whether you need to scissor out some repetition. I learned this little trick from Vance Packard, a colleague in the American Society of Journalists and Authors. He spreads his chapter across a tilted board especially made for this. I lay my pages out on an ironing board. My wife calls it "the battle of the board" because I'm always using it when she needs it. But we have reached a friendly solution. We now have two ironing boards—a "his" and a "hers."

43. *Polish the first and the last.* Give the first and the last of anything you write special effort. I mean the first and last sentences in a paragraph, the first and last paragraphs in a chapter, and the first and last chapters of your entire memoir. They deserve special emphasis. The first captures your reader, the middle develops your thought and the last clinches what you have to say, providing you have said it skillfully and with punch.

44. *Learn some of the editing marks.* They will save you time and energy as you polish your copy. These copy marks are simple enough and they are accepted and understood by editors, printers, and most typists. Many dictionaries list them (in the front or the back) as "proofreaders' marks." Here are some that you should learn to use:

To indicate a new paragraph use either one of these paragraph marks: ¶ ⌐

¶ We moved to Chicago in 1965.
⌐ We moved to Chicago in 1965.

To insert words in a sentence use the caret:
                    to Chicago
    We moved∧in 1965.

To connect one line with the beginning of another, pencil in a line as follows: I will never forget the aromas that⟩
⟨came out of Mother's kitchen.

Use this delete sign ℒ to eliminate words in a sentence. I will never forget ~~as long as I live~~ the aromas that came out of Mother's kitchen.

To transpose words put a curved line under one word and over the next: I loved play⁀to the organ.

A small vertical line between two words means that you want them separated by a space: I will|never forget.

To indicate that you want two parts of a word to be run together without a space in between use short curved lines: mem‿oir.

To change a letter from upper case to lower case draw an oblique line through it thus: The M⁄ain A⁄rgument was.

To do the opposite, to change a lower-case letter to a capital, place three little lines under it: The m̲a̲in a̲rgument was.

A circle around a number or abbreviation means that it is to be spelled out: She was ⑤ feet ④ in. in height: she was five feet four inches in height.

To do the opposite, a circle around a word means to abbreviate it, and a number that is spelled out means to return it to a numeral.

24

The Three Indispensable Pages

❧

THERE ARE THREE pages that are a must for any memoir. Together they round out your memoir package and add a great deal to the impression it will make. You will find these three pages in all non-fiction books, including this one. I will take them up separately.

THE TITLE PAGE.

This will be the first page seen after you open your cover. It will repeat the title on your cover, if you have one there, and it will show your by-line as the author.

Keep your memoir title simple and brief. It can be a phrase or thought that personally appeals to you. Sometimes you can lift a phrase right out of your manuscript that will make a suitable title. Strive for a title that makes a clear, informative statement rather than one that is too clever or romantic. At this time, before you "go to press," set aside a page near the front of your notebook to scratch out some titles. Put down a half dozen or so "possibles"; add to this list as you get other ideas. Then come back and pick out your favorite.

Ideas for your main title are unlimited. Here are a few interesting memoir titles that I have seen or written that may help you to spark your own:

>   *The First of Four*
>   (She was the first of four daughters.)
>   *It Was Worth It!*
>   *How Dear to My Heart*
>   *Random Thoughts*
>   *"Born Alive"*
>   (A phrase from his birth certificate.)
>   *Ponderings on My Past*
>   *The Relay Race*

(One generation handing the baton to the next)
I Remember, I Remember
Between There and Here
A Tale of Sixty Years
My Yesterdays
Holding Up the Mirror to Me
A Son Remembers
A Look over My Shoulder
All These Gifts

You may also find it helpful to see how famous people have titled their published memoirs. Here are a few such titles I've liked: *Something of Myself* (Rudyard Kipling); *Out of My Life and Thought* (Albert Schweitzer); *The Times of My Life* (Betty Ford); *Josh: My Up and Down, In and Out Life* (Joshua Logan); *Bubbles: A Self Portrait* (Beverly Sills); *I Didn't Do It Alone* (Art Linkletter); *A Backward Glance* (Edith Wharton); *The World of Yesterday* (Stefan Zweig); and *The Summing Up* (Somerset Maugham).

THE TABLE OF CONTENTS.

This follows the title page and it gives the reader an overview of the chapters to come. You should start a contents page now. Write the word CONTENTS at the top of a page in your notebook. Then, one after another down the page, list the titles of episodes you have already written. Number them with Arabic numerals on the left. As you finish writing each episode add its title to the contents page. Watching this page grow will give you a sense of accomplishment. After the memoir is typed in final form you can insert the proper page numbers on the right.

THE INTRODUCTION.

This important personal statement (it can run one, two, or more pages) serves as a bridge that leads your reader into your memoir. I call it the "introduction" in this book rather than the "foreword" because in publishing the latter has come to signify a preliminary statement written by someone other than the author. However, you should call it what you like—foreword, introduction, preface, or prologue.

You can accomplish a great deal with your introduction and it deserves special attention. For one thing it will set your memoir in time, and place because you will end your introduction by signing it and by indicating the date of completion and the place where you lived at the time (name, date, and place). Start now to scratch out some thoughts for your introduction. When you have completed all of the episodes you want to include, come back and write these important opening pages.

Here are some ideas you may want to consider for your introduction and they may, in turn, spark other thoughts you will want to include. I certainly don't expect you to cover all of them.

1. You can explain why you decided to write this memoir.

2. You can explain how you gathered your material and how you went about writing it.

3. You can explain your title if you think it necessary.

4. You can suggest that perhaps your family will find it interesting to read about life as it was lived in another time, your time.

5. You can mention that perhaps there are parts of your life your family is not familiar with and that this memoir will help to fill in those gaps.

6. You can point out that this memoir was written candidly, that it describes your way of life the way it really was, and that you have included the tears as well as the laughter.

7. You can explain what your memoir is not: that it is not an encyclopedic collection of everything but rather a selection of remembrances that highlight your life, episodes that you hope your family will find to be informative as well as interesting. You can explain also that it is not a genealogy.

8. You might want to remind your family that you are writing this memoir at this particular time when you can reflect on your life with greater serenity and objectivity.

9. You can express the hope that your family will get as much enjoyment out of reading your memoir as you have out of writing it.

10. The pages of your introduction would be an appropriate place for you to dedicate your memoir to people particularly dear to you; also to give credit to those who gave you a helping hand along the way. If you wish to do this with greater emphasis you could do it on a separate page, as has been done in this book. Here are the words one man used to dedicate his memoir:

> To my Mother and Father:
>   How can anyone ever adequately thank their parents for their love, sacrifice, understanding, guidance, patience, their always helpful hand, all of which seemed to flow without end?
>
>   From a grateful son—*Thank You.*

Following are forewords that I have seen used. Note how they take on the tone of a personal letter. I want to leave this subject with one final thought: Avoid making any apologies in your introduction for your life, for your writing, or for anything else. You are better than you think. So be positive.

FOREWORD

These memoirs are written with the hope that they may prove not only interesting to read but that they may also give you, our children and relatives, a better understanding of where you come from.

I have tried to describe the life of former days truthfully so that you may feel a part of them. Even more I have wished to make your ancestors come to life as real people, experiencing joys and sorrows, success and difficulties, as we all do.

Writing this memoir has been a rewarding experience for me and I hope each of you will enjoy it and find it of value.

With
love,

[Name]
[Date]
[Place]

FOREWORD

With love, I truly thank my mother for the challenge she left me when her memoirs were written at the age of 78 in 1945, and with most of her eyesight gone. She died in 1953 at the age of 92.

Many times since I retired from the Foreign Service, after serving in the interesting countries we lived in, people would say "why don't you write about it."

I read about Frank Thomas and his Memoir Classes at the University of South Florida, took the course, and resolved that I would write a memoir, not only from a personal standpoint, but also about the experiences my wife and I had in over 40 countries with their different customs, languages and religions.

I wish to express appreciation to the American Red Cross and especially to the lady in Tampa who, as a Red Cross contact, took a deep interest in my desires and made it possible for me, a seventh grader, to eventually attend the University of Florida. This in turn made it possible for me to write these memoirs.

I appreciate the assistance given by my daughter in rearranging, correcting and typing my original drafts. I also want to thank my younger sister who was a great source of information on family events, via long distance telephone. I give appreciation, too, to my son for his services as a critic on parts of this memoir.

This is my memoir, but I would not have had so many episodes to write about if my wife had not taken part in them. In many of our experiences around the world she personally participated with the native women in wedding and death dances, feasts, and in visiting native homes. It was she who provided the hospitality of our home. I thank her for being part of me.

I dedicate this memoir with affection to my children, grandchildren and great-grandchildren, and to the people of the lands we loved, lived and worked in for 12 years who gave us understanding and valued friendships.

Sincerely,

[Name]
[Date]
[Place]

FOREWORD

This memoir with its title "A Rugged Road to Progress" is dedicated in loving memory of my parents, my grandmother and my favorite teacher Sister Mary Felicite. It is further dedicated to my daughter, sisters, nephews and nieces.

First of all I want you to understand that I am not a professional writer. Secondly, I never dreamed of writing my memoirs as I thought I had nothing to write about.

Then one day my sister Hazel, who had been digging up our family "roots" for the past three years, asked if I would join her in taking a course in Memoir Writing at the University of South Florida. "If we take it I'm sure it will enable us to do a better job of writing our family's history," she insisted. As a result of this, and our inspiring instructor, I am proud to present you with a copy of my memoirs.

-It is hoped that as you read this humble script you will look beyond the blood, sweat, and tears, and profit by the following teachings and precepts of our forefathers:

"Love thy neighbor" is a precept that could transform the world if it were practiced universally. Love is interracial, interreligious, and international.

Our parents were imbued with faith, faith in God, · faith in their fellowman, and faith in themselves. With faith nothing is impossible.

Our parents had racial dignity. Color never destroyed their self-respect, nor did it cause them to conduct themselves in such a manner as to merit disrespect of any person.

Faith, courage, dignity, brotherhood, ambition, responsibility—these are needed today as never before. We must cultivate them as tools for our task of completing the establishment of equality for all.

As the poet Henry Wadsworth Longfellow has said:

Lives of great men all remind us
We can make our lives sublime,
And departing leave behind us
Footprints on the sands of time.

Children, have fun reading my memoirs. I hope this little book will inspire you to write yours so you, in turn, can hand it down to your children.

[Name]
[Date]
[Place]

25

Writing Bite #12—100 Bonus Topic Ideas for Variety

❦

THE TOPICS FOR EPISODES that one can choose out of a life are infinite. This final Writing Bite chapter lists more than 100 ideas that can be developed for a memoir to add variety. Some have been suggested by the Memory Sparkers of previous chapters. Others have been chosen by beginning memoir writers in my classes, or have been written by me.

Study this list. What subjects, besides those you have completed, do you think you would like to add to your memoir to round it out? Jot down the titles of these extra episodes at the top of separate sheets of paper and from time to time scratch out thoughts for them. Some of these thoughts will come out of your own memory. Others, requiring some hard facts such as names, dates, places, and people, will come out of your family's memorabilia.

I am listing these ideas for memoir episodes through the language of titles because I believe that will serve to dramatize the subject as well as the effectiveness of good headlines. Also, starting with a title will help you to focus down more sharply on your subject. Use your own titles or these or any variations of these. An asterisk (*) preceding a title indicates an episode that appears in this book.

My Lucky Break—A Turning Point
The House That Was Home for 50 Years
A Career That Chose Me
Surviving the Great Depression
Christmases I Remember
I Remember Pearl Harbor
My Favorite Vacation Place
Sayings My Family Lived By

My First Six Years
U.S. Presidents I Remember
How I Became a Teacher
My High and Mighty Teen Years
I Wasn't Born a Boy, But They Kept Me
*My Father—A Man Born Too Soon
Seven Children—Seven Blessings
I Remember V-E Day
Food I Remember in My Family
The Three Wars in My Life
Our Courtship and Marriage
"Darkness Brings Out the Stars"
I Remember Castor Oil and Camomile Tea
The Travels in My Life
We Had Very Little but I Never Felt Poor
*I Remember Armistice Day in WW I
I Found a Career by Accident
*I Was an April Fool's Child
Values My Parents Taught Me
California Here I Come
The One Place in My Life I Would Like to Go Back To
A Disappointment That Turned Out to Be a Blessing in Disguise
My Home Sweet Homes
I'd Like You to Meet My Dad
*The Walk That Changed My Life
On Not Becoming an Old Maid
My Other Mother
My Other Father
Fads I Remember in My Day
History and Me
Toys I Cherished as a Child
Our Cottage on the Lake
My Second Career
Nicknames I've Been Known By
The Career I Sometimes Wish I Had Chosen
I Was Brought Up on "Waste Not, Want Not"
The Job That Became a Career
My Best Friend
This I Believe
I Was a Late Bloomer
Jobs I Worked at After School
The Teacher That Influenced Me Most
The Songs That Were Popular Then
How I Learned to Drive a Car
My School's 25th (etc.) Reunion

The Home I Loved the Most
The Best Trip I've Ever Taken
My First Full-Time Job
My Week on Campus at Elderhostel
The Most Difficult Job I Ever Tackled
My Favorite Foods
The Best Present I Ever Received
The Event That Most Affected My Life
The Books I Read When I Was Young
Toys I Played with As a Child
We Did the Charleston Then
The Subjects I Liked Best in School
What Friendship Means to Me
My Favorite Sport(s)
The Wedding Anniversary I Remember the Most
Slang Expressions We Used in My Day
*I Remember, I Remember
*My Voyage to America
Dear Old Golden Rule Days
Our Honeymoon
Games We Children Played
My Father's Unfulfilled Dreams
I Remember V-J Day
*My Midlife Crisis and How I Coped
WW II—The War That Changed Our Lives
My Father—Ingenious and Ingenuous
I Remember My Grandparents
From Crystal Sets to AM-FM
I Met My Wife but Didn't Know It
I Remember the Stock Market Crash
*Our Family's Health History
*I Chose My Own Career
We Were Wiped Out by a Hurricane
Home Remedies Used in My Day
No Rocker Required
My Love Affair with Music (Etc.)
*My Preschool Years
I Remember the Most Important Day of My Life
*Our First Family Car
Looking Back on 50 Years of Marriage
Our Farm Neighbors
*Mamma Mia
My Experience in the Military
Tracing Our Ancestors Through Genealogy
Inventions I Remember

An Accomplishment I Am Proud Of
My Young Adult Years
Sometimes It Pays to Miss a Train
People Who Have Influenced My Life
The Teenage Street I Once Knew
You Pick Your Friends—Not Your In-laws
The Day Before Christmas on a Wisconsin Farm
My "Irresponsible" Son, Jim
My Auntie Grace
Papa as I Remember Him
Southward Journey
Memories of My Elementary School Days
My Sisters and Brothers
The House I Was Born and Raised In
My Report Card Years
The Family I Came From
What Friendships Have Meant to Me
My Mother—She Showed Her Love Through Food
The Pets I Loved the Most
The Farmhouse Where I Was Born
My Faith and What It Has Meant to Me
My Great Grandma
My First Day of School
Retirement—A Shift in Lifestyle
My Thoughts on Living and Dying
I Leave You My Faith in God
P.S. More Things I Forgot to Mention

A MEMOIRIST WRITES:

Rare is the home where children have not been admonished by parents through homespun sayings and quotations. That is why this thought was included in one set of the Memory Sparkers in this book. This memoir writer, born and raised in Canada where she went on to become a family physician, has vividly recalled many of these phrases her family lived by. She writes well and with great enthusiasm about them. She not only remembers them clearly, but she shows through the use of a number of anecdotes, how they continued to give counsel to her throughout her life. She has added another interesting and revealing chapter to her memoir.

"Sayings My Family Lived By"

My Mother had a saying for every situation in our lives. "Honesty is the best policy."; "A penny saved is a penny earned."; "All work and no play makes Jack a dull boy."; "Let not the sun go down on thy wrath."; "Handsome is as handsome does.", and its twin, "Actions speak louder than words."

These were the black and white painted posts on the highways of our days that prevented us from making many mistakes. Many modern marriage breakdowns could be avoided by the tolerance derived from these pithy words of wisdom.

"Anything worth doing is worth doing well." This was the rule of our home. I think perhaps it is ingrained in teachers. My Mother was a teacher and though she is long gone, at various times in my life when I have been tempted to do less than my best, her voice comes back to say, "Anything worth doing is worth doing well."

This adage saved the life of at least one of my patients. When she was 60 a woman came to me for a complete pre-retirement physical. She planned to take a long-anticipated trip around the world. She had no complaints. It was 5 p.m. on a Friday and I had had an exhausting week. I checked her over and came at last to the pelvic examination. All looked healthy and I thought, "She's okay so I'll skip the Pap test." Then I heard my Mother's voice saying "Anything worth doing is worth doing well" and I did the test. The next morning a telephoned report stated that the test was positive for cancer. Two days later she had a hysterectomy. There were no complications. Two years ago, when she was 86, she died of a heart attack after 26 healthy, happy retirement years.

"No work is demeaning unless you do it poorly." "A good workman takes pride in his work." "A good workman never blames his tools." These three teachings of my parents made it possible for me to earn my way through college as I took on any job that came up. I swilled out hotel garbage, scrubbed "glory holes" (closets full of filth and junk), house-cleaned, worked on farms and did other "menial" jobs. We children learned early the satisfaction of a job well done and the confidence of having a new accomplishment added to our potential usefulness in this world.

Of course as we children grew older we became as facile

as Mother with the apt reply. It became a game for us to respond with an exactly opposite saying which made Mother look as stunned at her unruly offspring as a Spanish bull when the matador sinks a barb into its shoulder.

Mother: "A stitch in time saves nine."
We: "Take no thought for the morrow. Behold the lilies of the field. They toil not neither do they spin . . . "
Mother: "Never put off to tomorrow what you can do today."
We: "Patience has its own reward."

Poor Mother! We impishly baited her, wondering out loud how, as a teacher, she had controlled a whole classroom when she couldn't control three of her own children.

But all teasing aside, Mother's aphorisms appeared like life preservers in our times of stress or indecision. "Make it do or do without," when teamed up with "Where there's a will there's a way," provided us with most of our major toys and sports equipment as children. Those sayings taught us ingenuity in solving problems that persist to this day.

"If at first you don't succeed, try, try again," kept me going many times but especially against tremendous health odds when I lost my heaviest year in medical school due to blood poisoning and subsequent myxedema.

"Actions speak louder than words," was an arresting, consoling thought when one was crying out for words of affection or appreciation from one's undemonstrative family.

"You can move a mountain with a teaspoon," my Father told me when as a four-year-old I looked out at the threatening Rocky Mountains surrounding our city. That thought has given courage to me, my family, and my patients in tackling what seemed like overwhelming odds.

"Where every prospect pleases and only man is vile," rises to my mind to further stimulate my urge to promote preservation of the ecology and the beauty of this world. Combined with "Where there's a will there's a way," a solution can be found to using the earth's material resources while still retaining its beauty.

Some time-honored sayings aroused in me feelings of frustration and discomfort. Mother's repeated "A woman's hair is her crowning glory," gave me a baffled girlhood. *My* crowning glory was a thick waist-long mop of heavy brown hair. Years later I recall a barber saying: "I've cut bailing wire less tough than your hair." I swore my Mother combed it by pulling the comb through it while pushing herself backwards from me. It hurt!

As a small child, dampened strands were wrapped around rags, knotted and left overnight to become curly ringlets the next morning. But sleeping on these knotty bumps, after crying as I acquired them, was difficult. Mother would encourage me with the saying "Pride suffers pain." However when I flaunted my painfully acquired curls the next day I was deflated by "Vanity, vanity, all is vanity," or "Pride goes before a fall," or most often "Beauty is as beauty does."

As I reached my teens and tried putting up my hair I was, as usual, campaigning to be allowed to have it cut. I never seemed to have any luck at this for if Dad agreed Mother wouldn't. But one Easter Mother was on my side. Style decreed a center hair-part with braided coils of hair covering the ears. This made my size 23 head so enormous that the only headgear I could find was a crocheted hat which I stretched tightly across my hair-swelled head. My Dad was a minister and it was his rule that his family must sit in the front seats at church so that the rest of the congregation would fill in behind us. So my hat and I sat there before him. He could not fail to see his 17-year-old daughter in her hideous headcover while all about her the ladies nodded and bowed their flowered and beribboned Easter bonnets.

At dinner that day my Father said very forcefully: "Mother, take that girl and get her hair cut. She's breaking the Sabbath!" So on Easter Monday morning my head dropped forward as the last strands of my hair fell to the floor of Eaton's downtown store in Toronto.

Incidentally, Mother kept her hip-length "crowning glory" until shortly before she died when surgery weakened her arm so she could no longer make the sweeping strokes of the brush necessary to keep it well groomed.

"A whistling girl and a crowing hen always come to a bad end" is a proverb which has roused my resentment from early childhood when Father taught me to whistle, a gratifying experience at that time. "Whistle when you are sad" has served me well all my life, and now that the vocal chords begin to hoarsen, it's a cheerful way to express my musical feelings. Besides, it's fun titillating the birds around me.

But there is one family saying which always brings a smile to our faces. Back in the early Twenties my brothers and I played in an orchestra. With no mechanical music except hand-wound gramophones (remember the little white dog on the RCA Victrola?) live musicians were greatly appreciated. On the night in question our group of eight put on a concert in a church basement in a tiny suburb of Toronto. After the attentive audience had finished applauding and we were gathering up our instruments, a small lady came up to us. Beaming with good will she exclaimed: "Youse done swell!"

To this day that is our family's supreme accolade.

WRITING POINTERS: 45-50

45. *Explain the terms of your generation.* Occasionally terms dropped in passing in a memoir may be familiar to the writer but not to your descendants. Pausing to explain these not only makes it easier for your reader, but such explanations often add interest and color to the writing. Your children and grandchildren, for example, may not be familiar with such terms, fads, and names as: the lamplighter, the New Deal, Lucky Lindy, hobble skirts, corsets, the Gibson Girl, the snood, the Rough Riders, the Charleston, the Shag, the Tin Lizzie, arc lights, or crystal sets.

46. *Go back to the beginning.* Whenever you are involved in a lengthy creative effort over a period of weeks, whether it be writing a memoir, a book, or an article, it is wise to go back to see if the beginning of your work has the same quality as the rest of it. Usually, if you are like most writers, you start such a project slowly. You gradually develop your style and get your "second wind." By the time you are halfway along you have hit your stride. Now you are writing more fluently and with greater confidence.

Go back and check your first few chapters, the ones you wrote weeks ago. Did you find your writing to be a bit stilted or lacking in candor? Were these chapters written haltingly as you searched for your particular way of communicating with your reader? Can you now, with the warmer, more relaxed style you have developed, make these early chapters more interesting? Let your early chapters harmonize in tone and quality with the later ones.

47. *Style is you.* Memoir writers in my classes are often surprised when I tell them that I see something of a style in what they have written, even though they are beginners. Perhaps this is because I have always advocated that they be themselves and not try to imitate anybody else. In his useful little volume *Writing and Selling a Nonfiction Book*, Max Gunther says: "The individuality of a writer's style—the personal element that distinguishes it from other writers' styles—is one of the things that make it attractive."

What you write, your choice of words, how you arrange them, will reflect your own personality, your own way of thinking. That is why, in editing a manuscript, I endeavor to touch it as little as possible. I want the individual to shine through. So there is no need to look high and low for a suitable style. It is near at hand. It is within you as long as you write simply, naturally and lucidly what it is you want to say to your reader.

48. *Editing your copy.* Someone has said that you haven't learned how to write until you've learned to rewrite. It is not easy to revise something you have written. It is especially difficult for beginners who may have fallen in love with their first draft. You should edit your own copy with as much courage as you would were it someone else's. Throw out fancy phrases, cut down on 60-word sentences, eliminate repetition, replace general words with specific words, and long words with short ones. Remove anything that slows your story down or that does not add to it. After you've done that, retype it. You'll be pleased with the way it looks.

Ernest Hemingway once said that he rewrote the ending of *A Farewell to Arms* 39 times before he was satisfied. "What was the problem?" he was asked. "Getting the words right," he replied. I certainly do not expect you to change anything that many times. But a little careful editing has never hurt any piece of copy.

49. *About rules.* You know the saying, rules are meant to be broken. There are no rigid rules in writing. Just suggestions and guidelines and that is the spirit in which I have presented them. I certainly do not regard anything I have said as sacrosanct. Unquestionably the more skilled you become the more you will experiment. On the other hand the beginner will be more cautious. It has been said that writing is an act of faith. I believe this. You must first have confidence in yourself. Given that, regardless of what anyone else may say, you need to listen to but one voice—that little voice inside of you. Learn to trust it.

50. *Symbol for "The End."* Since this is my last numbered writing pointer it is appropriate to remind you that you should always let your reader know when you have come to the end of each episode or of the entire memoir. To do this, drop down two or three spaces from your last line and write either "The End" or use the symbol -O-. In journalism we use -30-, the sign-off that telegraphers once used to indicate that they had come to the end of the message they were transmitting.

26

Expanding to a Family History

ONE DAY MY PHONE rang at home and it was a woman who had tracked me down after seeing the announcement of my memoir writing course in a university catalogue.

"If I take your course," she asked, "will it allow me to also write about members of my family?"

I assured her that my bite-by-bite, chapter-by-chapter approach would certainly permit this. I am so happy she called me because she later turned out one of the finest memoirs I have seen. Her descendants will treasure it for generations. In it she included revealing chapters about her parents, her maternal and paternal grandparents, and a rare portrait of her great-grandmother who was 75 years old when my student was four. She has permitted me to reproduce this chapter in the pages that follow.

Many memoir writers have the urge to include material about family members who have preceded them, and also, in some cases, about those who have proceeded from them. In writing about your life you may already have written episodes about your parents and grandparents. In that case you are now acquainted with the how-to of expanding to a family history.

Now, if you decide to write about more distant relatives virtually every chapter in this book can be helpful to you. First you need to dig out the facts, whether they come from family documents, photos, letters, relatives, tombstones, or genealogy. A family tree is one thing (and it certainly can be included in your memoir) but obtaining the narrative and anecdotal material that is needed to bring those names to life is another. You won't know how far back along your ancestral line you can write about until you start piecing together the precious bits of family knowledge you will need. Fortunately, the woman who wrote the episode that follows, "My Great Grandma," persisted in her search for material.

As you research you will find the Memory Sparkers in this book especially helpful. These will help you to frame the questions you will need to get the answers about your ancestors at each stage of their lives. Information such as birth, schooling, marriage, children, occupation, military or civic service, location of homes, travels, religious leanings, later years, and the date and circumstances of their death. Naturally, at this late date, you will have gaps in your material that you will have to write around. Where an important fact is missing, do not hesitate to explain to your family that though you have searched you were unable to obtain it. Remember, too, that you can insert important dates and events relating to your ancestors in your chronology, ahead of yours.

Some memoir writers I have known have been fortunate to have had ancestors who also prepared memoirs that were handed down. In these happy circumstances the present-day memoirist has either quoted passages from one written by an ancestor or reproduced all of it as a separate part of the memoir package, duly making note of this in the introduction and the table of contents.

One woman, blessed with a copy of her mother's memoir, combined it into a mother-daughter dual autobiography with the title "This We Remember." The introduction explained that her mother's memoir, written 44 years before, would precede her own.

While searching for facts in family records and documents be sure to interview living relatives. See how much your parents can tell you about your grandparents and other relatives. If your parents are not living, go to your oldest living relatives, or friends of the family. Take notes, or tape your conversations.

In the book she has written with Dora Flack, *Preserving Your Past*, Janice Dixon says, "Your family can become closer and more unified when you search out your family stories by asking family members what they remember, when you share the information you gather, and when you gain strength from establishing your own ties with your ancestors."

Who is it in your family that knows the stories that have been handed down? In his book *Roots*, Alex Haley talks about the "griots" of Africa who helped to fill in the missing links in his genealogy. These were the gifted men and women who lived centuries ago in African tribes. There being no written language in the tribes, the griots were trained from childhood to memorize the tribe's history. Today it is said in Africa that when a griot dies it is as if a library has burned down.

Treasure the "griots" in your family and lose no time in eliciting from them what they know about your ancestors. I remember Dorothy who cried on my shoulder one day. Dorothy had an invalid aunt living in Arizona who had always told many fascinating stories about the family's relatives in Ireland. Wanting to gather these stories for a family history she sent off a tape recorder to her aunt requesting that the dear lady talk her stories onto tape. But the feeble aunt found the "contraption" too difficult to manage and her stories died with her. The telephone or a personal visit would no doubt have produced better results.

A MEMOIRIST WRITES:

Here's how this woman wrote about her Great Grandmother. She has produced an excellent chapter here working from memory, from stories that had been passed down in her family, and from her research of family photos and documents. Gradually a clear picture of her Great Grandma emerges. Note the easy flow of her language and of the feeling you get of the times in which her relative lived.

"My Great Grandma"

I think that the first time I became aware of my great grandmother as a person, separate and distinct from my casual acceptance of her as grandma, was on her birthday in 1918. She was 75 then and I was almost five. Somewhere in the box of family pictures there is a faded black and white snapshot of a tiny little lady with snow white hair. She is wearing her white linen apron trimmed with hand-made tatting, sitting beside, but almost dwarfed by, a huge birthday cake with 75 lighted candles. Being newly aware of numbers, I remember being awed and entranced by a birthday cake with 75 candles on it though I could not, of course, have any idea of what those 75 years of living had meant.

The picture was taken on the front porch of our home in Wauchula. Grandma had come with us to Florida when we moved from Oklahoma the previous year. She had been widowed while young and for many years had been living with her son Walter (my grandfather).

My first wondering about time and growing older was inspired by grandma and began, perhaps, that day. One of the conclusions I had come to about growing older turned out to be false. Since grandma was much the smallest adult that I knew then, and also much the oldest, I concluded that one reached a zenith of height and stature at some point in life and then, in some cases, the reverse process of growing smaller began.

Grandma was born in Hull, England. Counting back from that birthday that I knew, would place her birthdate in 1843. Her birthday was in September but I have forgotten the exact day.

I have an envelope labeled in my mother's handwriting, "grandma's wedding dress." The envelope contains a square of brown silk taffeta, a handmade lace hankerchief and a moth-eaten remnant of wool plaid. I was told that the not very pretty tan and red plaid was our Tartan, part of a wool tie that had belonged to grandma's son Walter when he was a little boy.

I know nothing of grandma's parents. That the scrap of wedding dress was brown and not white tells me that they were probably not affluent, that even a wedding dress would have to be practical. I know that she came to this country when she was in her teens. I assume that she came with parents though I do not know that, nor why. I know that she married my great-grandfather in southern Illinois when she was still young. How sad that so much is lost because I was not old enough to remember and no one troubled to write it down.

My great-grandfather was a coal mining engineer, a graduate of Glasgow School of Mines, from the mining districts somewhere near Edinburgh, Scotland. There is a tiny hamlet in Scotland that bears the family name. One of the family who has visited there tells me that it lies in the raped and ruined landscape of the mining country. The origin of our name has to do with sheep and sheepherding which was an occupation of many of the early Scots. Our Tartan does exist though I have never been able to locate a swatch of it. The earliest record of the family name is in Leith in the 15th century.

My great-grandfather was a middle-aged widower with a grown family when he married grandmother. It is easy to understand that the vast undeveloped lands of the middle west presented beckoning opportunity and this brought him to America. And opportunity there indeed proved to be for he later became a very wealthy man. I never saw him, as he died many years before I was born. The picture of him shows a bearded, stern and unsmiling face, revealing the Calvinistic old Scotsman that family legend paints him.

Our family moved to Clearwater in 1920, grandma along with us. My sister Jeanette, born on May 24th of that year, was a young baby and grandma's special charge. For the next several years after we moved, most late afternoons would find my brothers and me in grandma's room where she kept us amused by telling us "long ago" stories. (I realize now that one of the ways an elderly, dependent relative could help to "pay her way" in the family was by keeping the young ones out from under foot while dinner was being prepared. But that does not lessen the enjoyment of the stories she told us.)

Since our family circumstances at this time were modest, grandma's stories of her beautiful home, of the richness and color of her early married years seemed to me like stories about a princess.

It was not hard to imagine her as a beautiful young woman as she was still beautiful as I remember her. She was small and delicately boned with skin, though wrinkled, softly pink and white. Though she worked at any household chores that mama would allow her to do, I have no recollection of her when she was not immaculately groomed. I remember her as smelling faintly of lavender, her white hair neatly coiffed and always wearing, whether with a house dress or Sunday best, her white linen apron. Her aprons were trimmed, as were all her baby clothes, with hand-made tatting which she continued to make as long as her eyesight allowed.

I see her as she looked so many afternoons, sitting in her bedroom rocker with the late afternoon sun making a halo of her hair. Usually she had the baby Jeanette on her lap while my brothers and I sat at her feet.

Among the few pieces of furniture that grandma kept was a square hollow-box footstool with a removable lid. It sits now in my living room covered in green velvet. But in those afternoons when I sat on it in grandma's room it was upholstered in black leather. The stool has become a sort of talisman from grandma to me. Re-covered many times, it has traveled with me to all the homes I have had since those childhood days.

How I wish I could remember more of the stories she told me. She had seen Lincoln's funeral train and described being part of the grieving crowds when the train passed through her town.

Her husband was a very wealthy man and though he allowed grandma no partnership in the marriage nor any knowledge of his business affairs he was very indulgent to his pretty young wife. They had a beautiful home set in several acres of landscaped grounds. Grandma made trips to England to buy silver, china and linens and made periodic visits for clothes for herself and the children.

My great-grandfather, with his two partners, operated a large mining company which controlled the mineral rights to much of the farmland in southern Illinois during the middle and later 1800's. This was a time of great industrial development in the U.S. and coal was one of the most important commodities and a means to wealth for those who controlled it. Whether my grandfather's partners, were simply greedy and unscrupulous men, as the family legend would have me believe, or whether there were more legitimate reasons for the severe disagreements between them and my grandfather, is now lost in time.

In an effort to undermine his authority and gain control of the company they secretly fomented fear and resentment among the landowners to whose property the company held the mineral rights, persuading the ignorant farmers that mining under their farms would cause the land to cave in. So successful was the ploy in generating fear and anger among them that a small group of men attacked my grandfather one night. He was beaten severely and left wounded on the railroad track in the expectation that his death would be called an accident. His unconscious body was discovered by a friend and moved to safety before the train came. Although he lived for a year or two he had suffered such severe brain damage that he was never rational again.

The world of women in which my grandmother lived then, a little more than a century ago, was so different from the one my granddaughters know as to be almost unimaginable to them. Grandma had been taught the skills and graces of women of her time—fine sewing and knitting, tatting and embroidery, cooking and housekeeping. She liked to read and had read the classics of her day and the Bible daily all her life. But I doubt that her formal education went beyond grammar school. But worst of all she had no knowledge of her rights of property, no knowledge of the law or the business world and without a male relative to protect her she was helpless in a world of men.

During the two years my grandfather lived, after his accident, she lost everything. By one immoral, though perhaps not illegal, means my grandfather's partners exploited her ignorance and helplessness. They persuaded her to sign papers whose content she did not understand. By the time her husband died she was to discover that she had signed away her rights to everything he owned including the family home.

From being a protected and indulged wife she suddenly became a penniless widow with young children and two step-daughters as helpless as she. She sold the personal household effects, realizing what she could from the silver and linens. All that survives of those now is one silver cream ladle which has come down to me.

I know little about those years following her husband's death. I cannot remember that grandma talked of them at length or perhaps it is just that they were not dramatic enough for me to have remembered. I know that they were very difficult years for her and that she did whatever she could to provide food and shelter for her children. In the beginning she was reduced to doing only the things that she knew how to do—sewing and hand laundry for others. Her sons went to work at a very early age to share in the family support.

Though she spent some time with my grandparents after they moved to Florida, grandma continued to live with us most of the time. She corresponded with her son, Rob, and daughter, Anna, but she never saw them again. Travel was difficult and expensive in those days. When a family member moved to another part of the country, it often meant a permanent separation.

As many women of her time were forced to do, grandma had learned the art of being the extra woman in a household. She was always alert to contribute what she could. She shelled peas, churned butter, washed the dishes, did the darning and mending and helped to care for the children. But seldom did she express an opinion of her own. She avoided any part of a family disagreement and was careful never to suggest a better way of doing something to my mother.

Grandma had what the family thought of as her "English sense of humor" and my father liked to tease her about it. I think that often she was not sure whether he was teasing or telling the truth. He had built the first radio set in the neighborhood in the early days of radio. He listened to it late in the evenings, trying for distant stations across the country. When he put the headphones on grandma and told her that what she heard was coming from Pittsburgh, Pennsylvania, I don't think she quite believed him.

She never quite believed the telephone and she never

saw an aeroplane, though she had, of course, seen pictures and read about them. The automobile and the
train were as far as she ventured into the twentieth century and she would have been happier in a carriage.

She had lived to be much older than any of her family
before her and was always a little surprised about it. For
the last ten years of her life each new dress that she had
was chosen, in part, as one in which she felt would be
suitable for her to be buried.

Grandma's life and my own overlapped for a period of
only ten or eleven years but those years did much to help
me achieve a sense of myself, not only as an individual,
but as an individual who is part of the continuity of a
family. She provided my first understandings of growing
old and my first experience of death. Years later when I
was to read the poem "Thanatopsis" for the first time,
the often quoted last lines brought a surge of memory
and a more adult understanding of this lady of gentle
grace who had been my great grandmother.

So live, that when thy summons comes,
approach thy grave,
Like one who wraps the drapery of his couch
About him, and lies down to pleasant dreams.

Grandma lived secure in her simple faith that Heaven
was waiting for her and, fittingly, death came to her quietly in her sleep.

27

Writing Your Ending

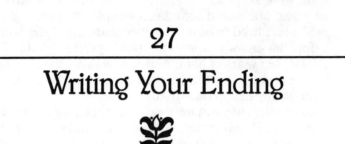

EARLIER I POINTED out that every good story has a beginning, a middle, and an end. Your introduction was the beginning, your prologue. The chapters about your life that followed were the middle. Now you have an opportunity to add a final touch to your life story with an ending, your epilogue.

It is true that sometimes the best things said come last. Your ending need not be lengthy, but surely you will want it to come from the heart. How have you viewed your life? Can you sum it up philosophically? Have you, now, come to terms with it? Are you satisfied with your accomplishments or would you have done it differently if you had your life to live over again?

Do you have personal beliefs, some values you hold dear that you would want to pass along? How do you perceive your generation? How would you contrast it with the present generation? Do you wish to pay tribute to your family and to others who gave you a helping hand along the way? Do you wish to express your hopes and goals for the future?

What are your reflections on religion, on death and dying, eternal life? One man wrote a spiritual will for his children that was read at his funeral. It said in part: "I leave you faith in God. Please keep it, use it, cherish it, and pass it on. This inheritance of faith far surpasses any other possession I could leave you."

Your ending, stated simply with affection, can take you wherever the spirit moves you. Here are three endings written by memoir writers I have assisted. Note how they have chosen to speak to their families. You may get more "sparks" from their words:

"Love and Prayers Go with You"

> We drop a pebble into a pond and the ripples spread on and on indefinitely. Our smile lights up the face of a pas-

serby who a moment before was depressed, and he smiles at the next passerby. We teach a child to love, and he responds warmly to those about him. So our lives go on touching one person after another—who knows how far.

Just so our ancestors touch our lives not purely by the genes we have inherited but also with the precepts passed down through the generations. We, in turn, shall influence those to come for countless years in the future.

You have a strong family ancestry and from all I've seen you will pass it on in that condition to your descendents.

Our love and prayers go with you.

(Signed)

"I Pass My Torch on to You"

It has been a good race; it has been a good time to live. The best of all times for me.

We accepted the torch of this relay race from our predecessors and sped on, stumbling at times but never quitting, never losing faith.

This lap has brought us far. From gaslights and kerosene lamps to electric lights, and to neon lighting that makes the skies over cities glow at night. From slow-moving horse and buggies to luxurious automobiles, speeding diesel trains and planes that streak across the skies. We have gone into outer space and put men on the moon to walk and discover more miracles for the benefit of mankind.

Communications have advanced from the printed newspaper to the radio and on to the television that brings news, entertainment and education into our homes around the clock.

Our medical discoveries have extended life expectancy. From the wood stove we have moved to gas, oil and electric heat to electronic systems controlling temperature and the air quality of our homes. We have gone from laundry tub and corrugated scrub board to the washing machine. A lively interest in the arts and crafts has been revived. This is good. Man does not live by bread alone. These are but a few of the achievements I have seen in my lifetime.

But now this lap of the race is almost finished and I

pass my torch on to you, my beloved family. May you carry it forward. I have tried to instill in you a sense of purpose, of self-sufficiency so you may do well in this race. You have accepted this better than I had dared hope. You are most capable of carrying on. I am proud of you.

We as a generation have accomplished many things, but there is much more for you to do. In some areas we have barely scratched the surface. There are many more mountains to climb and, as Robert Frost said, "Many, many more miles to go."

There are many problems yet to be solved; human frailties make it so. Hopefully, we have laid some of the groundwork for you to go forward to find solutions.

May you accept your torch with courage, strength, high ambition, confidence in your God-given gifts, and with the same faith that our forefathers passed on to us centuries ago. God bless you all.

(Signed)

"To Love and Be Loved"

My parents were neither rich nor famous as the world judges. But their lives were rich and full. Their beginnings were humble but their reach was ever upward. They accepted the responsibility of their own lives, meeting the problems of daily living with integrity and courage, and these were the values they taught their children. During many of the years of their marriage they worked hard and had few of life's luxuries. But even in the most difficult years they found time enough, and love, to reach out to those whose lives touched theirs.

They are gone and I am bereft. Never again will I have that secure and unchanging love which a good parent gives a child. To love and be loved. We seek it all our lives. But if one cannot have both, to be loving is the better. That is the heritage my parents left me. They taught me how to love.

(Signed)

Part Two

How to Package Your Memoir

We all come from the past, and children
ought to know what it was that went into
their making, to know that life is a
braided cord of humanity stretching up
from time long gone, and that it cannot
be defined by the span of a single journey
from diaper to shroud.

Russell Baker, *Growing Up*

Oft in the stilly night,
Ere Slumber's chain has bound me,
Fond Memory brings the light
Of other days around me.

Thomas Moore

One must wait until the evening to see
how splendid the day has been.

Sophocles

28

Before You "Go to Press"

YOU HAVE FINISHED writing your episodes. You have organized them so they flow in a pattern that suits you. Now, before you "lock up" your creative product, take a few minutes to examine this list to be sure you haven't overlooked anything of importance:

A "WHAT'S MISSING?" CHECKLIST

1. *Up front* (Chapter 24)
    Have you set up your three indispensable pages?
      The title page
      The table of contents page
        With chapter numbers and titles on the left and page numbers on the right.
      The introduction
        Have you concluded it with your name, place, and date?
        Be sure to list your introduction in the table of contents.
    Have you decided to dedicate your memoir to one or more people in your life either in your introduction or on a separate page preceding it?

2. *Photos*
    Have you chosen your most important photos and decided where to place them? You can spot them in chapters relating to them or group them together in the middle or at the end of your memoir.
    Be sure the photos you choose will reproduce well. You can test this by having them photocopied.
    Have you identified each photo with a caption showing the names of people appearing in them, and when and where they were taken?

3. *Documents*

Do you intend to reproduce any documents dealing with your life (diplomas, birth certificate, marriage certificate, award certificates, special letters, etc.)? These can be positioned in appropriate chapters or in your appendix.

4. *The Chronology*

Have you prepared one? If so, you can place it at the beginning of your memoir or in your appendix.

5. *Ancestral Chart*

If you have decided to include a family tree of your immediate family, it can be placed at the beginning, in the middle, or in the appendix.

6. *An Ending*

Have you written one?

7. *The Appendix*

If you intend to use one, be sure to list it in your table of contents. This is a handy place to position additional useful information you have not used in the rest of your memoir such as your chronology, your ancestral chart, maps, more photos, copies of family documents, family letters, wedding invitations, and certificates of award.

8. *Miscellaneous*

Have you been specific throughout as to names, places, and dates? Your memoir constitutes an important family document of record.

Have you included your full name and the date and place where you were born?

Have you included the full name of your parents, grandparents, brothers and sisters, children and grandchildren with birth dates and birthplaces? Remember, they love to see their names.

Have you included the full name of your spouse with date and place of marriage?

Have you included the full names of relatives and friends, either in the text or in your chronology?

In the episodes you have written, have you (where possible) included the names and locations of your schools, your teachers, and organizations you have worked with or belonged to?

In your text, where you have discussed them, have you been specific about naming the towns, cities, and states where you have lived?

Do you think you have answered most of the questions that your family might have asked about your life?

PREPARING YOUR MANUSCRIPT

> Wanted: skilled, accurate
> typist, to type manuscript.
> Must be neat. Call 000-0000.

Now to give your memoir that final look. You have checked it for spelling and grammar, accuracy and clarity. You have edited out the extraneous. You are ready for the final typing. Regardless of what format you choose for packaging your memoir (see next chapter) you will want to have a neatly typed final draft.

Yes, neatness does count. You should want a good-looking, easy-to-read manuscript. If you don't type, find a typist to do it for you. Perhaps you have a friend or neighbor who is a good typist. If not, in some communities, typists advertise their services in the local paper. If you read writing periodicals such as the *Writer's Digest,* you will find state-by-state listings of typists who advertise their services. It is handled by mail. Many are using word processors. Typists usually charge by the page. It may be possible for you to get a lower rate by negotiating a price for your entire package.

Whether you do it yourself or have it done for you, here are some guidelines for setting up your manuscript.

First, however, a word of *caution.* If you plan to have your memoir printed, or photocopied and bound to a special size, be sure to consult with your printer *before* you have your manuscript typed. He will specify the size of page, margins, spacings, etc., in order to best facilitate the printing job.

Note that I advocate typing your original draft on one side of the paper only. That's fine for the original draft. However, when you are having your photocopied or printed memoir run off you may want to use both sides of a page in order to save space and expense, assuming that the paper can handle it. Consult your copy center or printer about this.

> Use white, unruled, 8½ × 11-inch paper of a reasonably good quality. Try, if you can, for at least 25 percent rag content.

> An electric typewriter produces a neater, straighter line.

> Use pica type (normal size) which is slightly larger than elite type. It is easier to read.

Use only one side of the paper on your original draft.

Use double spacing, or at least one-and-a-half spacing.

Make one or more copies.

Keep margins to at least 1 ½ inches on the left and 1 inch on the other three sides.

Be sure that a good, dark *black* typewriter ribbon is used.

Indent paragraphs uniformly at least five spaces.

Number your pages (using Arabic numbers) in the upper right-hand corner, or at the bottom center of the page. Start your numbering with the introduction and go on through to the appendix.

Place an ending symbol -0- after each chapter to indicate that there are no more pages to follow in that particular segment.

29

Ideas for Reproducing Your Memoir

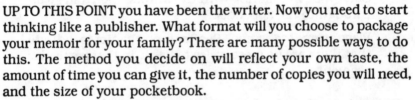

UP TO THIS POINT you have been the writer. Now you need to start thinking like a publisher. What format will you choose to package your memoir for your family? There are many possible ways to do this. The method you decide on will reflect your own taste, the amount of time you can give it, the number of copies you will need, and the size of your pocketbook.

Although, ideally, you would want your final product to be easy to handle and read, practical and durable, the important consideration is that you *do pass your life story on.* Here are a number of options for you to consider for reproducing your memoir, ranging from the simplest and least expensive to the more complex and costly:

1. *The staple.* I have seen the memoir pages photocopied, stapled together in the upper left-hand corner, and handed out in that form to family members at a reunion.

2. *The no-cost option.* Here the parent, because of location in an area inaccessible to facilities, or because of age or financial circumstances, simply turns the completed manuscript over to a son or daughter and asks that it be reproduced and distributed to family members. Most children would do it gladly.

3. *The folder.* Check your stationery store for a three-post clasp binder folder. They come in different colors. Some have a transparent cover allowing the title page of the manuscript to be seen at once. Use 8½ × 11-inch paper and have it three-hole-punched to fit the clasp binders. This is a good size for a bookshelf.

4. *A three-ring loose-leaf notebook.* I have found this format to be the most popular among memoir writers I have worked with. These hard-cover notebooks come in attractive colors. Red is one color often chosen. Be sure your pages are neatly typed with generous margins so that they will reproduce well when you photocopy them. Unless you are going to photocopy your black-and-white photos, you will need to have as many prints of your photos made as you have books. Individual prints should be mounted on pages of a slightly heavier stock. Hang on to your original manuscript. You may decide to update your book later, or to have more copies made.

5. *Self-publishing.* This option might be worth looking into, if you have the time and patience to apply yourself. It will cost more than the options previously mentioned, but you will have the creative satisfaction of taking part in each step of the process. Thus, in the end, your book will reflect your own standards.

Whether you print your life story from camera-ready typewritten pages or have it typeset, you will find it to be an absorbing experience. You don't have to be an expert and you don't have to do it alone. You can edit your own copy. A printer with an art department can get you through such steps as design, layout, typesetting, paste-up of each page for the camera, proofreading, printing, and binding. You may want to take on some of these steps yourself.

Ask around about a good printer in your area, or consult the yellow pages. Many weekly newspapers also run job shops and have had experience with books and brochures. They offer a variety of printing services from quick copy to offset printing and binding. Many quick copy centers can also provide some of these services. But before you go near a printer you should read at least one of the self-publishing books recommended in the Writing Bibliography so that you will be conversant with the various steps involved.

If you choose to self-publish from typewritten copy, you should hold off on your final typing until you have consulted your printer or copy center. You and he must first determine the size of your book before your pages are typed. I have seen some with soft cover in an 8½ × 11 size. Another size favored is 5½ × 8½, arrived at by folding an 8½ × 11 sheet in half. This is approximately *Reader's Digest* size.

To keep your costs down you should get bids from at least three printers. Ask for samples of work they have done for others. Once you've chosen your printer, determine the size and whether you will print from typewritten pages or typeset pages. Ask him about the difference in cost. Ask to see samples of the paper stock for the cover and the inside pages. Discuss with him the artwork for the cover, how he will handle photos, the numbering of pages, and the type of binding you will get. Be sure in your own mind that you will end up with an attractive book design.

Once you have agreement on the total number of copies to be printed, and the total price of the job, try to pay only a third up front, another third on submission to you of proofs (sheets showing an impression of each page), and the remainder when the job is completed.

6. *The subsidy publisher.* The ads beckon "the unpublished author" in newspapers, magazines, and on radio and TV. The sponsors are most often subsidy book publishers, the so-called "vanity" presses. The subsidy publisher differs from the trade publisher who sells his books mainly through retail stores. He doesn't pay you, you pay *him* to have your book published. Many flattering inducements are advanced, many promises are made, and the contract you are asked to sign can be elaborate, if not ambiguous. I can only say "Let the buyer beware." If you want to have your memoir published in hard cover with the idea of making a profit then this option is not for you. Few books handled by subsidy publishers are money-makers, and most fail to return even a fourth of the author's investment.

Unless money is no object it is hardly worth an expenditure in the thousands of dollars to have your memoir printed in this way when there are so many other options open to you. However, should you wish to look into this avenue further I would suggest that you first write to *Writer's Digest* (9933 Alliance Road, Cincinnati, OH 45242) and request its reprint "Does It Pay to Pay to Have It Published?" You may conclude that it does not after you have read the answers to many questions posed in this article about subsidy publishing.

Additional Notes

Handling your photos. Remember that many black-and-white photos can be photocopied using the darker setting. If you can do it this way it will cut down on your photo expense. The IBM Copier 11 and the Xerox 9500 models do a passably good job with black-and-white photos, especially where the originals are sharp to begin with. Oddly enough I have seen some old, yellowed black-and-white photos that came out looking better on the copying machine than the originals did. Test your photos on a copying machine using the darker setting. If you're not satisfied with the result, then have prints made. I do not advise photocopying color photos.

Incidentally, you should take time to get acquainted with some of the expanded services available in some of the large photocopying centers in your area (sometimes called quick-copy or duplicating centers). Many can not only reproduce your pages, they can do the entire job—collating, selecting and printing your cover, and providing the needed binding.

If you are going to have your memoir printed, then all you have to do is take your photos to the printer and he will make halftones from them. From these he can run off as many copies as you need for your books. The halftone is a printing plate made by a process that transforms the photograph's image into a series of small dots.

Paper selection. You should discuss the quality of paper stock with your printer or copy center. It is worth a few cents more to get a better grade that will preserve your memoir longer. Some papers are more suitable for photocopying and others for printing. Bond paper is sold according to grade number, the #1 grade being the best. Bond paper with a rag content is more durable than paper without rag content. If your printer or copy center does not have bond paper with rag content you can buy it in a stationery store and have him run the job on it. But check with him first to learn whether his equipment will reproduce well on that kind of paper. All legal documents are printed on paper of 25 percent rag content or better.

The binding. If you get into a format where you need binding you have choices of varying cost. Here are some: The simplest is the staple binding. Sometimes, depending on the thickness of the book, a staple and tape binding can be used, the tape running along the spine of the book. Another less expensive binding is the plastic spiral binding, also called comb binding. Many cookbooks are bound this way so the pages can be laid out flat. Wire spiral binding serves the same purpose but you may have difficulty finding someone who can do this. Paperbacks are "perfect bound" using an adhesive applied to the spine and cover. Hard-cover "case bound" books require extra steps and this method is far more expensive.

The cover. If you are using a three-ring loose-leaf notebook or a clasp binder folder for your memoir you have no need for a special cover. If you have your memoir printed and bound in soft cover you will need art for your cover. You will also need to choose a heavier paper stock for it in a color to suit your taste. The art can consist simply of the printed title and your name. You can go beyond that with a drawing of some kind. One man I know simply had his family crest reproduced on the cover below his title and name.

Any local freelance artist can design a cover for you if you point him in the right direction. Have him submit a rough sketch before he finalizes it. If you don't know an artist you can check with the president of a local art club, or look in the yellow pages for one. Very often a printer will have an artist on staff, or on call, who can take on this assignment. You can have a lot of creative fun giving birth to your finished book.

30

More Questions I Am Often Asked

Can I update my memoir from time to time?

Certainly. Consider doing it annually or every two, three, or five years. Use the same technique of separate episodes dealing with new highlights in your life. Having written your life story to date it will be easier for you now to sift out what is more important and entertaining. Your three-ring loose-leaf notebook will come in handy for this updating. Keeping a journal or diary will also be helpful. The notes you jot down in your journal about significant changes or events in your life will make it easier for you to do the updating later.

Also, why not urge the younger members of your family to start a journal now so they can draw on it later when they, too, prepare their memoirs for their descendants?

Should I have my memoir professionally typed?

Yes, if you wrote it in longhand. I would say yes also if you do not have a typewriter with a dark ribbon that can deliver sharp, readable letters or if, as a typist, you use the biblical "seek-and-ye-shall-find" two-fingered method of typing making many strikeouts. Of course, if you have a word processor with a letter-quality printer (or know someone who has), then you are in a most fortunate position to get many copies made of your memoir. If you want to read how a professional writer made a transition from the typewriter to the computer, read William Zinsser's book *Writing with a Word Processor.* "There's no limit to the variety of projects that a word processor can help a writer to write," says Zinsser.

Should I copyright my memoir?

If you place the copyright notice at the beginning of your memoir as soon as you have created it, you have already copyrighted it. The notice consists of three elements: the word "Copyright" or its symbol ©, the year, and your name. Thus: "Copyright, John Doe, 1985." Copyright is a form of protection that gives you the exclusive right to print, reprint, sell, or distribute your creative work.

However, if you wish to officially register your copyright, you must send two complete copies plus (at this writing) a fee of $10 to the Register of Copyrights, Library of Congress, Washington, DC 20559. If your memoir is unpublished, you need send only one copy. To get the information and application form you need, write to the Register of Copyrights and ask for circulars R1 and R99, and for form TX. Your application, copies, and fee must be mailed in the same package. Later you will receive a certificate verifying your copyright.

Be sure to place the copyright notice on your copies *before* you distribute them and *before* you send copies to the copyright office. I recall one man who turned out an excellent memoir running 120 pages, 8½ × 11 size. It had a specially designed cover, a section for photographs, and a number of reproduced documents. He contracted with a local printer for 85 copies, but not knowing copyright procedure, he omitted the copyright notice. He later learned that he could no longer copyright his memoir and that it had fallen into the public domain.

A Writer's Guide to Copyright, edited by Caroline Herron and published by Poets & Writers in New York is a clear manual on copyright law especially as it pertains to writers.

Can I break into print with my life story?

I have never discouraged anyone from trying. If you feel that your story can grip the reader and inform and entertain him or her, there's always a chance. That is, provided you have a thick skin and you apply the tried and true virtues of patience and persistence. Had I not used a full measure of both, this book might not have seen the light of day.

In what follows I will discuss the possible placement of part or all of your memoir on three levels.

1. *Your local newspaper.* Make no mistake about it, writing your life story for your family and for yourself has to be one of your proudest accomplishments. In her book *How to Write and Sell Your Personal Experiences,* author-teacher Lois Duncan writes about a student who believed that a written record of the most interesting events in one's life is "the most important legacy a person can leave future generations."

The recording of your life memories for your descendants is a newsworthy event. A number of my memoir writing students have been interviewed by their local newspapers. In some cases, newspapers selected and ran entire memoir chapters of particular interest. So once you have your life story neatly printed or packaged, don't hesitate to get in touch with the local editor. If yours is a small weekly newspaper, telephone him, or visit his office and show your "pride and joy." Point out some of the highlights to him. Tell him why you decided to write it and how you went about it.

If your local newspaper is a large busy daily, then I would suggest that you use a device the professionals use—*the query*. It is your sales letter to the editor. Call the newspaper, get the name of the feature editor or the managing editor. Then write him or her a letter of one page (preferably typed) or at the most, two pages. Here's a sample of what you might say:

> *Dear (name of editor):*
>
> *I am 65 years old and have just completed one of the proudest achievements of my life—my life story. I am about to present copies of it to my 12 children and grandchildren so they and future generations may know about the times in which I lived and some of the events that shaped my life.*
>
> *My book includes chapters about my early schooling and the games we played then, life on a Pennsylvania farm where we made our own butter and cheese, an account of a visit to our village blacksmith, a story about our family's first car, and vignettes of my mother and father.*
>
> *My book has 125 typed pages taking me from birth to my recent retirement as a supermarket manager. There are 11 chapters and 18 photos in it. It took me seven months to write it. There are many things in it that may interest your readers.*
>
> *I will be glad to come to your office with a copy of my memoir, or to be interviewed by one of your reporters in my home. My phone number is 000-0000.*
>
> > *Sincerely*

2. *Magazines.* First, let us take a look at what it is you have to "sell." Then I will suggest how you might go about "marketing" your "product."

What are the chapters in your life story that are most apt to interest magazine editors? Here, for our purposes, are four categories I have chosen that I think have possibilities:

Chapters tied to events. An editor might consider using pieces out of your memoir, such as the following, provided they are well written and vividly recalled. Also, provided you get to him early enough in his publishing schedule: "I Remember the Day We Put a Man on the Moon," "I Remember V-E Day," "I Remember the Stock Market Crash," "I Remember Pearl Harbor," "My Voyage to America," "I Remember the Day President Kennedy Was Shot."

Chapters tied to seasonal holidays. Does your memoir tie in with such holidays as Mother's Day, Father's Day, Memorial Day, Christmas, New Years', and so on? Then such episodes as the following might interest an editor: "My Father—A Man Born Too Soon," "My Mother—She Showed Her Love Through Food," "My Father's Unfulfilled Dreams," "Mamma Mia."

Bear in mind that consumer magazines work at least six months ahead; in the case of seasonal material as much as a year ahead. So be sure to time your query accordingly.

Chapters of an inspirational or religious nature. If your memoir includes an experience that profoundly changed your life, one that brought you closer to your Maker, you have another placement opportunity. Editors of inspirational and religious magazines are always on the lookout for writers willing to share such experiences. Here are some examples in this category: "My Midlife Crisis and How I Coped," "Darkness Brings Out the Stars," "Values My Parents Taught Me," "A Disappointment That Turned Out to be a Blessing in Disguise," "The Walk That Changed My Life," "We Were Wiped Out by a Hurricane," "My Faith and What It Has Meant to Me."

Today there are magazines for almost every interest, and for every magazine, an editor who is looking for well-written new ideas. These magazines range from regional publications you have seen, usually named after your area, to national consumer publications, such as the *Reader's Digest, Redbook, Ladies' Home Journal, Good Housekeeping, Life, 50 Plus,* and *Modern Maturity.*

There are some excellent directories for studying magazines and their requirements. *Writer's Market,* published annually, lists magazines in every category, including consumer, regional, and religious, with addresses of the publications, the names of editors, and publishing interests. *The Writer's Guide to Magazine Markets: Non-Fiction* lists 125 of the top consumer newsstand magazines with detailed information on the kinds of material editors look for. *The Religious Writers Marketplace,* by William Gentz and

Elaine Colvin, lists more than 1,500 publishers and publications in the religious field.

Narrow down your choice of magazines that appear to best suit the particular memoir chapter you have in mind. Then study them. Pick them up at your local newsstand, or go to the magazine rack of your local library. Some publications offer free sample copies if you write for them.

Next, prepare your query to the editor along the lines of the sample I've given you under newspapers. If possible, include an anecdote or two from your chapter. Give the editor an idea of its word length, and if you were written up in your local paper, be sure to attach a tear sheet of the story to your query.

Incidentally, many of these chapter ideas would also appeal to your local newspapers should you be unable to place particular ones in magazines.

3. *Book publishing.* There are a number of ways to approach a book publisher. The most unproductive way, to my mind, is the one thousands of unpublished writers use. They pack their precious pages into an envelope and ship them, unsolicited, to the address of a publisher picked at random. Ralph Daigh, in *Maybe You Should Write a Book,* points out that the larger book publishers admit to receiving more than 10,000 book manuscripts annually from unpublished authors. These go into a so-called slush pile, and most go unread or are returned unopened.

A more sensible way to approach the publisher is to use the query method and to use it after you have carefully selected a publisher prospect. Nor is it necessary to go after the "big guns" in publishing. A good memoir, taken as a whole, is much more likely to be considered by one of the regional presses such as those listed in the *International Directory of Little Magazines and Small Presses* than by a major publisher. This volume gives names and addresses, the material the publisher uses and a geographical index.

"The regional press," says Richard Balkin in his informative book *A Writer's Guide to Book Publishing,* "resembles the commercial trade house and differs primarily in the limited scope and size of its list, its expectations, its overhead and expenditures . . . . For the author whose book may have a limited audience, the regional press may be an ideal solution."

Another source for looking up book publishers is *The Literary Market Place* (LMP), a comprehensive directory of American book publishing found in most libraries.

Having decided on your publisher target, prepare your query carefully. Keep it to two pages or under. Be sure to tell him how many chapters there are in your book and its approximate word length. Ask if you may submit one or two typical chapters (if he says yes, be sure to enclose return postage). Include a thumbnail bio on yourself in your query and mention any writing credits you may have. If your local paper wrote you up, attach a clipping to your query.

Should you receive a reply from the publisher indicating interest but suggesting that certain revisions might make it more acceptable, count your blessings and comply. If you are turned down by one publisher, go on to the next. To quote author Dean Koontz, this process calls for a "vast reservoir of determination."

Should I try to get the help of a literary agent?

Unless you are a published writer and have been published with some consistency, I would not advise taking this route. Remember that literary agents, also known as authors' representatives, make their living on sales—almost always 10 percent commission on what they sell in the United States and more on foreign rights. Naturally, they earn more income from professionals who write regularly. That's why I believe you have less chance of getting an agent than a publisher.

Some writers I know feel that they do not need an agent. No agent, no matter how good, can sell an unsalable manuscript. On the other hand, it is hard to believe that a superbly conceived and crafted work could not make it on its own merits given the author's persistence. After all, as the saying goes, aren't editors paid to seek out publishable manuscripts?

If you feel you have the qualifications to interest an agent and neither the time nor the know-how to sell your special material on your own, then try approaching one. But do it the same way you would approach a publisher, by using the query method before you send in your manuscript.

A discussion of what agents are and what they do, plus the names and addresses of many, can be found in *Literary Agents: A Complete Guide*, Poets & Writers, Inc., 201 W. 54 St., New York, NY 10019. Also, *Literary Agents of North America*, Author Aid/Research Associates, 350 E. 52 St., New York, NY 10022, lists over 450 agents in the United States and Canada indicating the specialties, requirements, and policies of each.

A word of caution. Most recognized agents have the professional integrity and ability to handle a writer's work effectively. However, there are a few on the fringes of this field who have been described as "predatory sharks" who bilk the unsuspecting. These self-styled "story doctors" are the ones that also advertise widely and make a living from charging beginning writers exorbitant "reading fees." They may flatter your work and promise that they can place it providing you let them rewrite it—for a fee. One memoir writer who consulted me, unfortunately after the fact, told me she had lost $1,400 to such a "literary service" without any result.

Some agents may charge a reading fee for unsolicited material but refund it in the event of a sale. Most recognized agents do not charge a reading fee believing that editing should be done by editors after the book is sold. In all cases where fees are involved, you should ask in advance for a written explanation of precisely what the fee will be, what you will get for it, and whether it is a one-time fee only.

Can I become a writer?

I am sometimes asked this question in my writing classes by people who have had a taste of creative excitement. I never discourage them. But I do ask this question in turn: "How badly do you want it?"

The famed late Notre Dame football coach Knute Rockne was once asked what he most looked for in a football player—was it weight, speed, or brains? He replied, "None of these. I look for a *desire* to play football."

No one can tell you positively whether you can or cannot become a professional writer, and you should not let anyone do it. You learn by writing. You should get better as you go. To begin with, you can profit from the techniques used by other successful writers. After that you are on your own.

In his book *A Professional Guide to Marketing Manuscripts*, Paul R. Reynolds expresses his belief that success for the writer depends to a considerable measure on two attributes: "a compelling urge to write, and a great belief in oneself." If you have these, a typewriter, a ream of paper, and a willingness to learn from your mistakes, then neither rain, discouragement, writer's block, or rejection slips can stop you.

I would like to put a P.S. on this. Should circumstance prevent you from pursuing a writing career long enough to become a full-time professional, be consoled in the knowledge that creative expression in writing is as good a part-time hobby as any, and more personally fulfilling than most. Good luck.

Author's Postscript

A BOOK SUCH AS this, dealing with human lives, deserves the best an author can give it. I have endeavored to anticipate your needs for this worthwhile project—that of putting down an account of your life as a gift of love to your family. But whatever has been written can be improved and I will welcome any comments, ideas, or suggestions that I can pass on to others who also wish to write their memoirs.

When you have completed your memoir, if you feel I've been helpful and if you have an extra copy, I'd appreciate receiving it, autographed, for my prized collection. Address a note to me c/o Writer's Digest Books, 9933 Alliance Rd., Cincinnati, OH 45242. I'll get back to you with a forwarding address.

Congratulations, and I hope you have found creating your memoirs one of the more rewarding experiences of your life. May I ask that you consider bringing this book to the attention of your descendants so they, too, will be encouraged to leave their imprint on the history of your family?

Sincerely,
F.P.T.

appendix

A SELECTION OF 100 AUTOBIOGRAPHIES

Adams, Henry. *The Education of Henry Adams* (American historian and scholar)

Andersen, Hans Christian. *The True Story of My Life* (Dutch author of fairy tales)

Angelou, Maya. *I Know Why the Caged Bird Sings* (American singer, actress, playwright)

Bacall, Lauren. *Lauren Bacall by Myself* (American actress)

Bailey, Pearl. *Talking to Myself* (Singer)

Baker, Daisy. *Travels in a Donkey Tray* (Author)

Baker, Russell. *Growing Up* (Journalist's Pulitzer Prize-winning memoir)

Belli, Melvin. *Melvin Belli: My Life on Trial* (Lawyer)

Berle, Milton. *Milton Berle: An Autobiography* (Comedian)

Bok, Edward. *An Autobiography* (Author, philanthropist)

Borland, Hal. *High, Wide and Handsome* (Nature writer)

Bourke-White, Margaret. *Portrait of Myself* (Photographer)

Bryson, Dr. J. Gordon. *One Hundred Dollars a Horse* (Physician)

Burns, George. *Living It Up: Or They Still Love Me in Altoona* (Comedian)

Catton, Bruce. *Waiting for the Morning Train* (Historian)

Cellini, Benvenuto. *Autobiography* (Italian sculptor)

Chevalier, Maurice. *I Remember It Well* (French actor, singer)

Christie, Agatha. *An Autobiography* (English mystery storywriter)

Churchill, Winston. *My Early Life* (British statesman)

Clark, Kenneth. *Another Part of the Wood—A Self-Portrait* (Art historian)

Clemens, Samuel. *Mark Twain's Autobiography* (Author)

Colette, Gabrielle Claudine. *My Mother's House* (French novelist)

Croce, Benedetto. *An Autobiography* (Italian philosopher)

De Mille, Agnes. *Dance to the Piper* (American choreographer)

DeMille, Cecil B. *The Autobiography of Cecil B. DeMille* (Movie director)

Douglass, Frederick. *Narrative of the Life of Frederick Douglass, an American Slave, Written by Himself* (Abolitionist, journalist)

Du Maurier, Daphne. *Myself When Young: The Shaping of a Writer* (Author of *Rebecca*)

Durant, Will and Ariel. *A Dual Autobiography* (Philosophers, authors)

Ellington, Duke. *Music Is My Mistress* (Pianist, composer)

Fitzgerald, Zelda. *Save Me the Waltz* (Wife of author F. Scott Fitzgerald)

Ford, Betty. *The Times of My Life* (President's wife)

Frank, Anne. *The Diary of a Young Girl* (Teenager hiding from the Nazis)

Franklin, Benjamin. *The Autobiography of Benjamin Franklin* (American statesman)

Freud, Sigmund. *An Autobiographical Study* (Founder of psychoanalysis)

Gandhi, Mohandas. *Autobiography: The Story of My Experiments with Truth* (Architect of India's freedom)

Gaulle, Charles de. *The War Memoirs of Charles de Gaulle* (soldier, writer, statesman)

Getty, J. Paul. *As I See It* (Millionaire)

Gibbon, Edward. *Autobiography* (English historian, author of *The Decline and Fall of the Roman Empire*)

Gilbreth, Frank B. *Time Out for Happiness* (Author of *Cheaper by the Dozen*)

Grant, Ulysses S. *Personal Memoirs* (U.S. President)

Greene, Graham. *A Sort of Life* (Novelist)

Hart, Moss. *Act One: An Autobiography* (Playwright)

Hayes, Helen. *On Reflection* (Actress)

Herriot, James. *All Creatures Great and Small* (Veterinarian)

Jefferson, Thomas. *The Autobiography of Thomas Jefferson* (U.S. President, author of the Declaration of Independence)

Johnson, Josephine W. *Seven Houses: A Memoir of Time and Places* (Actress)

Jung, C. G. *Memories, Dreams, Reflections* (Swiss psychologist)

Kazin, Alfred. *A Walker in the City* (Writer, professor)

Keller, Helen. *Story of My Life* (American blind deaf-mute, author)

Kingston, Maxine Hong. *Woman Warrior: Memoirs of a Girlhood Among Ghosts* (Teacher)

Kipling, Rudyard. *Something of Myself* (English writer)

Lawrence, T. E. *The Seven Pillars of Wisdom* ("Lawrence of Arabia"; British archaeologist, soldier, writer)

Levenson, Sam. *In One Era and Out the Other* (Humorist)

Lindbergh, Anne Morrow. *Hour of Gold, Hour of Lead* (Author, wife of Charles Lindbergh)

Lindbergh, Charles. *We* (Aviator)

Linkletter, Art. *I Didn't Do It Alone* (Broadcaster, lecturer, businessman)

MacArthur, Douglas. *Reminiscences* (Soldier)

Martin, Mary. *My Heart Belongs* (Musical comedy star)

Maugham, Somerset. *The Summing Up* (English author)

McBride, Mary Margaret. *A Long Way from Missouri* (Broadcaster, journalist)

McCarthy, Mary. *Memories of a Catholic Girlhood* (Author)

Mead, Margaret. *Blackberry Winter: My Earliest Years* (Anthropologist)

Meir, Golda. *My Life* (Israeli prime minister)

Mill, John Stuart. *Autobiography* (English philosopher)

Muggeridge, Malcolm. *Chronicles of Wasted Time* (English journalist)

Newman, John Henry, Cardinal. *Apologia pro Vita Sua* (English theologian, writer)

Oursler, Fulton. *Behold This Dreamer* (Author)

Preminger, Otto. *Preminger* (Film director)

Quinn, Anthony. *The Original Sin: A Self-Portrait* (Actor)

Reagan, Ronald. *Where's the Rest of Me?* (Actor, U.S. President)

Reed, Gwendolyn. *Beginnings* (Writer, compiler of early lives)

Rice, Grantland. *The Tumult and the Shouting* (Sports columnist)

Riis, Jacob A. *The Making of an American* (Journalist, social reformer)

Robertson, A. M. *Grandma Moses: My Life's History* (Painter)

Rogers, Will. *The Autobiography of Will Rogers* (Humorist)

Roosevelt, Eleanor. *The Autobiography of Eleanor Roosevelt; On My Own This I Remember* (Wife of U.S. President)

Rousseau, Jean Jacques. *Confessions* (French philosopher)

Russell, Bertrand. *The Autobiography of Bertrand Russell* (English philosopher)

Saint-Exupéry, Antoine de. *Flight to Arras; Wind, Sand and Stars* (French aviator, poet, philosopher)

St. Johns, Adela Rogers. *The Honeycomb* (Journalist)

Sandburg, Carl. *Always the Young Strangers* (American poet, historian, novelist)

Santayana, George. *Persons and Places* (Poet, philosopher)

Schweitzer, Albert. *Out of My Life and Thought: An Autobiography* (Physician)

Selye, Hans. *From Dream to Discovery* (Authority on stress)

Stein, Gertrude. *The Autobiography of Alice B. Toklas; Everybody's Autobiography* (American author)

Steinbeck, John. *Travels with Charlie* (Author)

Thomas, Lowell. *Good Evening Everybody* (World traveler, radio commentator, author)

Thomas, Piri. *Down These Mean Streets* (Author, started writing in prison)

Tolstoy, Leo. *Childhood; Boyhood; Youth; A Confession; Recollections* (Russian novelist)

Ustinov, Peter. *Dear Me* (Actor)

Van Gogh, Vincent. *Dear Theo: The Autobiography of Vincent Van Gogh* (Dutch painter)

Vining, Elizabeth Gray. *Quiet Pilgrimage* (Novelist)

Washington, Booker T. *Up from Slavery* (Educator, reformer)

Welk, Lawrence. *Ah-One, Ah-Two: Life with My Musical Family* (Bandleader)

Wells, H. G. *Experiment in Autobiography* (English novelist, historian)

Wharton, Edith. *A Backward Glance* (Novelist)

White, Theodore. *In Search of History* (Political journalist)

White, William Allen. *The Autobiography of William Allen White* (Editor, journalist)

Wilde, Oscar. *De Profundis* (Irish poet, wit, dramatist)

Wilder, Laura Ingalls. *On the Way Home* (Author)

Wright, Frank Lloyd. *An Autobiography* (American architect)

MORE MEMOIR EPISODES WRITTEN BY OTHERS

"Our First Family Car"

Soon after we moved to Buffalo, New York, in 1921 Dad decided that we should have a car. I don't recall anything of the procedure of shopping for the car but I do remember that Dad was dead set against a sedan because he felt that when riding in a car one wouldn't want to be all cooped up.

So our new car was a Ford Model T Touring Car. As I recall it, the price was $450 which included a couple of optional extras such as a "self-starter," spring steel bumpers, and a horn button on the tip of the gasoline feed lever.

An explanation of the operation of a Model T will clarify the advantage of a horn button on the end of the gasoline feed lever. Actually there were two levers on the steering column just under the steering wheel. There was the spark control on the left which adjusted the timing (used only when starting the engine) and the gas control on the right.

Since the gas control regulated the speed of the car, just as the foot accelerator does in today's cars, it was desirable to keep the right hand on this lever most of the time. With the horn button at the tip of this lever you could blow the horn without removing your hand from the gas lever.

Incidentally, this gas lever would hold in whatever position it was set. Thus on highway driving you could set it at the desired speed and use both hands for steering. The car's highway speed was a maximum of 40 m.p.h. but we rarely exceeded 25 m.p.h.

Although Dad was eager to have a car, even to the point of going to night school and taking a course in auto maintenance, once he had the car, he was somewhat less than enthusiastic about driving it. I remember vividly how cautious he was. He preferred to drive only on weekends when the traffic was very light. Perhaps he was never very keen about driving because of the way you operated the car.

Our Model T had three foot pedals in the floor. The left pedal operated the forward motion of the car, the center pedal was the reverse, and the right pedal was the brake. In addition, there was a hand brake on the left side.

The left pedal was the most difficult one to learn to use. It had three positions. In the mid position the car was in neutral; in the full forward position it was in low gear and in the full back position it was in high gear. To run the car you pushed the left pedal forward to low gear while at the same time you fed the gas with the hand lever to rev up the engine. When the car gained sufficient speed you let the pedal come all the way back into "high." This took a lot of practice.

Driving backward was a two-foot operation. You had to hold the left pedal in neutral with your left foot while you activated the center pedal with the right foot and, of course, you controlled the speed with the right hand. This took a lot of practice, too.

Mother, however, looked forward to the prospect of driving with keen anticipation. Soon after we got the car she learned to drive. Women drivers were a rarity in those days but Dad never objected to Mother's learning.

I never will forget one of the first practice trips that Mother and I made. Her instructor had told her that she should get some practice in city driving so we went to the Broadway city market. Because of the way the stalls of the market were arranged the streets through the area were very narrow. I recall Mother's nervousness (and mine, too) as she threaded her way through these narrow lanes at slow speed. Now driving a Model T at slow speed is rather tricky because of the need to down shift to low gear with the pedal while at the same time co-ordinating the gas feed. Mother would be looking at her feet to be sure she was pressing the correct pedal and forgetting about feeding the gas evenly. This caused the car to jerk and jump all over the street. Needless to say we were both relieved to get home safely from that trip. Eventually Mother became a very good driver to the point that Dad always turned the driving over to her. One of the things we kids looked forward to during the summer months was the "Sunday afternoon drive." We never went very far but it was always fun.

A Model T Ford touring car was then essentially a fair weather vehicle. But driving in the rain was kind of fun. Side curtains, which were included in the original equipment, were kept rolled up under the back seat. When the rain started you had to pull over to the side of the road and all hands helped to get the curtains up and fastened. As I recall, there were four sections—two for each side. The door portions were supported by steel rods that were inserted into holes in the top edge of each door. Even though they leaked a bit, the curtains did quite a good job of keeping the rain out. Inside you had that cozy feeling like being in a tent during a rain storm.

Yes we did have a windshield wiper but you had to operate it by hand. The wiping blade was attached to an arm, the top end of which came through the top frame of the windshield. On the inside you had a little crank that you turned which moved the wiper blade back and forth. In a light rain, the driver would just give the wiper an occasional swipe but in a downpour the front seat passenger kept the wiper going. You should understand, however, that the whole rain operation, curtains and all, was more of an emergency procedure. If rain was predicted, or if it just looked like rain, you would not start out in the first place.

During the winter months most people left their car in the garage, feeling that driving on snow and ice was much too hazardous. We did likewise. With the approach of winter we would jack up the car and put it on low steel stands which Dad made—one under each axle. Dad always felt that letting a car stand on the garage floor for such a long period of time was not good for the rubber tires. Additional precautions included draining the radiator and removing the battery and taking it into the basement of the house.

One year, during the winter season, Dad decided that the car needed painting. To simplify the job, we unbolted all four fenders and lifted off the engine hood and carried them to the basement where we sanded and painted them. The color? Black, of course. Painting the car body had to wait until the weather warmed up in early spring. The paint job turned out quite well but we were a little late getting the car into service that spring.

It is interesting to note that although Dad took the night school course in car maintenance, I can't remember his ever doing a thing to the engine. Perhaps the course taught him that the best thing to do with an engine is to leave it to a trained mechanic.

We drove that car until 1928 when we traded it in on a Pontiac sedan—a real beauty!

"I Remember, I Remember"

When I was a child we lived in the country in a suburb of Lowell, Massachusetts, where we had several large meadows to play in. There was a brook and we had a forest all our own where we spent many happy hours at play.

One of my earliest memories was of my brother who was two years older than I. We had been playing together and he climbed a tree and in the attempt tumbled to the ground. I remember running to him crying. He had sustained a deep cut in his forehead and blood was streaming down his face. I was terrified for the moment. Then someone came along and took care of him. To this day he still wears the scar of that childhood injury.

I remember a very happy occasion when friends of my father came to dinner. Among the guests was a little girl of my own age who many years later was in my graduating class in elementary school. I never forgot the pretty white tablecloth and my mother's best china which were used only for guests and special holidays. This was my introduction to social events in the home and I loved it all.

Soon we moved to another house nearer to my father's work. It had an even larger garden. It was in this new house that my brother Frank was born. I hardly remember the occasion. I was sent out to play. However, it was no fun because I was alone. Frank was born on the birthday of the patron saint of Ireland, so he was named Francis Patrick. Later it would become just plain Frank. My most vivid memory of Frank was that he was "all red" and that he cried a lot.

One of the most beautiful memories of this period of my life centered around the small apple orchard between our house and our neighbor's. It was spring and I was playing alone. The trees were covered with lovely pink and white blossoms. The grass was wondrously green and the fragrance was almost overpowering. It seemed to my childish imagination that this must be a fairyland.

I can remember some of the hardships that my mother endured. I recall her going to the well in our yard to pump water. Later the pump was moved indoors to the sink. I remember washdays on Monday. There was an old-fashioned wringer and wash and rinse tubs on either side. The copper boiler on the kitchen stove was fired with wood. It was here that the white clothes were boiled white. Bleach was unheard of in those days. I remember the clean laundry on the lines, flapping in the breeze.

I remember the kerosene lamp on a bracket on the wall with its glass chimney so bright and sparkling. Still another lamp shone from its perch on another table.

A parlor stove set on a bright tin mat radiated its warmth over us children while we played around it on the floor. Mother was often with us darning or sewing. Occasionally she would feed the stove more logs and we would then get a glimpse of the brightness within. These were happy memories of warmth and security which the newer methods of heating never have been able to supplant.

This was the era of the horse and buggy and the horse and wagon. They never ceased to fascinate me. Our beloved Dr. O'Connor and our Pastor always traveled in this fashion from the city.

I remember the year I had an almost fatal case of pneumonia. But for the loving care of my mother and our wonderful doctor I might well have passed away. As I began my period of recovery I remember a few chocolates left on the mantel each day by our doctor for a "good little girl."

I remember the old talking machine and the concerts by John McCormack on Sunday afternoons. I remember our delightful front porch with its rockers and neighbors stopping in to visit us there. It was a wonderfully happy time for me.

I remember my grandmother coming to visit us only once. She was quite old and not in very good health and the distance in those days was great. I recall her black-beaded bonnet with ribbons tied beneath her chin and her heavy black cloak. I used to wish she could come more often to see us. I remember when Grandmother died. I went to the wake with my mother. The older ladies were all wearing snowy white aprons. There were some flowers and a sheaf of wheat which attracted my attention. I felt very sad and after the funeral I cried with my mother as she mourned for grandmother.

I remember the jolly times we had at Thanksgiving and Christmas. The turkey would be delivered by horse and wagon the day before the holiday and mother would start at once to prepare it. She would bake a half dozen pies and a cake and Irish potato cakes and Irish bread. At Christmas the grocer always sent a tall, white candle to be placed in the window to welcome the Christ child.

We hung our stockings in the parlor and each child received candies, an apple and an orange. Also one present each such as a doll or a toy horse and cart. No one would be happier than we children were at the holiday season. Relatives would drop in later to wish us a Merry Christmas. Then it would be bedtime and we would relive the day again in our dreams.

"My Auntie Grace"

I once cut out a quotation from something I read saying: "Some things we think we do not know how to do we find we can do by trying. By stretching out one withered hand it becomes useful."

This was so true of my Auntie Grace. She had a withered hand but could do so much that was useful. She was so important an influence in my life that she deserves a special place in my memoirs.

She was born in Schenectady, N.Y., in 1861. When she was two she had polio. This was long before there was a Salk vaccine. Her left arm was partially paralyzed and she was always lame. Both her arm and hand were withered. But the skin remained like baby skin.

She was sent to a nearby Catholic school where patient nuns taught her all kinds of handwork—sewing, use of a sewing machine, crocheting, knitting and embroidery. She learned to support her work with her left hand while working with her right.

She had a tricycle which she rode all over in downtown Schenectady. She belonged to the First Presbyterian Church when Dr. Stevenson was pastor.

When my father built the Stratford Road house she had to ride her tricycle up the Union Street hill. She said someone always pushed her. People were kind. There was little car traffic in those days.

Auntie Grace and her Mother, my Grandmother, came to live with us when I was two. After Grandma's death Auntie Grace's income was only about $300 a year.

She used to sit in a comfortable chair with wide arms by a window box. Always there was a Bible, the *Outlook* (a magazine which no longer exists), and the *Atlantic Monthly.* Hanging on a little knob was a crystal set radio with earphones. She was interested in sports and listened to reports and games on her radio. When I was a teenager my boyfriends always liked to talk about sports with Auntie Grace. I never cared for sports. I think they came to see her, not me.

When I was little I used to get in bed with Auntie Grace and hold and pat her "little hand." I'm sure she liked this. I surely did.

Auntie Grace always fixed the vegetables, set the table and washed the dishes. My brother Dawson and I dried them and put them away in the pantry. She dusted the stairs every morning. She had a stick, made smooth with use, and a big square of hand-hemmed cheesecloth. She backed down the stairs and dusted each one carefully. Then she would shake the dust cloth out of a window on the landing on her way up.

She had a single brass bed, a bird's eye maple bureau and desk and a sewing table with two layers. Everything was neat and in place. She helped me with lessons at this desk.

She must have had headaches. She kept Bromo Seltzer on a shelf in her closet. I loved the fizzy drink mixed with water. She let me taste it sometimes. She never complained.

In the summer all the Stratford Road children gathered at our house and on the wide front porch she taught us all to knit, crochet, embroider, and sew. While we were making things for the fair we had at the end of the summer, she read to us, checking now and then for mistakes in our handwork. We had to rip out if there were any. "Anything that is worth doing at all is worth doing well," she would say.

Every Saturday we studied my Sunday School lesson. I was a prize pupil in my Sunday School class. Many friends came to see her. If Mother went shopping she would leave lemonade or iced tea in the icebox and cookies or tiny sandwiches that Auntie Grace could serve. She and my Mother got along very well.

If someone did something that was below her standards she would say to me, "Winifred, you know what is right. Don't do things because so and so does it."

Even on cold days in the winter she put on her Treadwell dyed sealskin jacket, mittens, a little hat, and walked up and down the front porch. The lovely brown color of the sealskin is now a lost art.

There are so many little things I could have done for her that I never thought of when I was growing up. I'm sorry.

She sent to McCutcheon for samples and together we would choose my dress material. She made my petticoats—rows of tucks with handmade lace on the bottom. She made warm mittens and scarfs for Dawson and me.

When I was in High School, my Mother gave me $4 to buy a spring hat by myself. I went to our three department stores and found none I liked. Then on the way home I went to Mrs. Heinz's millinery shop and there I found a hat I loved. It cost $6 and had daisies on it. I came home without a hat. I told Auntie Grace there wasn't one I liked that I could afford. Having a new Easter hat in those days seemed very important. Auntie Grace took $2 from her purse and said "Go—get that hat." So I walked all the way back to Jay Street and came home with my hat. She loved it. My Mother did, too.

Auntie Grace was the only one who approved of my nursing career. We had many long talks about it. She understood that I did not care for office work.

I hope I wrote to her often while I was in training but I don't remember.

She died in November, 1927. She had dusted the stairs as she always did and said, "Etta, I don't feel well." She sat on the davenport in Mother's arms and quietly breathed her last breath. She was no trouble to anyone, ever.

She was the most perfect person I have ever known.

"Our Voyage to America"

This memoir writer was born in the United States of British parents. When she was four she was taken to England to live. In the following episode she describes her return to America in 1922 at the age of 12 on the steamship Haverford. *Her vivid recollections of the voyage, and of the immigrants aboard who came to our shores for the first time, provide many interesting insights.*

We left Britain on May 11, 1922, at 5:00 P.M. on the *Haverford* bound for America. The previous evening we had had one long party! Friends, relatives and neighbors came and went, hugging, kissing and crying, and wishing us well with love and small gifts. After many hours the children were put to bed; we had to rise at 4:00 A.M. the next day for the trip to Liverpool, which was to be made in Mr. Hanson's touring car. Mother stayed up all night with her Mother and sisters.

The trunks had been picked up a few days earlier so we needed only a few suitcases. We were sailing on the *Haverford* again because it was the only ship that my Mother trusted. Mother and my brother, Larry, had sailed on the *Lusitania* on her maiden voyage and she often talked of this beautiful ship; but after its disastrous sinking in 1915, which was a personal tragedy to her, she would sail only on the "tried and true" which she knew.

We traveled second class. There was also a first class and steerage. The first and second class boarded first and the steerage last. We watched them embark. These people looked pitiful and poor. We were told that they had come from many European countries to Liverpool for their passage to America. Many were dressed in black; others wore very dark clothes, even the children. The women wore scarves and shawls on their heads. They looked sad, strange and frightened, and seemed always to huddle together.

Our steward found us and took us to our stateroom. It contained two lower beds and two upper ones. Larry and I claimed the "uppers." We had to climb a small ladder to get into them, and we could look at the sea through the porthole while we were in bed.

We went back to the rails to call back and forth to our friends on shore. Soon the gangplank was lifted, the engines rumbled, the ship blasted its loud whistle and we began to move slowly away from the land that we had called home for the last eight years. We stood at the rail waving our handkerchiefs and crying a little, too. Our friends waved frantically back to us, and we watched and waved until they looked like tiny dolls on the distant dock. Finally we could no longer see them, and we felt a little forlorn.

The steerage people were down below on a large wide deck and we would watch them from over our deck rail. We couldn't understand their language or gestures, but they were interesting and we were curious. The sailors called them the "immigrants." When we waved to them at first they just stared up at us, but after a few days they began to wave back and even smile. We weren't allowed on their deck, nor they on ours, so we never got to know any of them. There were so many of them. They stayed in clusters and their deck always looked crowded.

Larry wanted to see the engines and had been constantly bothering our steward about it. One day he came by and said that he would take us down to the engine room. We trotted after him from lower deck to lower deck until we came to the very bowels of the ship.

We stared in awe at the yellow bulbed ceiling, the big fat pipes all around, and the glowing fire in the furnace. We had to stand behind a rail to look down at the stokers, as they shoveled the coal and threw it into the gaping open mouth of the furnace. They were proud of their job. They worked quickly—their upper bodies bare, and the sweat glistening on their faces, arms and torsos. They would rest after a while and two others would replace them. It was very hot and we wondered how they could stand the heat day in and day out, year after year!

We knew where the life jackets were kept, but never had a boat drill on the whole trip. With gray blankets over their knees, the grownups sat in deck chairs chatting; the children made their own fun. Hide and Seek was a great game on board ship—there were so many hiding places! We imitated the sailors and we all took turns playing Captain. Jump-rope was also popular, except when the sea was rough and the ship rolled. Then it was impossible to play!

The weather was still cool when we left Britain, but now it was getting warmer. We shed our woolen dresses and were wearing cottons and sweaters. We had been at sea for ten days and had seen nothing but the great expanse of water on every side. Now we were beginning to see land, faintly at first and then as we came closer (for we were nearing the Hudson River) we could see trees and green grass, and the land looked beautiful to us. This was *my* America.

We steamed into the southern end of Lower Bay where all ships stopped, for this was the quarantine area. Harbor pilots now boarded the *Haverford* from the Ambrose Lightship stationed in Ambrose Channel. Two doctors and an immigration inspector also boarded. Passports were routinely checked, and all cabin class passengers were examined by the doctors, all except United States citizens who were exempt. My sister and I did not have to attend, but Mother and Larry did because they were still British subjects.

The cabin passengers passed in single file for examination and were quickly checked by the doctors. The "immigrants" would have their examinations later at Ellis Island.

Those who had boarded now climbed down the ladder to their waiting cutter and the ship began to move again. It steamed slowly northward through the Narrows and soon the harbor and tip of Manhattan Island came into view.

Our "immigrants" crowded their deck. There seemed to be hundreds of them now. They were eagerly watching and excitedly gesturing at the new land that they could now see. Dimly outlined against the sky were many large skyscrapers that looked much like the backdrop of a stage.

We were now sailing up the Hudson River and we crowded the ship's rails. One could feel the excitement sweeping through the ship. The many chattering tongues of the "immigrants" were beyond recognition or reproach. They spoke, it seemed, in awe, disbelief and joy. They hugged and kissed one another and outwardly sobbed as they gazed at the beautiful Statue of Liberty standing 300 feet above the water, holding her torch aloft and welcoming our ship to her shores. This she had done since the year 1886 when she had been placed upon her pedestal on the little island of Bedloe in New York Harbor. She had been a gift to America from the French.

Why were they sobbing? Was it for all the loved ones left behind? Was it for the promise of a new life for them? Was it for the fear of living in an alien land among strangers? All these and many more thoughts must have crossed their minds. This was the land of my birth, and I knew it not. I was excited and curious, but I was fearful, too!

Just beyond the Statue of Liberty was Ellis Island, the end of the journey for many, and as we continued our piloted way up the river we saw the large buildings on the lower end of Manhattan more clearly in all their awesome majesty.

We were now preparing to dock. Passengers had collected all their small baggage and bundles. The "immigrants" were each wearing a tag with their name and manifest number on it which served as their identification for the processing at Ellis Island. They looked uneasy and frightened, and yet expectant.

The ship coughed, shrugged, creaked and struggled as she fought to get into her proper position in her berth at the pier. As she made it, the hawsers were thrown by the ship's sailors, caught and secured to the moorings by the longshoremen, and we were finally docked in New York.

As the gangplank was put into place the cabin passengers began to disembark. They passed through customs and had their baggage and passports checked. At the same time the steerage passengers were leaving the ship by another gangplank near the stern. They poured to the end of the pier where the barge to Ellis Island would stop for them. They carried their strange-shaped bundles and rolled-up mattresses with them. Most of them had slept on the deck and had supplied their own bedding. The baggage was also removed at this time and transferred to the barge which made a great many trips back and forth to Ellis Island that day.

I learned sometime later that an average of 5,000 aliens were processed daily for 100 consecutive days during February until May of 1920. A quota system was established then in June of 1921 through May, 1922, the month that we came. The "rush" lasted until June 30, 1924. On July 1, 1924, the quota was reduced to two percent of foreign born people as determined by the 1920 census.

We four—Mother, Larry, Alice and I—had watched from the rails and were now readying for the completion of our voyage. Soon all were disembarked. Trunks, baggage, boxes and imports of all sorts were removed from the ship's hold and the gangplank was lifted.

The *Haverford* steamed out of the Hudson River, released her harbor pilot, turned into the Delaware River and picked up her second pilot. Then she steamed grandly to her berth at Market Street in Philadelphia. She docked at 4:00 P.M. on May the 23rd in the year of 1922, the day of a new beginning.

We were home at last. We were eagerly waiting to see this bright new country with its bustle and noisy cheerfulness, especially the clanging trolley cars.

"This is my country," I thought; "I hope I like it." Because we had to come home I had given up a scholarship that I had worked hard for, and I had been angry and rebellious. I wanted to go to the preparatory school. I did not want to come to America; therefore I arrived full of misgivings. Perhaps the long voyage had helped to some degree because I was now ready to put things back together again. Like our "immigrants" we were anxious to start our new life, too.

And the very first new thing we did was to eat a double-dipper ice cream cone. Vanilla!

"Mamma Mia"

One of the few early snapshots of my mother Virginia shows her scrubbing clothes on a washboard in a big round zinc tub. She and the tub were in the yard of her first home in Rockland, Massachusetts. She was in her middle 20's, the mother of twin boys, George and Lawrence, and a third little one, Alfred. The year was 1915 or 1916. The war in her native land of Italy and Europe was rumbling in the distance.

Mamma Mia was a tiny woman of about 90 pounds at the time and only 4'10" tall. She was very pretty, with dark hair falling in ringlets and wisps around her face. She was wearing a long apron almost down to her shoes. She was squinting into the sun but still you could see that she was pretty.

As I remember it, she was always working. I never knew her to go out for an evening's relaxation until her family was all grown up. She had told me, though, that in the early years of her marriage my father used to take her into Boston by train occasionally. The big treat for them was to feast on the delicacies of the sea offered at the famous Union Oyster House in the North End of Boston.

From the very beginning my mother lived the work ethic. When she was a little girl in Italy she was sent to a convent for schooling and training in the domestic arts. There she helped embroider the priests' vestments. Little Virginia's well-trained fingers were employed even before she was ten years old. She helped her mother embroider and trim fine clothing for the wealthier citizens of her Italian village near Naples. Sometimes she made Belgian lace for trousseau adornments.

In her later years she made each of her children an exquisite lace dining tablecloth. Heirlooms every one of them, they were crafted only after countless hours and years of labor of love. She completed the first one for Lawrence, one of her firstborn twins, as a wedding gift. Each of us received ours as she finished them, either on the occasion of a wedding anniversary or as a Christmas gift or at some other special time. My mother set to work on my treasured white lace cover 11 years after I was married when Bob and I had our first dining room. It took her four years to complete since we needed an especially large one to accommodate our growing family.

Mamma Mia has not overlooked her grandchildren. Many of her two dozen are the proud owners of one of her handsome afghans. It is easier on her eyesight and arthritic hands to work on smaller projects now so she contents herself with making ski caps for her great-grandchildren.

Soon after the death of her father, the Mayor of her town, my mother's family left Italy. My grandmother boarded a ship bound for the United States, in the year 1900. With her were my mother, her sisters Amelia, Ella, Celia and Mary and two brothers, Richard and Lawrence.

When my grandmother arrived in Boston, Louis, evidently previously known to her, was waiting for her arrival. They were married almost immediately. In a very short space of time my mother had been adopted by a new country, a new father, and was thrown into a new way of life. They lived on Hanover Street in Boston (my mother still has strong reminiscent nostalgic feelings about that famous Italian settlement) and later moved to Rockland, Massachusetts.

My mother went to work in a stocking factory in South Boston. This required taking a ferry which cost one cent each way. It was the only money she was allowed to keep from her pay.

Mamma Mia remembers that her stern stepfather never allowed her to dance. She used to watch longingly from her second floor window while other young people held dances in the street below. Musicians set their stage in front of one of the local bars and played for the dancing. Popular at the time was the dance called the Cake Walk.

My mother worked most of her married life in shoe factories stopping only long enough for the occasional birth of a child. My parents never had a car. One of the clearest pictures of her in my memory is that of her carrying two heavy bundles of groceries home from town after a day's work. The bundles were almost as big as she was. She worked in shoe factories until she was 72 years old. Then she retired.

My mother was the silent partner in our home. My father was the social one. He customarily insisted on each of us coming home with our spouses for Sunday dinner. In true patriarchal style he presided over the dining table, a privilege he obviously relished.

As young adults we did not fully realize the strain this must have been for Mamma Mia. After she worked all week I doubt if it was fair to have her spend the biggest part of Sunday preparing a banquet of five or six courses for a dozen or more hearty eaters.

The meal always began with a soup such as chicken and spinach, followed by spaghetti or shell macaroni or some other pasta, with meat balls. Alongside there was always a tossed green salad or antipasto.

Then we got to the serious part of the meal with a roast of chicken, beef, ham or veal and the accompanying delicious roast potatoes. I think her specialty must have been stuffed leg of veal. Nowhere else have I ever found that same unique flavor of stuffing made of bread crumbs and eggs seasoned with "a pinch of this and a pinch of that." She was one of those cooks who was hard put to give you a recipe—she seldom measured any of the ingredients. I had to stand by her to figure out a recipe. Otherwise her culinary achievements would have been lost to me and my children. As it is I still cannot duplicate the subtle flavor of her bread-stuffed peppers although she has coached me time and again. You will find a few of her recipes at the end of this chapter.

Her usual scrumptious mince or apple pie finished off the meal. Sometimes my father produced a pitcher of his homemade wine from the modest wine cellar under our front porch. His muscatel was my favorite.

The meals during the week may have been meager, pasta e fagiole, peas and eggs, or a giambotta of mixed vegetables in one pan. But Sunday dinner was always a feast.

I recall special Sundays when we were young and my mother made the macaroni, cavatelli (meaning little hole or hollow) from "scratch," as the saying goes. On a pastry table she heaped a mound of flour excavating a hole in the center like Vesuvius. Into this hole she broke and dropped a couple of eggs and some water. She mixed the liquids with the inner edge of her crater gradually nibbling away at the mound until the mass of ingredients was combined.

She mixed and kneaded and kneaded and thumped until she had a shimmery satiny smooth hill of dough. This she divided into small fist-size portions. Each portion was then rolled by her deft hands. She stretched and coaxed the dough until it became a two-foot cylinder, three-eighths of an inch in diameter. This she cut into three-quarter inch pieces.

This is the point at which we younger children went into action, becoming "pasta machines." I get a pang of nostalgia as I recall her training us to hollow out the short pieces of dough. We would put the tips of our index and middle fingers into the top of the piece of pasta dough, pressing gently as we rolled it on the floured surface. Result: a beautiful, little creamy colored canoe-shaped cavatelli. We continued in assembly line fashion until we had completely covered the floured tablecloth spread over a card table with 200 to 300 pieces depending on how many would be gathering for dinner.

Then Mamma Mia gathered them up to drop them into a large kettle of boiling water to cook for about 20 minutes. How yummy they tasted, slightly chewy and smothered with Mother's incomparable Italian tomato sauce!

On very, very special occasions my mother made delectable ravioli, a little tartlet pasta stuffed with the best tasting ricotta cheese and egg mix imaginable. Here the children's role was to seal the edges of the tartlet with a floured fork, depressing the two layers of dough together firmly so the precious filling would not ooze out in the boiling process. Oh, those were the days, my friend!

Mamma Mia loved gardening. She used to spend an hour or so on pleasant evenings, spring and summer, caring for a little flower garden at the side of the house. I never understood where she got the energy after a hard day's work at the shoe factory to do the difficult bending, digging and weeding. I know now it had to do with the relaxation, peace and serenity one finds only in bending close to the earth.

Needless to say her patience and endurance were tried over and over again by five sons and three daughters. There was a son's brush with the law when in his teens, another's rebellious departure for New York and independence. Especially trying was my sister Mary's ten-year bout with tuberculosis. It began at the bloom of her life when she was 20, a tragedy for her and another ordeal for Mamma Mia.

I, too, added a few gray hairs to my mother's crowning glory. I recall so vividly her stinging, "Lady Jane, why did you come in so late last night?" From the time I was a little girl through my dating years "Lady Jane" was the signal that Mamma Mia was angry at me. Not until our own youngest daughter at 18 years of age began doing the same did I understand the anguish I had caused.

I cannot remember my mother ever complaining about the hardships of her life to us children. It is as though each successive putdown she endured merely made her stronger and more resilient. Just before her 90th birthday another upsetting crisis occurred in our family which disturbed her deeply. It involved a serious difficulty one of her grandchildren was enduring. The bad news really overwhelmed her for a day. But the next day she rallied and called me on the phone to say, "I'm like the tree in the forest. I will not fall."

Lest one begin to feel sorry for her (she couldn't stand that) there have been rewards. She is admired and adored by each of her children, and her grandchildren think she is very special. My children see her as a very wise woman who comes out with unexpected gems of wisdom now and then. She has a fine sense of humor, too.

Another trait of Mamma Mia's, though perhaps not as remarkable, seemed uncanny to me. It was how she always remembered where everything in the house was. If one of us asked where our books were she would say, "See on the buffet in the dining room." And that's where they would be. If Joan couldn't find her sweater, Mamma would say, "See on the chair in the hall." That's exactly where she would find it. If my father complained that one of the boys had misplaced his hammer, she would say, "See on the shelf in the cellarway." Sure enough, the hammer would be there. It was incredible to me that she could be away from the house all day at work and yet know when she came home where everything was.

At about age 72, this very independent lady, my mother, began her travels. After never having left Massachusetts for 60 years she flew twice to California to visit one of her sisters. Even more amazing, later at age 76, she took the trip my father had always dreamed of taking. She flew to Italy for a three week tour with the Sons of Italy organization. Somehow I feel she took that trip for my father because he did not live to do it himself. He had died several years earlier at age 73 after a lengthy period of poor health.

Until one year ago, at age 92, my mother lived alone in her beloved home on Beal Street in Rockland, Mass. She did much of her own housework and cooking. She continued with her needlework although admittedly she took on "simpler, smaller projects." Until recently her favorite activity was a shopping excursion and luncheon out with me. Now she prefers to eat at home and have her errands done for her. The arthritis in her knees has slowed her down. My sister Mary now lives with her and helps care for her.

My mother has always made it a practice to read the daily paper and an occasional book. Her television set is not only a companion to ward off loneliness but also she says, "to keep her knowledgeable."

When I go to visit my mother, only once a week now because I live 50 miles away, she wants me to sit and talk with her instead of rushing around to do some household chore for her. It is as though each moment is too precious. She wants to say the things that are on her mind and learn, too, what Bob and I and our children are doing.

Mamma Mia is becoming or has become a bit of a legend, I believe. She is the last remaining member of her generation who made up the Little Italy of Rockland, Mass., in the early 1900's.

My mother has changed in appearance. She is probably four feet nine inches tall if she stretches very hard, and is round of figure. Her full head of hair is creamy white, neat and in place to this day. Her face has a soft roundness that doesn't let you notice the wrinkles. For many years she has been taken for a woman 10 to 15 years younger than she actually is.

Though her looks have changed she has never changed from being a loving mother in every way. She has never stopped being concerned about her children whether that child is 49 or 67. She is always ready when any one of us needs help, whether it is a bit of mending, a place to sleep overnight, a ten dollar loan, or a bit of advice.

Mamma Mia is truly a remarkable woman, made of sterling, with a heart of gold. As I sit back and reflect on her life, I realize something I never put into words before. Mamma Mia is my idol!

A Few Family Recipes

Ravioli

Ravioli Shell

4 cups all-purpose flour
2 eggs, lightly beaten
2 Tbspn oil, vegetable or olive
1 tspn salt
¾ cup water

In a bowl or on a pastry board, hollow out center of flour mound. Add the other ingredients in the hollow all at once. Stir in with fork or hand from center until flour is moistened and combined. Knead lightly and briefly until it is smooth and satiny. Roll very thin, about ¹/₁₆". Dough may be divided into 2-3 pieces.

Ravioli Filling

1 lb. ricotta cheese
2 eggs
1 tspn salt
¼ cup grated Italian cheese

Blend eggs with ricotta until creamy and smooth, adding salt and grated cheese as you blend. Place by spoonfuls on rolled dough. Fold dough over to form turnover shape. Cut around and seal edges with floured fork, crimping edges together.

Boil ravioli in large kettle of boiling salted water for about 20 minutes or to taste. Serve with Italian tomato sauce.

Giambotta

2 Tbspn olive oil
½ medium pepper, diced
1 small onion, diced
1 lb. green beans
1 lb. zucchini squash
3 medium potatoes
1 can whole or chopped tomatoes
Salt and pepper to taste
1-1½ cups water

Heat oil over moderate heat. Cook peppers and onions until tender but not brown. Add green beans and potatoes and water to barely cover. Simmer till nearly cooked. Add zucchini and tomatoes and seasonings. Cook 10 minutes longer.

Stuffed Peppers

½-1 cup water to moisten crumbs
6 medium to large peppers
2-3 cups coarse bread crumbs, preferably dry Italian
8-10 black olives, chopped
2 Tbspn olive oil, 1 mixed in, 1 to drizzle over top
Season with garlic salt, oregano, salt and pepper

Remove stems and caps of peppers. Discard seeds but chop white fleshy part into stuffing. Parboil peppers and caps 3 min. Drain. Stuff. Bake 30 min. at 375° with or without caps.

"Surviving the Great Depression"

This memoir writer, then a girl of 14 living in Minnesota, vividly recalls how she and her family managed through the Great Depression of the 1930s. Using her flair for dialogue and description she makes her episode come alive by taking the reader there.

"There's some bad times ahead, there is," Dad said gloomily at the supper table. "Everybody's going to have to do some sacrificing."

I helped myself to another of Mom's freshly baked scones and worried over Dad's somber tones. What would we have to sacrifice? It seemed to me that as it was we didn't have a lot of things other people had.

We had adequate clothing, but Mother made most of it. And there was always plenty of good food. But these were necessities. Our only luxury was the old upright piano that needed frequent tuning.

It was October, 1929. That enormous black economic cloud that had been over the United States and Europe finally vented its fury in the form of a stock market crash and the ensuing Great Depression—a depression that was to plague people for the next ten years.

Heavy stock market investors lost everything; they went from riches to rags overnight. As the gloomy days wore on, offering no hope of a quick recovery, a pall of hopelessness settled in. The despair generated a rash of suicides.

A panic rush on the banks preceded the closing of all financial institutions across the country. When the banks reopened, only about ten percent of the investor's savings and checking account was recovered.

But Dad was not a loser. He didn't believe in putting his money in the bank. "I'll take care of my own money," I heard him say to Mother several times. Now he said, "See? I told you them banks were no good. This would never happen in England, believe me." Then he chuckled and added, "Now who's the smart one?"

He didn't think he was going to be a loser in the work area, either.

"We're better off than a lot of 'em, we are," he said. "Being on the railroad makes a difference. The railroad's the backbone of the country. They can't get along without 'em. The railroads will always run."

But he didn't realize how deep the economy would fall. He had not anticipated that by 1932 one out of every four workers in the U.S. would be out of work, or that in that same year world trade would drop by fifty percent. Factories closed their doors, one by one in quick succession, some of them never to reopen.

Because St. Paul was largely a clothing manufacturing city, it became a ghost town. But the ghosts, all very much alive, stood in the bread lines awaiting their daily stipend. The lines grew longer every day, as did the lines of those looking for work.

Repossesed homes went begging on the open market. No matter how attractive the price and terms, no one had the money to buy. Bread dropped to five cents a loaf, and milk to five cents a quart. The streetcar fare was five cents, and twenty-five cents bought a large piece of round steak. But low prices mean little to an empty purse.

Payments on mortgages already in existence did not drop, no matter how badly the paycheck shrank. Eventually almost the entire paycheck, when there was one, went to pay the mortgage and the electric bill. For many it became a choice between those two items, so that in time electric service to many homes was cut off.

With all the business failures, the need for railroad service dropped. Dad's five day work week dropped to four, then to three, and finally to only seven days a month. Then the days were cut to five and six hours instead of eight. Still, he was one of the fortunate ones who at least had some work.

We worked the little backyard garden for every ounce of food it could possibly produce. Mother canned and preserved everything that didn't go on the daily table, plus whatever she could manage to buy at the farmer's market.

In 1930 I was attending Monroe Junior High School, about ten miles from home. One night after I had gone to bed, I overheard another of those jolting conversations.

"Ellen will just have to quit school," Dad said. "Carfare is just too expensive to spend on her running to that school. She should be working and helping out, anyway."

Where would I, just turned fourteen, find work when so many experienced men with families to support couldn't find jobs? And what kind of work could I do? I lay there not daring to breathe for fear of missing Mother's reply.

"We can't do that, Dad. The law says a child must stay in school until its sixteenth birthday."

I relaxed. Thank heaven for the law. And again for the fact that Dad was a law-abiding man.

"It's a lot of poppycock, that's what it is! It's foolish to waste schooling on girls in times like these. They're all just going to get married and have babies anyway. They don't need an education for that!"

I lay there and worried. Maybe, somehow, he'd manage to get special permission to keep me out of school. He was always good at getting his own way, it seemed.

That I wouldn't finish school had never occurred to me. I could accept the clothes repaired over and over again, and the dime-store rubber soles covering the holes in the bottoms of my shoes—but quit school? Never!

The next morning at breakfast my father said, "You get right home from school today. We're going to get some wood, you and I. Can't afford coal this winter."

When I came home from school, Dad was waiting for me, his corncob pipe between his teeth. No matter how hard the times, he couldn't give up his pipes. He also had a wheelbarrow for himself and our large coaster wagon for me. In the wheelbarrow lay an axe and a two-man crosscut saw.

I changed my clothes and we started out. I had no idea of our destination; I just followed along, glad of the opportunity to court his favor.

His course led us to the bridge, then left along the ridge of the high river bank. I was puzzled. I couldn't see any usable wood around there. The only wood was the dense growth of tall trees all the way down the cliffs and steep banks to the river's edge.

"Why are we stopping here?" I dared to ask.

"Because this is where the wood is."

"Where?"

"Down there!" he snapped, pointing down the 75-foot embankment.

Down we went, grasping tree trunks and limbs for support as we descended. Our first tree was one that had already fallen; another lay nearby.

After close inspection, he said, "These'll do. Haven't rotted yet." He looked at me. "Well, c'mon, put that axe down and take hold of that end of the saw."

Thus I was introduced to the handling of a crosscut saw. I tried hard to keep to his rhythm.

We cut the two fallen trees into three or four-foot lengths. He then took one length, balanced it on my shoulder, showed me how to hold it steady and said, "Git up there now, it's gettin' dark, it is."

I looked up that steep embankment feeling as if I had the weight of the world on my shoulders and wondered how I'd ever make it. I'd spent many hours with school chums picking ferns and wildflowers on some of these banks, but never in my wildest dreams had I ever imagined them with a log on my shoulder.

But the experience of those flower-picking jaunts served me in good stead now as I sought familiar footing and branches with which to pull myself up. Down and up we struggled until all the logs were piled on Dad's wheelbarrow and my coaster wagon. It was dark when we got home.

The next day every muscle in my body moaned and groaned in agony. How could one body have so many muscles? But I was ready for school on time.

"Get home a little faster this afternoon," Dad said. "It's gonna take a lot of wood to keep this place warm all winter."

I groaned inwardly. Did he really think he was going to fire that furnace with wood all winter? Winters are long and cold in Minnesota. That furnace had to be in use for nine months, and we had long sieges of below zero weather during those months. I could see what I would be doing all through the long winter ahead, and the prospect didn't intrigue me a bit. The only glimmer of encouragement was that maybe he'd be pleased with me and I would be able to stay in school if I made like a woodcutter.

After a week of chopping, sawing, and hauling, Dad came up with another project. He offered no further explanation, but I looked forward to a day free from carrying logs up that steep bank. It had snowed several times by this time, making it harder than ever to get up that rugged, slippery cliff.

However, on Monday after school I was dismayed to find him waiting once again with the wheelbarrow and the wagon. Had he changed his mind? But when we started out, I noticed that the axe and saw had been replaced by large burlap sacks.

Our destination this time was the railroad tracks. We walked along picking up the coal that fell from the coal car behind the train's engine and putting it into a sack slung over our shoulder.

"We need this to bank the fire at night," Dad explained.

When we stepped aside for a passing train, we would be covered with soot from the engine's black smoke.

These excursions continued all through the winter; it was the only way to keep up the supply of fuel. We pushed through heavy snow, bucked the icy winds, slid on ice along the railroad tracks, and skidded and puffed our way down and up the slippery Mississippi River banks, and kept the house warm all winter.

But this did not increase the cash income. Something more had to be done.

One day in late spring Dad made his announcement at the supper table. "I've started an egg route."

"An egg route!" Mother gasped. "We don't have chickens!"

"Don't be foolish, woman!" Dad said. "I know that. I'll *get* the eggs."

"How?" I dared to break the rule that children should speak only when spoken to, especially at the table.

He explained, "I'm going to use my railroad pass to go down to the little town of St. James, south of here. That's poultry country, and I can get the eggs there at wholesale. I've already talked to some people, even a couple of restaurants, that'll buy eggs from me."

I welcomed this news. The wood and coal hauling would come to a stop, at least for awhile.

He brought the eggs from St. James in two large, oblong suitcases, the eggs nestled in light cardboard egg dividers he had managed to acquire somewhere.

Then in June, just at the close of school for the summer, Dad came home with two more old but intact suitcases.

"Where'd you get them?" Mom asked. "Whatever are they for?"

"At a secondhand store," Dad replied impatiently. "They're for Ellen. She can go with me now, and there'll be more eggs to sell."

Two suitcases full of eggs were heavy, and they had to be handled gently, but this was still much easier than hauling logs and coal.

I enjoyed the streetcar ride to the St. Paul Union Depot. The early morning was cool and fresh. The trees, the grass, and the wild flowers all sparkled with a special kind of newness.

Sunrise was like a rebirth of the world. Birds sang as if they had discovered their voices for the first time. What had been just a bud yesterday was suddenly a beautiful flower.

The Union Depot, the central terminal for all the railroad lines, was fascinating in an entirely different way. The huge, high-domed brick and concrete building that occupied two square blocks looked as if it should have been a state capitol building.

For me the place had a certain kind of mystique about it. Such a variety of people in their equally varied modes of dress interested me a great deal. I studied their faces. Some looked worried, others bored, and still others looked happy. I wanted to ask them where they were going.

But Dad always hurried me along. "We want to be settled in before she starts," he'd say.

From my vantage point at the passenger car window I could watch the baggage men and the porters, "Redcaps" as they were called, pushing the cumbersome metal-wheeled, wooden baggage carts along the runway. I tried to read the colorful labels pasted on the trunks. I just knew they had been to mysterious, faraway places.

St. James was as far down the line as we could go and still catch a train back the same day. In fact, we had just one hour between trains.

The trip back was never as exciting. The heavy suitcases had to be handled with such care, and the walk from the train through that huge depot to the outside, and then three blocks to catch our streetcar, seemed to grow longer every time. But I never broke an egg, thank heavens.

I was never asked to accompany Dad on his egg route. My Saturdays were spent helping Mom in the house.

Until I left home, I managed to get additional small jobs such as helping the newsboy and his mother, or occasionally baby-sitting for an evening. The newsboy paid me one dollar a week; baby-sitting jobs paid fifty cents an evening.

By this process of groping, grasping at every opportunity, sometimes creating our own opportunities, we stumbled through the Great Depression and somehow landed on our feet.

"Our Family's Health History"

Our family seems to have enjoyed excellent health, generally speaking. The reason I say "seems to have" is that I'm not sure whether it has been our innate vigor or our attitude toward health that has kept us perking. My parents' response to sickness was, "Don't pay any attention and it will go away." They meant, within reason, of course. It was never spelled out to me that it was shameful to be ill, but somehow, in the way children learn attitudes, almost by osmosis, I perceived that to admit illness was to admit a fault or a weakness in one's character that ought to be overcome.

We kids were expected to be well, therefore we were. I have usually found that children tend to fulfill the expectations others have of them. My parents may have carried their expectations to an extreme. Certainly I remember times when I felt sick but never mentioned it.

On the other hand, some families seem to be so preoccupied with their physical state of being, and have so little faith in their bodies, that they cannot participate fully in a normal life. A third grade teacher I knew had the right idea. She would say to her pupils, "Hug yourselves. Hug your beautiful bodies. They are miraculous machines that work automatically for you. Treat them right and they will take care of you."

Most of my ancestors came from sturdy peasant stock, and were used to hard physical work. Success in this line does not allow for chronic ill health. Can you imagine a Wisconsin farm wife who must cook dinner for 35 "thrashers" taking time out for a headache or menstrual cramps?

When I was growing up in southwestern Wisconsin, our medicine chest's contents looked rather different from what I keep on hand today. There was a bottle of iodine, bandages and adhesive tape, alum, a bar of white cocoa butter for chapped hands, Mentholatum, liniment, Aunt Annie's salve (of course), quinine, aspirin, cascara for a laxative, powdered boric acid with an eye cup, Packer's tar soap for shampoos (to be rinsed out with a little vinegar, preferably in rainwater), and probably a few other innocuous items. After Orpha entered nurses' training, we became a bit more sophisticated. She introduced argyrol, albolene, and hospital-made sanitary napkins. First-year nurses had to make their quotas of these, and when I went to visit Orpha at the nurses' dormitory at the Lutheran Hospital in LaCrosse, she usually set me to work at that task.

A family such as ours that did not go running to doctors for every minor ailment, had to depend on certain time-honored practical remedies. One that we used with complete confidence was Aunt

Annie's salve. Aunt Annie was Grandma's unmarried sister. Because of her congenital lameness (hypothetical), she was advised by her parents not to marry. Although she had many suitors and was a pretty woman, she did remain single, and chose to support herself by being a practical nurse. Her mother had handed down to her a recipe for a drawing salve that had been used for several generations in Holland. Annie made, packaged and sold this fragrant brown salve all over the United States. She had many a testimonial letter from satisfied customers. She did not advertise. Simply by word of mouth, Annie's trade grew as large as she could handle.

The magic of the salve was that it drew prurient matter out of any infected part, such as a wound or a carbuncle. It would heal a severe laceration without a scar, if used continuously after the infection was gone.

Naturally, I always wondered what miraculous ingredients were in the salve. It was not until Aunt Annie died and left the recipe to Mother that the secret was revealed. Mother then disclosed the three, and the only three, ingredients as—white lead, camphor and beeswax. She cooked up a batch herself, but it didn't harden the way Aunt Annie's did, and that ended the salve story.

When I was in grade school there were cases of what was called "the itch." I believe it was probably a fungus infection, as it seemed to be contagious. Whatever it was, it caused ugly rashes on the skin, mostly on the hands. The treatment was to apply a mixture of powdered sulphur and lard.

Another home remedy I remember was the use of a double strand of yarn tied around the toes for relief of chilblains. It seemed to work, if only by the power of suggestion.

One rarely hears of goiter now, but when I was a child it was a fairly common condition, especially in southwest Wisconsin, where iodine is lacking in the soil. School children were regularly given iodine tablets.

In my childhood, "mastoid" was a word to strike terror in a mother's heart. Commencing from the common cold, infection from throats and nasal passages could spread to the inner ear where pain and inflammation resulted. In severe cases surgery was required. Inevitably, an unsightly scar along the neck branded a child forever as a victim of this dread disease. Before the discovery of penicillin and the sulfa drugs (about the beginning of World War II) a child with an earache evoked great concern.

The following anecdote illustrates the ineffective use of a home remedy and is also a little joke we used to tell on Grandfather Elmer.

When Gretchen was about four, we were at Hugh's parents' home when she developed an earache. As we discussed what to do, Dad suggested an old family remedy. We were to soak a raisin in hot water until it was plump and warm. Then it was to go down into the ear. As we debated the effectiveness of this procedure, Dad pointed up his argument with "That's what Uncle Will *always* did, and he had earaches all his life."

By the time our three children were born, medicine had come a long way. Gretchen, Chris and Cindy had the usual childhood illnesses—chicken pox, mumps and measles. Infants routinely got shots for diphtheria, whooping cough and tetanus. The development of Salk vaccine for polio was a major event for many an anxious parent in the 1950's. Dental care seemed to lag behind. Fluoride treatment began in earnest in the late '40's. Almost every adult in my grandparents' generation wore false teeth or perhaps should have. My parents were very particular about our dental care, even though it meant financial sacrifice somewhere else, and Hugh and I have followed the same policy.

It might be of interest to our later generations to know what their forebears on both sides of our family died of, or what frailties they may have carried in their genes. Thus I include the following: Paternal Grandfather Charles died of diabetes at age 69. None of his numerous progeny has had it as yet. My sister Orpha died of a stroke at age 88. Maternal Grandfather Frank died at 79 in his sleep. Maternal Grandmother Mary died at 88 of cancer. My father, John, died at 89 of leukemia. My Mother, Margaret, died at 83 of a heart ailment.

Hugh's Maternal Grandfather Fred died at 77; he fell over in the middle of a sentence. Hugh's Maternal Grandmother Elsie died at 90. No diagnosis. Hugh's Paternal Grandfather Emmons died at 82, cause unknown. Hugh's Paternal Grandmother Edith died at 85, cause unknown. Hugh's Father Elmer died at 72 of liver cancer. Hugh's Mother Lark died at 86 after having a stroke about two years earlier. We have had several cases of retinitis pigmentosa in our family and one of our great-grandparents suffered a spinal malformation.

I do want to add that this information must not be regarded as ominous or threatening. It is intended only as documentary material. Hugh and I are happy that our three children and four grandchildren are healthy specimens now and we presume the next generation will be likewise.

"My 'Irresponsible' Son, Jim"

This memoir writer, a dauntless spirit and the mother of seven childen, decided that she would include a chapter about each in her memoir, hardly an easy task. Before she reproduced her completed memoir, running 216 pages, she asked for comments from each child. Where they took issue with her observations she acknowledged this in the text, nevertheless holding to her own perceptions. Here is her profile on one of her children, superbly done.

When James Robert, our third child, arrived on September 28, 1948, we had settled into being a happy, healthy little family. Like Kevin, he, too, was born at South Shore Hospital in South Weymouth, Mass. With dark curly hair and dark brown eyes he was the first of our children to resemble me; still, except for a round face, he looked quite Irish, like Kevin.

From his early months Jimmy was quietly subtle about his needs. At a time when he was refusing solid foods, he drank bottle after bottle of milk. I would give him a filled bottle to drink in his crib while I went about my chores. If he wanted more, he would throw the bottle out to get my attention. When he had had enough milk the empty bottle would remain in the crib.

As a toddler he needed only to be near me in his playpen or on the floor, playing with his toys. If I gave him an affectionate smile now and then or a few moments of my attention, he was happy. When Marylou and Kevin were away at school or off someplace else playing, he would occupy himself contentedly by the hour. I remember his love for toy cars. He remembers his love for toy soldiers and that he fantasized himself as "a great soldier" until he was about 12.

From the time Jimmy was in the first grade he marched off to school in the most businesslike way. He would tuck his lunch box or school bag under his arm like a briefcase and clip right along at the heels of Marylou and Kevin. Despite his serious manner, he had a ready smile and was friendly with everyone he met.

During Lent I used to like to go to daily Mass. I would get breakfast ready and then wake the children. Jim, who woke easily and arose quickly, was mother's little helper in a special way by the time he was eleven. He would carry baby Teresa from her crib downstairs to her highchair as soon as she woke. While I was at church he amused her and gave her something to nibble on like toast or dry cereal.

Jim followed along after Marylou and Kevin to Holy Family School and then Cardinal Spellman High School. His marks were always high and we assumed he was a good student but he claims, "I never developed very good study habits anywhere."

He played some football at Spellman High but I seem to recall a head injury which at least interrupted his career on the varsity team. His high school was noted for its musical productions like "Sound of Music," and "The King and I." Jim had been taking piano lessons for a number of years and Dad and I were very proud when he was asked to accompany his classmates in the production of "The King and I." For him it was a good experience because so many of his friends were involved in the production.

Once upon a time Jim considered becoming a priest. He put it this way: "I considered becoming a Jesuit during senior year in high school on the rebound from a girl I liked who entered the convent. I was attracted to the priesthood because of the aspects of social service and moral philosophy, both of which still are very important to me. However, I always knew deep down, even when I was a devout Catholic, that I should not be a priest because the administration of the sacraments did not interest me." There it is. It speaks for itself.

Our childrens' turning from the Catholic faith has often caused Bob and me to wonder if we subjected them to too much parochial education. We will probably never know the answer to that puzzle.

From the time he was 16 Jim worked at a Supermarket in Holbrook, Mass. He was a short order cook and baker in the delicatessen department. His boss really loved him. Jim worked hard and diligently. Every time I came into the store Al would say, "If you have any more like him at home, send them in. I'll hire them all."

One of the foremost lessons I tried to teach our children was moderation. On weekends when they were allowed to go to a school function or to a friend's house party they were expected to be in by 11:00 P.M. or at midnight on special occasions.

Jim never could understand this rule. His friends often came to our house; they were fine young people and Bob and I were fond of them. Still, when he was out for an evening, we asked that he observe the curfew. Often he did not. I would have to ground him for the next weekend or two. Jim's response sounds defiant but it was simply stated: "That won't do any good. Your punishment doesn't make sense. We're not doing anything wrong so I can't see why you're so upset."

"But," I argued, "when young people stay out too late, too long, they are apt to get tired, quarrelsome or bored and restless. That's when the trouble starts."

"Not with me and my group," he persisted. So it continued through his senior year, one weekend out, one or two weekends in. How fortunate we were that this was his most serious offense!

Since Jim maintains that he never developed good study habits I must assume that it was his "talent and promise" which earned for him an outstanding record at high school. He achieved perfect and near perfect scores in his college entrance exams, 800 in the mathematics achievement test and 785 in physics. He was awarded scholarships to several colleges; he chose Boston College. He lived at home contentedly and commuted during his first three years of college.

In the spring of his junior year, Jim decided to quit and to enlist in the Navy. I gave him a ride one Monday morning to a recruiting office. I did not know where we were when I dropped him off because I was mentally and physically blinded by tears thinking of what he was planning to do. He said that his grades had been "sliding," so he had given up the idea of being a scientist and was "searching aimlessly for career goals."

Nonchalantly he called home a few days later and remarked, "Oh, I didn't sign up. The recruiting officer told me to finish college first and then come back. He said I would be more valuable to the Navy then." That wonderful unknown man! There are those who scoff at the power of prayer. Not I. Again God had answered a mother's pleading prayers.

It was during college that Jim became serious about running. In his teens he had run simply to get himself from one place to another. He ran off and on until he became a member of the track team during his freshman year at Boston College, and earned a varsity letter in cross country running as a sophomore. He had taken a 50-mile hike in 1963 with a friend which he thinks was probably an important "precursor" to the development of his enjoyment of running. They were 15 years old when, inspired by President John F. Kennedy's physical fitness program, they walked from Rockland to Plymouth and back in about 15 hours.

Jim met Peggy and they became good friends during his sophomore year. One of the first things we heard about her was that she made delicious stew, a clue to the now well known fact that she is a marvelous gourmet cook. At the end of their junior year they were in love and shortly after they had graduated, he from B.C., she from Boston University, they were married.

How well we remember Jim's "graduation" from college! It was one of those rare times when he upset us. There the whole family sat, in the hot sun with throngs of graduates and their families. He marched handsomely into the awards arena, capped and gowned and solemn. His name was called and we looked aghast at each other—no James. What could this mean? We never saw him leave his seat but he was not there.

Later, contrite and disturbed he explained. He had not finished a final paper. His professor had told him it was proper for him to receive his degree anyway and he could pass the paper in within a given time limit. Not Jim. That was not his way.

His conscience would not let him perform what he considered a hypocritical charade. He had left the ceremony nauseous, "suffering from the scars of the middle two years in college and my poor work habits."

Never mind. The wedding more than made up for the empty graduation day. Peg and Jim were married in a chapel at Boston College on August 8, 1970. Father Timothy O'Leary, curate at Holy Family Church, officiated at a wedding in the new tradition. There were readings from Kahlil Gibran as well as from the bible, read by members of the wedding party, our son Kevin and Jim's friend John. Allen played the guitar and our daughter Ginger played an organ piece. It was all very proper, nicely done.

John and Mary gave Peg and Jim a lovely wedding celebration. The feast was served outdoors to about 150 friends and relatives. With a festive tent on the lawn of their nicely landscaped home in Wellesley, Mass., and a three-piece orchestra for dancing, it was a gala event.

The bride and groom drove off joyously in their esteemed convertible Chevrolet Impala for a one-month camping honeymoon trip.

Then began Jim's 12 years of work and study for his doctorate. Their first year was spent in Hingham, Mass. They lived in a really antique Cape house nestled in a green field a long drive from the street and hidden from the view of passersby. I feel sure they will always treasure that very special place.

They enjoyed several happy years at the University of Massachusetts where both earned their master's degrees. They again found a cozy older home to live in, this time an apartment at the rear of a stately home totally surrounded by gorgeous plantings and trees. Again they were very fond of the rural setting. Dad and I enjoyed our visits to Amherst.

It was quite a change for them, then, when they moved to Cambridge so that Jim could continue his studies at Harvard. Peg, who had majored in psychology, had valiantly contributed to their support by working with the mentally disturbed in state hospitals both near Amherst and in Boston. Later for a change of pace she worked first as a pastry chef in a restaurant in Cambridge and then she cooked meals several evenings a week for a household of Jesuit priests.

The 12 years of Jim's studies were a period of hard work and a lot of doing without. Only two people with special qualities like Peg and Jim, with stamina, patience, endurance and determination and above all much love, could have held up for those 12 years. They are obviously remarkable managers judging from what they have been able to do with their minimal income. With a little assist from both sets of parents they were able to make a down payment on a home in Cambridge. Located one mile from Harvard where Jim was studying, their real estate consisted of two six-room units of an older row house. A very wise investment, it enabled them to live almost rent free, with the rental unit paying the mortgage. The property is perhaps two to three times what it was worth when they purchased it in 1977.

In spite of their bare bones budget, as they dub it, they saw their way clear to starting a family. Peg just missed her goal of having her first child before she was 30. Samuel Augustine, a very bright handsome little dark-eyed copy of his Dad, was born on May 24, 1978, seven weeks after her 30th birthday. Katherine Rachel, one year old on January 28, 1983, is just as Irish looking with her big blue eyes in a sweet pink and white round face, topped with strawberry blond hair, as Sam is Italian looking. They should make quite a picture of contrast as they walk to school together in a few years.

At last Jim's doctoral work is over. Much of the pressure is gone, both financial and mental, since the autumn of 1982. With his thesis passed in and approved and with an appointment to the research staff of Columbia University, there is a collective sigh of relief from the whole family. The University is in New York City but again Jim and Peg find themselves in a rural setting in a suburb of New York. The Lamont Doherty Geological Observatory where he is a research associate is nicely located on the western bank of the Hudson River, 15 miles north of the great city. Our little family occupies a handsome white Cape Cod cottage on the grounds while they look for their own housing, a fringe benefit of his new appointment.

We stopped there on our way to Florida in January, 1983, our third or fourth visit. Peg treated us to one of her superb dinners, a succulent chicken served so attractively with its accompanying vegetables. It was a bittersweet occasion for we were saying good-bye to them for three months, and young Bob was there for his last evening before flying back to California.

Their new life is taking shape nicely. Sam goes to preschool several days a week. Kate joins Peg as she does errands or visits friends in their recently purchased used car. They are happy to have a car after being without one for years; it is especially important to Peg. Jim is as always engrossed in his research but it seems easier to get his attention these days, to pull him from the depths of his thoughts to what is going on about him.

Jim still loves running. He usually runs five or six times a week, for a distance of five to eight miles or even more if he is in training for a race. Running was his salvation I think during the strained years of graduate research.

If running provides his mental and physical relaxation, then indeed Peg, Sam and Kate are the day-to-day source of the emotional and social levelers he needs. He has made it a practice to plan his time to allow for both kinds of relaxation. Sometimes his schedules go awry, I'm sure, because the demands of science are open-ended but he seems to be keeping a good balance most of the time. He and Peg say that many scientists overlook or neglect these areas of their lives.

Yet he causes me to wonder if he still thinks of himself as irresponsible; in his twenties he characterized himself by the theme song he had chosen, "Call Me Irresponsible." I wonder if he was thinking of himself as irresponsible when he wrote, regarding the first draft of my chapter on his life:

> "I encourage you not to try to protect my feelings in writing your memoirs. You'll end up with nothing but fluff. I really wish to encourage you to try to delve deeper in your vignette even if it hurts you or me."

My answer to that is I never thought of him as irresponsible. If he insists that I "delve deeper for new truths" I may find it necessary to indicate that I am disappointed and distressed, even unhappy, because he does not call himself a Christian. For that is the only thing that "hurts." No, I prefer to wait silently and pray inwardly. All his actions and attitudes are as loving and kind as those of any Christian I know.

It took 12 years for Jim to take his first step into the world of science research; what does it matter if it takes another 12 years to find that science and God are compatible?

"My Thoughts on Living and Dying"

Beside my mirror that hangs over my dresser is a prayer I read daily. It is not attributed to any author so I have made it mine. It reads:

> Lord, thou knowest better than I know myself that I am growing older, and will some day be old. Keep me from getting talkative, and particularly from the fatal habit of thinking I must say something on every subject on every occasion. Release me from craving to try to straighten out everybody's affairs. Make me thoughtful, but not moody; helpful, but not bossy. With my store of wisdom it seems a pity not to use it all . . . but thou knowest, Lord, that I want a few friends at the end.

Teach me the glorious lesson that occasionally it is possible that I may be mistaken. Keep me reasonably sweet. I do not want to be a saint . . . some of them are so hard to live with, but a sour old person is one of the crowning works of the devil.

Help me to extract all possible fun out of life. There are so many funny things around us and I don't want to miss any of them. Amen.

Writing my memoir has spurred me on to write what might be my final chapter. I have given the subject some thought and I have arrived at peace with myself and my Creator. I have prepared my last Will and Testament and I no longer feel it necessary to live in fear and trembling, feeling that everything that is fun is "immoral, illegal, or sinful."

I was more afraid of dying when I was young than I am now. I do not fear death. I have looked upon it many times when it has arrived as a friend to end suffering. I have held the hands of my own brother while he took his last breath and witnessed the sigh of relief as life left his body. I have also been called into homes where death has come in the night, silently. I have witnessed the anger mixed with grief in those who have been bereaved. When my time comes I only wish not to suffer a long time.

I feel that every day is a bonus to be enjoyed, not in idleness, but in accomplishing those things I was too busy to do when I was immersed in the business of making a living. Yes, I do feel a certain urgency in the way I live now because I know I have much less time left than I have lived.

My only dread, as time marches on, is that I may end up helpless and dependent; a burden. To that end, I have chosen to move into a total care environment where I know I shall be no burden upon our son and his family. I did this while my health is still good and the end looks a long way off.

I regard my body as something loaned to me for the period of time I am allowed to use it and have made provision at the end that some useful parts may be used to help those whose lives might be extended by their use. Then I would like to be cremated and my ashes scattered over the woods and fields where I have walked and romped with several dogs I have loved. To me, the birth of a baby, or a litter of puppies, or the dropping of a foal, are all miracles. They are clear evidence that our Creator intended that we should continue to exist.

Recently I found consolation in the words of Dr. Felix Montelbanez in his book *A Doctor Looks at Death*. "It might help to dissipate our fear," he says, "if we remember that, were we endowed with consciousness before birth, we would probably feel the same fear of the unknown when passing into the light world of noise and confusion. We ought to know how to leap into the unknown world of death just as we do into life at birth . . . particularly when we have a treasury of memories of tasks completed and affections fulfilled."

Finally, I wish to convey my sentiments on this subject to my loved ones through a poem I have always cherished. Though I have searched, the author is unknown to me:

Immortality

Do not stand
By my grave, and weep
I am not there,
I do not sleep—
I am the thousand winds that blow
I am the diamond glints in snow
I am the sunlight on ripened grain,
I am the gentle, autumn rain,
As you awake with morning's hush,
I am the swift, up-flinging rush
Of quiet birds in circling flight
I am the day transcending night,
Do not stand
By my grave, and cry,
I am not there
I did not die.

"The Day Before Christmas on a Wisconsin Farm"

This episode is an example of how vividly we can recall special moments in our lives. In a remarkable partial memoir focusing entirely on the days of his youth on a midwest farm, this memoir writer paints a nostalgic picture. He titled his memoir "Wisconsin Farm Boy" and prefaced the following episode with the words: "This story, a true one, is about one special day in the life of a farm boy, age nine—a day where memories were written in indelible ink on the mind and nature of that boy."

I awoke with a start, fully awake almost at once. The room was still semi-dark; dawn was just on the edge of breaking. Staring at the ceiling I wondered what it was that had awakened me so early. For the moment I could sense only that it was something good and bright. Then it flooded in. It was the day before Christmas; tonight was Christmas eve!

Quickly I brushed three homemade quilts aside. Shivering from the sudden sharp coldness of an unheated room I clutched my clothes and scrambled into them. It was not too early to be up because I could see light from the kitchen kerosene lamp at the bottom of the stairs. I could hear the familiar sounds of Mother making breakfast.

I took a quick look through the south window at the home of the nearest neighbor, the Christensen family, just one-third of a mile away. Peering through the gray light of dawn across the snow-covered field, activity could be seen there too.

I buttoned my wool shirt, pulled up the suspenders of my overalls over my shoulders and then clattered down the stairs, ready and eager for anything.

That day was to pass swiftly. There was much to do. First there was breakfast—oatmeal, applesauce made from apples grown in the farm orchard, pancakes, home-butchered side pork preserved over the winter months by being imbedded in lard in a huge crock stored in the summer kitchen, and fried potatoes, milk and coffee.

Then there were house chores—washing and drying dishes and always the many parts of the cream separator. Snow that fell during the night must be swept from four porches. Drinking water from the pump outside must be brought in, including enough to fill the stove reservoir. Then of course there was firewood that was needed both for the kitchen stove and the dining and living room heaters.

Barn chores meant milking 15 cows and feeding 40 head of cattle and eight horses twice each day. This involved digging out a huge pile of silage and pitching hay down from the mow. Each cow was fed silage and a ration of bran. Each horse was given a ration of oats. Hay, clover or alfalfa, was a basic food for both. Gutters and stalls needed to be cleaned daily and fresh straw for bedding was provided each day.

Our chores were hardly finished when Mother called George my oldest brother, age twelve, and told him it was time to get the Christmas tree. She told me to go along to help haul it home. She told us to look for the tree on the far side of the wooded hill or on the edge of the south marshland, and to be sure it was a balsam. Tommy, age four and one-half, begged to go too. Finally, Mother said, "Alright then, get along with you. But you older boys watch out for him. Keep him with you every step of the way."

George ran to the tool shed to get the axe and we were on our way. We trudged through snow down to the river, crossed the bridge and moved up to the adjoining field and on to the wooded hills.

We were three proud and happy boys.

This was an important mission. After all, this was the day before

Christmas. Tonight was Christmas eve, and how could there be a Christmas without a Christmas tree! Then, too, we were doing a job that Father always had done because of the need to select just the right tree, though of course one or two of us had always accompanied him. And finally, there was the fresh snow. I could hear the crunch of it under my boots, for it was cold. Evergreen branches wore mantles of white. Bare branches of oak, elm, and poplar trees and marsh brush were trimmed with snow. And the sun gave a glistening whiteness both to wooded area and to marsh cover.

Joy and purity were surely written large that day for all to see, and it was not lost on me for I was to remember it for over 60 years.

We found our tree, an eight foot balsam, fresh and vivid green. We cut it down and took turns pulling it home, leaving behind us a new trail in the snow. We continued on up toward the big red barn and white house glancing back only once while near the river to see if tracks of a muskrat or even a mink or otter could be seen along the banks. It was known that Alfred, the oldest neighbor boy, had trapped 110 muskrat and eight mink the winter before.

The tree was set up in the front living room near the bay windows and was trimmed in the early part of the afternoon. Most plentiful, because they were made at home, were long strings of popcorn and chains of colored paper rings made from remnants of wallpaper. But there were also red ribbons and balls, long lengths of silver and gold tinsel, wax candles set in their individual holders, and a silver star for the very top.

George, Tommy and I were then dismissed from the room; the door was firmly closed and Mother made it clear that no one was to "so much as breathe near that door until it was time."

At about four-thirty the magic time started. The boys had been told to "be in the house by that time, washed and cleaned up, with your good clothes on—and your hair combed!"

We were on time. I noticed that Mother was "dressed up" and even had on a necklace. More than that her face was bright and expectant as she moved quickly about the kitchen and into the pantries, making last minute preparations for Christmas eve supper.

All rooms that bordered the closed living room were lighted with kerosene lamps that gave a soft glow. Barney, our hired hand, came in from the barn and then Father arrived. Aunt Stina, Mother's older sister, had come down from upstairs looking more elegant than ever. Everybody was there, and excitement was now mounting.

The evening meal on Christmas eve was something very special. It was served only once each year. It was always the same. It was simple but wonderfully good to me. Oyster soup, with heaping dishes of small round oyster crackers, a huge platter of paperbread, and milk. These were the main features, along with light from the candles that gave a touch of warmth and festive atmosphere. All three boys had watched with intense interest the preparation of the paperbread, a Norwegian holiday bread considered to be the supreme treat in foods.

And now, finally, it was the time! Dishes were quickly washed and then as if drawn by a magnet, I moved into the dining room and toward that closed door. Absorbing books and favorite games of checkers, cribbage, and chess were now forgotten. I almost wore a path from that door to the windows, peering out into the dark of the early winter night, then to kitchen, and back again.

Then, in the stillness of that early winter night, came the crystal clear sound of sleighbells from somewhere in the front of the house, then a bang at the front door. Silence followed. Soon the bells were outside once more, going away and away and then no more.

Mother, cheeks flushed with excitement, came hurrying in from the kitchen saying, "Did you hear him? Did you hear the bells? Let's go in and see!"

The door was pulled wide open and there, on the far side of the room, was the Christmas tree, now transformed by lighted candles with their intermingling glow on branches and decorations.

Below, was a large array of packages, all sizes, wrapped in holly Christmas paper and tied with ribbons and colored cord. Adults and children seated themselves in a semi-circle facing the tree. Fascinated, I watched intently alternating my gaze from the beauty of the tree to the mystery-laden packages below.

One by one, the packages were delivered, opened, and examined with exclamations of appreciation and delight. With affection and light good humor, little jokes were made about Santa Claus, the presents, and about each other. I received a box of candy and nuts, an orange, a pair of wool mittens, a wool scarf (used to wrap around one's face for protection against sometimes bitter cold and freezing, skidding winds while walking across open fields on the way to school), flannel pajamas, a jackknife, four books (adventure and boy exploit books) and a pair of skis.

Piling my treasure neatly together, I basked for awhile in the warmth of busy and animated conversation and exchange of anecdotes. No single word was heard of dissatisfaction or disappointment. Shortly after, I went back into the dining room, found a good-sized chair near a light, opened up one of my books and was soon quite absorbed, although mindful and content with the buzz of talk and activity in the next room.

As I climbed the stairs that night on my way to bed, I took my presents with me. But pleased as I was with them, I took with me also a struggling, emerging conviction that I had received that day something of far greater worth—something without form or price.

My last duty of each day, my nightly prayers of "Now I lay me down to sleep. . ." and the Lord's Prayer, were not forgotten—the one for the child in me and the other for the young adult. Of late, I had slipped into the habit of saying these under the protection of the quilts, not on my knees, excusing myself on the grounds that thinking real hard about the words and their meaning might be considered more important than the position of one's knees, especially in a cold room.

The two prayers, somehow, seemed incomplete. They seemed to say nothing about my Mother, Father and brothers. I felt I had to say something to somebody about my overflowing feelings towards them.

The words that struggled through cannot now be remembered but the gist of that "third prayer," I remember well—gratitude (not for being given presents but for being given my parents and brothers to be with), affection and a fervent hope for good things to come to them.

I went quickly and easily to sleep.

U.S. PRESIDENTS AND THEIR TERMS OF SERVICE

President	Term of Service
1. George Washington	April 30, 1789-March 4, 1793
George Washington	March 4, 1793-March 4, 1797
2. John Adams	March 4, 1797-March 4, 1801
3. Thomas Jefferson	March 4, 1801-March 4, 1805
Thomas Jefferson	March 4, 1805-March 4, 1809
4. James Madison	March 4, 1809-March 4, 1813
James Madison	March 4, 1813-March 4, 1817
5. James Monroe	March 4, 1817-March 4, 1821
James Monroe	March 4, 1821-March 4, 1825
6. John Quincy Adams	March 4, 1825-March 4, 1829
7. Andrew Jackson	March 4, 1829-March 4, 1833
Andrew Jackson	March 4, 1833-March 4, 1837
8. Martin Van Buren	March 4, 1837-March 4, 1841
9. W. H. Harrison	March 4, 1841-April 4, 1841
10. John Tyler	April 6, 1841-March 4, 1845
11. James K. Polk	March 4, 1845-March 4, 1849
12. Zachary Taylor	March 4, 1849-July 9, 1850
13. Millard Fillmore	July 10, 1850-March 4, 1853
14. Franklin Pierce	March 4, 1853-March 4, 1857
15. James Buchanan	March 4, 1857-March 4, 1861
16. Abraham Lincoln	March 4, 1861-March 4, 1865
Abraham Lincoln	March 4, 1865-April 15, 1865

17. Andrew Johnson.....................April 15, 1865-March 4, 1869
18. Ulysses S. Grant....................March 4, 1869-March 4, 1873
    Ulysses S. Grant....................March 4, 1873-March 4, 1877
19. Rutherford B. Hayes ....March 4, 1877-March 4, 1881
20. James A. Garfield ....March 4, 1881-Sept. 19, 1881
21. Chester A. Arthur ....Sept. 20, 1881-March 4, 1885
22. Grover Cleveland ....March 4, 1885-March 4, 1889
23. Benjamin Harrison ....March 4, 1889-March 4, 1893
24. Grover Cleveland ....March 4, 1893-March 4, 1897
25. William McKinley ....March 4, 1897-March 4, 1901
    William McKinley ....March 4, 1901-Sept. 14, 1901
26. Theodore Roosevelt ....Sept. 14, 1901-March 4, 1905
    Theodore Roosevelt ....March 4, 1905-March 4, 1909
27. William H. Taft ....March 4, 1909-March 4, 1913
28. Woodrow Wilson ....March 4, 1913-March 4, 1917
    Woodrow Wilson ....March 4, 1917-March 4, 1921
29. Warren G. Harding ....March 4, 1921-Aug. 2, 1923
30. Calvin Coolidge ....Aug. 3, 1923-March 4, 1925
    Calvin Coolidge....................March 4, 1925-March 4, 1929
31. Herbert Hoover ....March 4, 1929-March 4, 1933
32. Franklin D. Roosevelt ....March 4, 1933-Jan. 20, 1937
    Franklin D. Roosevelt ....Jan. 20, 1937-Jan. 20, 1941
    Franklin D. Roosevelt ....Jan. 20, 1941-Jan. 20, 1945
    Franklin D. Roosevelt.............Jan. 20, 1945-April 12, 1945
33. Harry S Truman....................April 12, 1945-Jan. 20, 1949
    Harry S Truman....................Jan. 20, 1949-Jan. 20, 1953
34. Dwight D. Eisenhower ....Jan. 20, 1953-Jan. 20, 1957
    Dwight D. Eisenhower ....Jan. 20, 1957-Jan. 20, 1961
35. John F. Kennedy....................Jan. 20, 1961-Nov. 22, 1963
36. Lyndon B. Johnson.................Nov. 22, 1963-Jan. 20, 1965
    Lyndon B. Johnson.................Jan. 20, 1965-Jan. 20, 1969
37. Richard M. Nixon...................Jan. 20, 1969-Jan. 20, 1973
    Richard M. Nixon...................Jan. 20, 1973-Aug. 9, 1974
38. Gerald R. Ford.....................Aug. 9, 1974-Jan. 20, 1977
39. Jimmy (James Earl) Carter..........Jan. 20, 1977-Jan. 20, 1981
40. Ronald Reagan......................................Jan. 20, 1981-

A WRITING BIBLIOGRAPHY

Balkin, Richard. *A Writer's Guide to Book Publishing.* 2d ed. New York: Hawthorn/Dutton, 1981.
    A realistic clearly written book dealing with every phase of the author-publisher relationship including manuscript submission, contracts, publication, and marketing. A must for any would-be author.

Chickadel, Charles J. *Publish It Yourself: The Complete Guide to Self-Publishing Your Book.* 2d ed. Aurora, Ill.: Caroline House Publishers, 1980. Paperback.
    One of the better books on self-publishing. Gives much information on the production details of producing a book.

Dixon, Janice T., and Flack, Dora D. *Preserving Your Past.* Garden City, N.Y.: Doubleday, 1977.
    An informative volume dealing with personal and family history and diary writing. Has helpful material on researching and organizing and on preserving documents. Appendix lists genealogical how-to books, records-conservation supply houses, etc.

Duncan, Lois. *How to Write and Sell Your Personal Experiences.* Cincinnati: Writer's Digest Books, 1982.
    This well-known author and writing teacher reveals the techniques that have helped her in selling personal-experience articles and books. Stimulating and candid with many examples.

Hofmann, William J. *Life Writing: A Guide to Family Journals and Personal Memoirs.* New York: St. Martin's Press, 1982.
    A readable, practical guide to gathering the family's folklore and keeping it alive. Especially helpful chapters on selection of topics, how-to focus down on each, and rewriting.

Literary Market Place/Directory of American Book Publishing. New York: R. R. Bowker Co. Published annually.
    The best guide on book publishing. Has many useful sections on every aspect of the subject including yellow pages listing suppliers of services.

Newman, Edwin. *Strictly Speaking: Will America Be the Death of English?* Indianapolis: Bobbs-Merrill, 1974.
This TV network house grammarian, dry wit and independent observer focuses on the sorry state of the English language and makes a plea for more lucid, graceful and direct language.

Perrin, Porter G. *Writer's Guide and Index to English.* 4th ed. Chicago: Scott, Foresman, 1968.
A well-organized reference book devoted to better English with a handy alphabetical index to usage and grammar.

Poynter, Dan. *The Self-Publishing Manual: How to Write, Print and Sell Your Own Book.* 2d ed. Santa Barbara: Para Publishing, 1980.
One of the best for writers who want to investigate self-publishing. Poynter is a successful writer/publisher. Covers all aspects from printing your book to distributing it. Provides a checklist for the production process.

Roget's Thesaurus.
The famous book of synonyms and antonyms. Keep it near you.

Shaw, Harry. *Errors in English.* New York: Barnes & Noble, 1970.
A quick reference guide to correct common errors in English, alphabetically arranged.

Strunk, William, Jr., and White, E. B. *The Elements of Style.* 2d ed. New York: Macmillan, 1972.
This little gem, a best-seller, should be a must on your reading table. No book, in so few words, will help you more with English style and usage. An excellent addition by E. B. White.

Todd, Alden. *Finding Facts Fast.* 2d ed. Berkeley: Ten Speed Press, 1979.
Todd shows you how to find out what you need to know quickly and easily from many sources. His practical shortcuts evolved from his many years of researching and writing articles and books.

Weisbord, Marvin, ed. *A Treasury of Tips for Writers.* Techniques by members of the American Society of Journalists & Authors. Cincinnati: Writer's Digest Books, 1965.

> The talented members of this leading writing society got their heads together to provide valuable tips on every aspect of writing from generating article ideas on through each step of the writing process.

The Writer. 8 Arlington St., Boston, MA 02116. Monthly magazine for writers.

Writer's Digest. 9933 Alliance Rd., Cincinnati, OH 45242. Monthly magazine for writers.

Writer's Market. Cincinnati: Writer's Digest Books. Published annually.

> A standard book in the library of any writer who wants to sell. Lists thousands of publishing opportunities in the magazine and book fields. Includes tips on writing, and a section on services available to writers.

Zinsser, William. *On Writing Well.* 2d ed. New York: Harper & Row, 1980.

> You can't read this informal guide to writing nonfiction without learning something. Zinsser is an established pro and this book is a modern classic.

index